THE HAMLYN BOOK OF

WORLD SOCCER

THE HAMLYN BOOK OF

WORLD SOCCER

PETER ARNOLD / CHRISTOPHER DAVIS

HAMLYN

LONDON
NEW YORK
SYDNEY
TORONTO

Published by
The Hamlyn Publishing Group Limited
London   New York   Sydney   Toronto
Hamlyn House, Feltham, Middlesex, England
© Copyright The Hamlyn Publishing
Group Limited 1973
ISBN 0 600 33897 5

Text set in 8/9, 10/11 and 11/13 point
Univers Light Monophoto 685.
Captions set in 8/9, 10/11 and 11/13 point
Univers Bold Monophoto 693.

Printed in England by
Jarrold and Sons Limited, Norwich

The pictures in the preliminary pages
and end-papers are as follows:

end-papers
Wittman scores for Borussia
Dortmund against Everton in the
European Cup, 1970.

half-title
Denis Law shoots past Carvalho of
Sporting Club of Lisbon to score for
Manchester United in the
European Cup-Winners Cup
quarter-finals of 1964.

title-page
Torres scores for Portugal against
Bulgaria and ends in the net
himself (1966 World Cup
Finals).

these pages
Garrincha of Brazil beats a
West German defender.

CONTENTS

INTRODUCTION

About 20,000,000 people, in all corners of the earth, play organized soccer. They may not outnumber those who catch fish, or swim or play cards, but if one adds the number of people who watch and considers the strength of their feelings for the game, it is clear that soccer is the most popular sport in the world. With the modern aid of satellite-beamed television 500,000,000 people might watch one World Cup game simultaneously.

The reasons for this are not difficult to discern. A good match provides an exciting display of fitness, strength and physical commitment. It is an expression of national or individual character, of skill and ball control. It satisfies a more cerebral taste for tactics, strategy and pattern-weaving.

Soccer's top players are international properties which the whole world can appreciate and discuss. Pele has the stature to postpone a war: a truce was called in the Biafran struggle so that he could visit both sides in safety. Players who in world terms are in the second rank can become local heroes of astonishing dimensions. Jackie Milburn need never buy a pint of beer for himself anywhere in Newcastle. 'Second rank' is almost a blasphemous term to apply to Milburn; it is necessary only in order to say that he was not as great a player as Pele. Nevertheless, some talents he possessed, such as an exhilarating quickness off the mark and a sudden lethal shot, even Pele could not improve upon. This is another charm of soccer: the diverse opportunities it affords for a great variety of skills to be practised. John Charles is immortal because nobody could head a ball better, Greaves because nobody could scent a goal-chance quicker, Bloomer because he could shoot so hard, Bobby Charlton because his character shone through his play. 'Fanny' Walden and Alan Morton made assets of their smallness: they buzzed through defences like flies impossible to swat. By different methods five-foot-and-a-bit Harry Hibbs and 22-stone Willie Foulke both became top-flight goalkeepers.

Similarly, the game throws up incidents to be appreciated and wondered at by followers of all colours and creeds. Pele's shot from the centre circle in the World Cup finals of 1970 was applauded equally by exuberant Brazilians, reflective Scotsmen (reflecting on where their national talents had gone), dour Russians, bemused Americans, even momentarily scrutable Orientals. While any schoolboys of 1953 vintage still live, so will the memory of the 'Matthews Cup Final'.

The appeal of soccer knows no social or economic distinctions. A Professor of Logic at Oxford University can enthuse as much over the game as the man who goes straight from work to stand on the terraces. The views of both will be informed by an instinctive grasp of the finer points which is almost a British birthright.

Soccer has attained its position as the leading international sport after 100 years of continual growth. The Football Association was formed in 1863. It was quickly followed by others in Britain. Holland formed the first continental association in 1889; New Zealand, surprisingly, had a football association as early as 1891; Argentina led the way in South America by forming an association in 1895. International matches were played in the early days, and soccer was played at the Olympic Games of 1900, although this first Olympic match was an exhibition. The United Kingdom won the first full-scale Olympic soccer tournaments in 1908 and 1912. In 1904 FIFA (the Fédération International de Football Association) was formed in Paris by representatives from Belgium, Denmark, France, the Netherlands, Spain, Sweden and Switzerland. The British, founders of the modern game, remained aloof initially, but England joined in 1906 and D. B. Woolfall, the FA's honorary treasurer, was elected President. The other home countries eventually became members, but British associations have twice

resigned. After the First World War, in common with some continental allies, England declined to associate with Germany and did not rejoin till 1924. After the Second World War the situation was reversed, and Germany was not allowed membership. The British withdrew for a longer period (eighteen years) in 1928 over disputes about amateurism. The Football Association resolved its own problems over amateurism by announcing in 1972 that, as in cricket, all players, amateur and professional, would be known as 'players'.

FIFA is now the strong governing body of world soccer. It has six confederations, representing six soccer 'continents', and in 1972 140 national associations were affiliated. British influence on world soccer is indicated by the long Presidency of Sir Stanley Rous.

A threat to FIFA's authority has recently developed over the question of Britain's representation. There was opposition to the admission of the associations of Scotland, Ireland and Wales in 1910 as some countries considered them to be mere subsidiaries of the Football Association, and indeed the first two were refused admission in 1908. In 1972, Uruguay, as spokesman for South American and Asian feelings, was dissuaded only at the last minute from tabling a motion at the FIFA Congress designed to cut Britain's representatives from four to one. Had such a proposal been carried, it is likely that Britain and other European countries would have withdrawn. Europe still provides most of the top-class soccer nations, and any move to reduce its power in FIFA councils would meet with strong opposition.

It is to be hoped that harmony once more is established, because FIFA organizes the World Cup tournament, and dissension and withdrawals could only devalue what is arguably the greatest sporting event in the world.

The World Cup is the means of measuring the progress of soccer in various nations. It is the show-case which first presented to appreciative audiences the superb control which the Brazilians learnt on their native beaches and which they applied so

successfully on far distant pitches. But it was Uruguay who first demonstrated that football was flourishing in South America, when they won the Olympic tournaments in 1924 and 1928, and then went on to be victorious in the first World Cup in 1930. Uruguay, with a population considerably less than that of Greater London, and with a constant handicap of losing star players to the more lucrative leagues in Argentina and Italy, have a splendid record in world football. They have won the World Cup twice, been twice more semi-finalists and once quarter-finalists.

Losing finalists in the 1930 World Cup were Argentina, who have not won a World Cup or an Olympic title, but they have long been one of the stronger South American nations and a force in the world game.

Brazil are the third great soccer nation in South America and their exploits are well known. In 1970 they became the first country to win the World Cup three times, and the Jules Rimet trophy is now theirs. As the world's best footballers Brazil have had no need to play anything but an attacking game, and indeed if there is one weakness in their football it is an aristocratic disdain for the routine requirements of defence.

Lesser footballing countries in the South American continent are Chile, Paraguay, Bolivia, Peru (who show promise of joining the first rank), Ecuador and Colombia. Mexico, in Central America, have appeared seven times in the final stages of the World Cup, and they were hosts in 1970. Uruguay, Brazil and Chile have also staged World Cups.

North America is an enigma on the soccer scene. It might be thought that soccer would flourish in Canada, with its strong links with Britain, but although it was introduced by immigrants in the nineteenth century it did not take hold, except as an influence on Canadian football, a quite different game. There have been periods of enthusiasm in the United States, and the defeat of England in the 1950 World Cup should have established the game. The biggest boom, however, came after the 1966 World Cup when Americans saw on their TV screens just what it was that caused such excitement elsewhere in the world. Leagues were set up and businessmen poured much money and commercial expertise into teams and stadiums confidently expected to become investments. British experts, like ex-West Ham player Phil Woosnam, were engaged to advise and supervise. Soccer had plenty of well-wishers in the States as the established game of American football has its drawbacks. These include an emphasis on physical strength which makes padding necessary and causes it to be unattractive to less strong schoolboys, and its lack of grace and flowing movement. Nevertheless the enterprise failed. Perhaps a soccer tradition is more important to the enjoyment of the game than older soccer nations realize, and of course a tradition cannot be bought, even with unlimited wealth. The biggest disadvantage soccer has in the States may arise from another tradition, that of American supremacy in most of the sports they undertake. The putative American fan may not have the patience to support the game while awaiting the time when America can compete in the highest circles.

There is no reason why African countries should not reach the top in world football. A line of superb runners like Kip Keino of Kenya have shown that physique, natural talent and dedication are not lacking: what are, perhaps, are coaching and facilities. Eusebio, born in Mozambique, reached the very top in soccer with Benfica and Portugal. Ade Coker, a Nigerian, shows promise with West Ham United. But the progress of African soccer is best demonstrated by the comic announcement in 1972 that the winners of matches in Tanzania would henceforth be decided by judges rather than by goals scored! There is a strong interest in soccer in South Africa, where professionalism was allowed in 1959. South Africans have appeared internationally for England, Scotland and Ireland. Perry, who scored the winner in the 'Matthews Cup Final', was South African, and Charlton Athletic have fielded many South Africans, notably Scottish international John Hewie. Latterly famous English internationals Stanley Matthews, George Eastham and Johnny Haynes have coached and played for South African clubs. There is a South African FA and a Non-European Federation, but due to *apartheid* neither can be admitted to FIFA and there are no immediate prospects of South Africa appearing on the international soccer scene.

The West Indian countries, like the African, are rich in natural athletes but poor in soccer traditions. It is pleasant to note that members of the immigrant community are beginning to appear in English football. The most prominent is Clyde Best, who has played some outstanding games for West Ham United.

Soccer in Australia and New Zealand has faced competition from Rugby. That a lot of soccer is nevertheless played in Australia is shown by the way British pools firms use Australian matches to keep them going in the summer. The game is popular with European emigrants but has not managed yet to capture enough national enthusiasm to make Australia a first-class soccer continent. Rugby Union is easily the leading New Zealand game, but it faces the same opposition as American football does in the States: brawn is essential, skill less so. Consequently New Zealand schools are beginning to prefer soccer and an upsurge in popularity is likely.

To Western minds, Asian soccer until 1966 meant Russia, although in fact soccer-wise Russia is European, both the national side and the clubs appearing in European competitions. The success of the North Koreans in the World Cup of 1966 aroused curiosity about standards further east. North Korea's performance was not a flash in the pan — the game has developed into a national sport there. It flourishes, too, in Japan, while China has claims that football began there and more sporting encounters with the West might reveal a continuing proficiency. Certainly strong challenges from China, Japan and Korea would brighten world soccer, particularly as their small players would be unable to use physical methods, and might well develop exciting new skills and tactics.

Russian soccer has the reputation of being predictable and unimaginative. There is no doubt that Russian players are technically accomplished, that their combined play is of a high standard and that they have a fine appreciation of tactics. Yet they have consistently lacked the spark of inspiration needed to be world-beaters. They are perhaps too regimented. What makes soccer supreme as a team game is that discipline is not enough — the spice of flair and individual brilliance must be added to the collation of teamwork and planning for a wholly successful soccer feast.

Modern football began in Britain and spread first to the Continent. European soccer still has the greatest strength in depth and only South America has claims to parity with Europe as a soccer-playing continent.

The development and current strength of South American soccer emerges in this book in the section on the World Cup, where the performances of the leading countries are traced from tournament to tournament. The same is true of British and continental soccer, but in addition the home countries and their clubs and continental nations and clubs, because of the number and the fierceness of the competitions between them, are given sections of their own.

Where will football go now? In Britain early in the 1972–73 season the signs were disquieting, though possibly a shortage of good newspaper copy gave them an emphasis that was unnecessarily alarming. Journalists concentrated on the increased violence on the terraces and attempted to equate that with the falling gates. Random opinion polls did suggest sporadically that some people had stopped going to football because of the thuggery, but it was only part of the truth. Football grounds, like New York, are in practice not as alarming as the statistics suggest; they are both divided into areas so that, as a rule, only those who seek to consort with thugs need fear the consequences of thuggery.

More to the point, fewer people were going to football matches in 1972 because (*a*) they were fed up with football, and (*b*) the football they had seen had acquired a predictable sameness. Public interest has almost always moved in waves — in 1966 and 1970 it was on the crest; in 1972 it was in the trough, and not surprisingly. The previous season, including various European competitions and television coverage thereof, had dragged on into the middle of June. Then players flopped exhausted on Majorcan beaches and the readers of the sports pages gave a huge sigh of relief and dwelt thankfully on the gentler configurations of cricket. Not two months later the players, their knees and torsos impressively tanned, were photographed sweating the pounds off for the start of the new season. *Match of the Day* returned to the Saturday night set with unconvincingly self-generated enthusiasm, and the whole hysterical circus began again. It can, of course, be argued that football extended into the summer months in World Cup years and the

Eusebio playing in the 1966 World Cup for Portugal against North Korea. Born in Mozambique, he is the greatest footballer to have come from Africa so far.

public were not wearied by it the following August. But then the football was different. In 1971–72 British football itself went into the trough as Ramsey's worn-out destroyers capitulated to the streamlined new German battleship, as the Football League produced more and more football that seemed to be the same, as fixtures piled up one upon the other so that the matches with the most built-in excitement, such as the later rounds of the FA Cup (and their replays) were eventually being contested by teams too exhausted to climb yet another peak — and no

wonder. The physical and mental strains are genuinely crushing. Only the most resilient will survive long. The exhaustion communicates itself to the watching public and they stay away, too enervated to bother with getting involved again.

Football is crazy. The game itself has grown up and made spectacular advances, but the Football League management has not and the players themselves are still treated like prize children allowed out to play in an expensive nursery. As at least one writer has pointed out, the extra-ordinary situation exists whereby

highly paid performers are controlled on the field by a miserably paid part-time official, and are managed by a highly paid professional who is himself subject to the whims of the amateur collection of butchers, bakers and self-important worthies who sit in the directors' box. Perhaps if they all realized it there would be a revolution.

Football is mad. But it will survive. There may be a European Super-League; half the present clubs may go to the wall because of the lunatic financial exchanges in which even moderate players are now valued at more than the price of a country

1

2

3

estate; the gap between the star clubs and the others may grow huge; a few cities may control the destiny of the game; the World Cup, like the Olympics, might even become a platform for political protest; but one thing will ensure its future — the players themselves. Somehow or other, each year throws up its new gift to the grandstands, a new figure with which to identify, a new idol who can convert the frustrations of the mean streets into a brief bright dream of freedom, equality and, above all, of self-expression.

1. **Ninety minutes or so after this picture was taken the relationship between British and continental soccer had dramatically changed. Ferenc Puskas leading the 1953 Hungarian side which beat England 6–3.**
2. **Johnny Haynes, ex-England captain, playing for Durban City against Berea Park in South Africa in 1971.**
3. **Ex-Chelsea right half Ken Armstrong, who played once for England in a 7–2 defeat of Scotland, coaching in New Zealand in 1967.**
4. **The possibility of violence is a fact of life in South American soccer. Police guard the players of Universidad Catolica and Deportivo Cuenca in the Olympic Stadium, Quito, Ecuador.**
5. **Emergent soccer. Ghana champions Hearts of Oak play the National team of Congo Brazzaville in Accra.**

Stoke City's first honour: the Football League Cup of 1972. Skipper Peter Dobing holds the Cup. Other veterans to be seen are George Eastham (left) and goalkeeper Gordon Banks (rear).

THE BRITISH GAME

100 YEARS OF SOCCER

Modern soccer was a nineteenth-century British invention. It is impossible to say, of course, who first kicked a ball for pleasure and when, but it is known that a kind of football was played in China at about the time of the birth of Christ, and in Britain the game has been played for several centuries, often against the wishes of the reigning monarch. Laws banning it were passed by many kings, because of the rowdyism and violence it provoked.

In the nineteenth century the game was popular in the public schools and universities. Customs of play varied in each school and in many even a certain amount of handling was allowed. With the coming together at university of players from different public schools a standardization in rules was necessary and in 1846 the first soccer rules were written at Cambridge University.

On 26 July 1863, at a meeting in London, the Football Association was formed. Although no official representatives of the public schools were present, the rules drawn up were based on the Cambridge University rules. When the final draft was voted upon in November, holding, tripping and hacking, once universal tactics, were disallowed, and their advocates, mainly the Blackheath club, withdrew from the Association to develop the modern Rugby game.

The Football Association was the first of its kind, and its influence was immense, many other Associations throughout the world being modelled upon it. The Scottish FA was formed in 1873, the Welsh in 1876 and the Irish in 1880.

The FA instituted its Cup competition in 1871 and in early years many Scottish clubs took part. Much travelling was involved which stretched the meagre finances of clubs, and of course many clubs were eliminated at an early stage of the competition each year. A competition was needed which guaranteed clubs first-class matches throughout the season, and a Scot, William McGregor, who was associated with Aston Villa, circularized a few top clubs suggesting a league. The idea was met with enthusiasm, and on 17 April 1888 a twelve-club league was formed. The founder clubs were Accrington, Aston Villa, Blackburn Rovers, Bolton Wanderers, Burnley, Derby County, Everton, Notts County, Preston North End, Stoke, West Bromwich and Wolverhampton. Most of these clubs have an illustrious history and even in the 1970s only Accrington have no real prospects of further glories.

Amateurs dominated the early days of the Football Association, and professionalism was referred to by C. W. Alcock, the Association's President in 1881 as a 'problem'. It was legalized in 1885 however. Scottish clubs had already demonstrated a flair for the game and the influx of Scottish players into England seeking wages led to the spread of the 'Scottish style', based on passing rather than dribbling. These early professionals were the first of the 'Anglo-Scots' who have been moving south ever since, and who have made such a mark in the Football League.

The oldest Scottish club, Queens Park, formed in 1867, have remained true to the amateur tradition, and although they have never since reached the heights of 1872, when they supplied the whole of the Scottish side which drew 0–0 with England in what is now regarded as the first 'official' international between the countries, they nevertheless still compete with moderate success in the Scottish second division.

The Scottish Cup was first fought for in 1873 and the Scottish League in 1890, so by the turn of the century the principal Cup and League competitions in England and Scotland were well under way. The British International Tournament had begun in 1883, so until the advent after the Second World War of the Football League Cup and European and sponsored competitions, the pattern of the British season was firmly established.

From the very beginning of organized soccer, there were great teams and players still spoken of with awe, although they and the spectators have long departed for grounds six feet below the old ones.

In 1889, for instance, Preston North End, playing in the 'Scottish style' (there were, after all, six Scotsmen in the side) won the first League Championship without defeat. They also won the Cup without conceding a goal, and became the first of only four sides ever to complete the 'double'. Preston have been called 'Proud Preston' ever since, and that particular side was called the 'Old Invincibles'. One of the first of the outstanding players was Preston's John Goodall, an Englishman who learnt his soccer in Scotland. His brother, Archie, who later played with him for Derby County, played for Ireland.

Liverpool won the Championship without losing a game in 1892, but the side which inherited Preston's mantle was Sunderland, three times Champions in the 1890s, the 'Team of All the Talents'. Aston Villa took over from Sunderland and were Champions five times between 1893 and 1900, becoming the second side to perform the 'double' in 1897.

Amateurs remained a force in the game until the turn of the century, the best side being the famous public-school team Corinthians. They did not enter competitions, but would undoubtedly have won many trophies if they had, for they beat the Old Invincibles of Preston 5–0. C. B. Fry, perhaps the greatest-ever athlete (cricket and soccer international and world long jump record-holder), was a Corinthian. He said that the finest centre forward of the day was another, G. O. Smith, who himself was a good cricketer. What heroic figures they were! The England full backs were Corinthians — the Walters brothers, whose parents, in another age, might have written Goon Show scripts, for they gave their sons the initials A.M. and P.M.

In Scotland, the success of a Roman Catholic club from Edinburgh, Hibernian, in winning the Scottish Cup in 1887, led to Glasgow Catholics forming a club: Celtic. It wasn't long before Celtic won both Cup and League, their first success in each coming in 1892. They thus stole a march on Rangers, who had been formed in 1873 but whose only success was the sharing of the Championship in 1891. Rangers later were Champions four years running from 1898 to 1903, winning all their games in 1898. The long Glasgow rivalry was under way.

All Glasgow was saddened in 1902 when at an international between Scotland and England at Ibrox Park

The great Billy Meredith leaves a Brighton defender watching from the floor.

the wooden terracing collapsed and soccer had its first major disaster. Hundreds of spectators were injured when they fell through the debris; others were trampled in the flight. Twenty-five were killed. Terraces all over the country have been made of earth and concrete ever since.
In 1904 Celtic won the first of six consecutive Championships, followed by three for Rangers, then four more for Celtic — it wasn't until Motherwell won in 1931 that the Celtic-Rangers sequence was broken!

The great side in England in the early 1900s was Newcastle United: their record in the Championship from season 1903–04 ran: fourth, first, fourth, first, fourth, first, fourth — they obviously didn't fancy second or third. Their star players were Colin Veitch, Peter McWilliam and Bill McCracken who was to perfect the offside game. Manchester United won the Championship twice, in 1908 and 1911, and the Cup in 1909. They had a remarkable winger in Billy Meredith, a Welshman who always played with a toothpick in his mouth. He won Cup-winners' medals with both Manchester sides. Meredith was bow-legged, a great dribbler and an early exponent of the wall pass. His forty-eight internationals spanned twenty-five years, and he was in his forty-sixth year when he played his last in 1920. Meredith played for Manchester City for his final three seasons and in 1924 he made the winning goal in a Cup tie by outpacing the full back: it was during extra time and Meredith was nearly fifty!

Steve Bloomer began his international career in the same year as Billy Meredith. Slim and pale, he did not appear to have the physique to become an all-time great, but in fact his shooting was famous for its power. A perfectionist, he was, like Haynes fifty years later, openly impatient with the shortcomings of his colleagues. Bloomer scored 352 Football League goals, a record which stood till 1936, when Dixie Dean beat it. His total of 28 international goals was also a record. It was said that the only times he did not aim low to the corners of the goal were when he was facing Willie Foulke, the giant 22-stone goalkeeper of Sheffield United and Chelsea. Bloomer could not resist trying to knock him over!

Foulke, who won two Cup-winners' medals, was a very fine goalkeeper, despite his immense size. He was also a great character, prone to argue with referees, and stories about him are numerous, the funniest perhaps being of the occasion when he felt a referee had awarded an off-side goal against him. After the match, between stripping off his gear and getting dressed, Foulke decided to have words with the ref, and went in search of him. Forewarned, the ref locked himself in his dressing room. The sight of Foulke, 6 feet and 22 stones of naked manhood prowling the corridor and swearing vengeance, must have been hilarious.

Jesse Pennington, of West Bromwich Albion and England, the best left back of his time, would never have dreamed of questioning a referee's decision. The perfect gentleman, he would rather lose than do anything unsportsmanlike. In the Cup Final of 1912 West Brom were playing 'Battling' Barnsley of the second division. It was extra time in a replay and, during Albion pressure, a clearance left Pennington challenging Tufnell, the Barnsley inside right, near the half-way line. The way to goal was otherwise clear; a foul would have saved the day, but to Pennington it was unthinkable. The goal was scored and Pennington never won a Cup-winner's medal. It was in this match that Glendinning of Barnsley, off the field for attention to an injury, suddenly ran on wearing only one of his boots to thump the ball away from the Barnsley goal. This incident led to the rule that players returning to the field must first receive the referee's permission.

Pennington's partner at right back in nineteen internationals was Bob Crompton of Blackburn Rovers, one of England's best captains. Firm, capable, of imposing presence, Crompton dealt with forwards without fuss. Behind

19

1

INTERNATIONAL
FOOT-BALL MATCH,
(ASSOCIATION RULES,)
ENGLAND v. SCOTLAND,
WEST OF SCOTLAND CRICKET GROUND,
HAMILTON CRESCENT, PARTICK,
SATURDAY, 30th November, 1872, at 2 p.m.

—————•—————
ADMISSION—ONE SHILLING.

No. 806

2

3

4

5

them was goalkeeper Sam Hardy, another player who inspired great confidence. He was one of the breed of goalkeepers who rely on anticipation and positioning. Liverpool and Aston Villa found Hardy as dependable as did England.

Other great England players contemporary with these were 'Smiler' Wedlock and Vivian Woodward. Wedlock, of Bristol City, was a centre half of 5 feet 4½ inches! Of course centre halves were not stoppers in those days, and Wedlock was a human dynamo usually preferred to Charlie Roberts, his Manchester United rival, by the England selectors.

Woodward was the last great amateur player. A centre forward, he won twenty-three full caps and approaching forty amateur caps. He was in the hero mould of the Corinthians – slim, not unhandsome, an architect and cricketer, a man who played fairly and uncomplainingly, and above all played well, whether for Chelmsford, Tottenham Hotspur or England.

A great Scottish centre forward whose career ran parallel with Woodward's was Jimmy Quinn, of Celtic, a fearless player who accepted injuries as he accepted goals. He was flanked at inside forward for Celtic by McMenemy and Somers, a peerless trio who swept opposition aside from 1904 onwards, and who helped Celtic, in 1907–08 to win every competition they entered.

'Fanny' Walden, a Spurs winger, won England caps before and after the First World War, and being only 5 feet 2 inches and less than 9 stone was a great favourite with spectators, who loved to see him trick full backs much bigger than himself.

The first official home international match was in 1872, between England and Scotland, and the result was 0–0 (a score not to be repeated for ninety-eight years). England won the return, but Scotland then had a period of superiority, losing only once more in the next fifteen years. England have never caught up in the matter of wins, although in 1969 they finally overtook Scotland in the number of goals scored. Wales played her first match with Scotland in 1876 and with England in 1879, Ireland soon joined in, and in 1883 the International Championship was started. In 1886 the International Board was formed, and caps were awarded for matches. There were many goals scored in the early games, perhaps none better than that scored by E. C. Bambridge for England in a 5–4 win over Scotland in 1879 – he dribbled the ball the length of the field.

In 1882 England beat Ireland 13–0 in the first meeting between the countries, still the record score in home internationals. Ireland achieved a great success just before the First World War, however, winning the Home International Championship outright for the first time. With a man off injured for most of the game, they opened their programme by beating Wales 2–1. Having beaten England for the first time in thirty-two attempts the previous season, Ireland then repeated the treatment 3–0. A draw against Scotland was needed to win the tournament – a defeat would leave Scotland champions. A record Irish crowd of 26,000 turned out to watch the game in a rainstorm which had begun the day before. The ground was covered in water. One Irishman, McConnell, soon went off injured, and then McKee, the goalkeeper, hurt in the first half, had to leave the field just after half-time. McConnell, the first invalid, then took McKee's place in goal. So Ireland fought on with nine fit men plus an injured make-shift goalkeeper. Scotland scored. On a stamina-sapping pitch, the Irish summoned their remaining strength and eight minutes from the end Young equalized. At the whistle the emotional spectators poured on to the quagmire, and drenched and cold, but warm inside, they carried the players to the dressing-rooms.

Soccer very quickly got under way again after the war: the third divisions (south and north) and Scottish second divisions were founded in consecutive years from 1920. In 1919 Motherwell outside left Ferrier played the first of 626 games for the club – a Scottish record. In 1920–21 Burnley went a record 30 games without defeat to win the League Championship. Missed penalties had decisive effects on the records of two clubs. In the last match of the 1923–24 season L. Davies missed a penalty for Cardiff City in a 0–0 draw with Birmingham. It lost Cardiff the Championship, which was decided on goal average for the first time. Cardiff scored one more goal

1. Ticket No. 806 for the first-ever international match.
2. Steve Bloomer of Derby County in 1911.
3. The wrecked terracing after the Ibrox Park disaster in 1902.
4. England captain Bob Crompton in 1913, near the end of his international career.
5. Liverpool goalkeeper Elisha Scott.
6. Vivian Woodward, amateur and professional England centre forward.

1

2

4

5

than Huddersfield and conceded one more, the difference in average being two-hundredths of a goal! Two years later Manchester City missed a penalty in the last match against Newcastle and lost 3–2. This miss meant relegation to the second division. The following year City missed being promoted back by an even closer goal-average decision than Cardiff's, five-thousandths of a goal: 1·7705 to Portsmouth's 1·7755.

Cardiff had their best side in the twenties, with a great centre half in Fred Keenor. Keenor played for Wales thirty-two times from 1920 to 1933 when Wales had their best-ever teams, winning the International Championship four times during this spell. His greatest day was for Wales against Scotland at Ibrox Park in 1930. It was a year when many League clubs refused to release players for international matches — the FA could demand the services of English players, but the Welsh and Scottish FAs could only request. Keenor was captain of a Welsh team labelled 'Keenor and Ten Unknowns'. The team is worth recalling in full: Evans (Cardiff City); Dewey (Cardiff Corinthians), Crompton (Wrexham); Rogers (Wrexham), Keenor (Cardiff City), Ellis (Nunhead); Collins (Llanelly), Neal (Colwyn Bay), Bamford (Wrexham), Robbins (Cardiff City), Thomas (Newport County). The players came from the second and third divisions and minor leagues.

Previous page
The Huddersfield Town football team of 1927. Having become the first club to win the Championship three times in succession, they then finished second in 1926–27 and 1927–28. The team is *left to right, back:* **Alex Jackson, W. H. Smith, E. Taylor, R. Kelly, S. Wadsworth, E. Barkas, A. Taylor.** *Front:* **L. Redfern, D. Steele, Clem Stephenson, F. R. Goodall, G. Brown, John Chaplin (manager).**

1. David Jack introduces Harry Hibbs to the Duke of Gloucester before the England-Scotland match at Wembley, 1930.
2. Joe Hulme scoring for Arsenal against Sunderland at Highbury in 1932.
3. 'Wee Blue Devil' Alan Morton, Rangers and Scotland.
4. Alex James of Arsenal and his famous long 'shorts'.
5. Ted Drake, Arsenal, attempts a flying header.
6. Dixie Dean leads out Everton at Highbury in 1936.

Three were amateurs. Wales should have lost by a cricket score, but inspired by Keenor they went to Glasgow and drew 1–1.

There were three great teams in the twenties: Glasgow Rangers, Huddersfield Town and the Scottish 'Wembley Wizards' of 1928. Rangers won all but two Championships in the twenties, and indeed between the 1919–20 season and the outbreak of the Second World War won fifteen times out of twenty. Rangers' greatest player was Alan Morton, the 'Wee Blue Devil'. He was only 5 feet 4½ inches and less than 10 stone, which helped him to be beautifully balanced. His ball control was magical and he was very fast. Like Finney later, his right foot was at least as strong as his left, which meant that as a left winger he could go inside or outside the back and centre with either foot. He was one of the Wembley Wizards who defeated England in 1928 by 5–1, a match older Scotsmen are still inclined to rate as the greatest exhibition of football they've seen. The team was: Harkness (Queens Park), Nelson (Cardiff), Law (Chelsea), Gibson (Aston Villa), Bradshaw (Bury), McMullan (Manchester City), Jackson (Huddersfield), Dunn (Hibernian), Gallacher (Newcastle), James (Preston), Morton (Glasgow Rangers). England had Roy Goodall, an immaculate right back, Willis Edwards of Leeds United, one of the greatest of right halves, Joe Hulme and Dixie Dean.

The game might have been quite different. In the opening minute England hit the post and the ball flew across the empty goal. Within three minutes Scotland took the lead. Morton went away on the left, centred, and opposite winger Jackson scored the first of his three goals. Just on half-time Alex James beat three defenders and fired in from the edge of the area. Playing brilliant combined football Scotland took their score to five before England, having missed in the first minute, finally scored in the last.

As well as Morton, three other members of Scotland's scintillating forward line are among the immortals of the game. Alex James, another small man, as famous for his long pants as his dazzling footwork, began his career as a scorer but became the mid-field general of the Arsenal side of the thirties. James was the greatest 'scheming' inside forward — the tactician who made the goals for the others to knock in.

Hughie Gallacher was only 5 feet 6 inches, but many rate him the greatest of all centre forwards. His size did not prevent him being superb in the air, and on the ground his

swerve, speed and control were of the highest class. A capacity for firing the ball in from any angle with great force made him the complete centre forward. He was a hard competitor who sadly took to drink and died a lonely man.

Alex Jackson was the only forward of the Wee Blue Devils over 5 feet 6 inches. A fast-dribbling, goal-scoring winger he was a member of the Huddersfield Town team which won the League Championship three times running from 1923–24 to 1925–26. Huddersfield were the third great team of the twenties. Their first Championship has already been described as Cardiff's misfortune – the next two were more decisive, and were followed by two seconds. The man who built Huddersfield was Herbert Chapman. In 1921 Chapman bought Clem Stephenson from Aston Villa to organize his team. Many thought Stephenson had already seen his best days, but he was an inspired buy (as was Buchan when Chapman bought him for Arsenal in similar circumstances years later. Chapman and Buchan are discussed in the section on tactics). Huddersfield won the Cup in 1922 before beginning their League run. Stephenson was an inside forward who kept the ball on the ground and did the simple thing quickly and well. That he won only one cap is one of soccer's mysteries.

There was some prolific scoring after the change in the off-side law in 1925. Dixie Dean scored 82 goals in 1927–28 including a record 60 for Champions Everton in the League. Dean, a tremendous header, scored 379 League goals in his career, a record at the time but since beaten. At the other end of Liverpool Elisha Scott's job was saving goals. He was extremely dependable, and made many spectacular last-ditch saves. Despite the interruption of the war he made

428 appearances for Liverpool and 30 for Ireland. Billy Walker, a stylish inside left, played 532 times for Aston Villa between 1919 and 1934 and shares the club's aggregate goal-scoring record with the tough and ultra-aggressive Harry Hampton.

Jimmy McGrory of Celtic scored eight goals in a Scottish first division match in 1928 against Dunfermline – eight of 550 that he scored altogether. He is the only player in British football with a personal goal average of over one per game. A goal-scoring oddity of the 1928–29 season was the position of Cardiff City at the foot of the first division. They had the best defensive record in the division, conceding three less goals than the Champions, Sheffield Wednesday! However, they themselves scored only half as many as Wednesday.

In May 1929 Spain became the first foreign side to defeat England – by 4–3 in Madrid. In 1931 the return match was the first of some notable matches against continental sides. The main attraction was the appearance in England of the fabulous goalkeeper Zamora. Thirty-four times an international, he was claimed to be the best and highest-paid goalie in the world. Alas, in the third minute, he slipped on the muddy pitch and missed the first shot aimed at him. Demoralized, he soon missed another. In all, he conceded seven. One of the greatest of players, he is remembered in England as a somewhat comic figure.

Next year Austria's *Wunderteam* came to Stamford Bridge, outplayed England for long periods, and lost 4–3. In 1934 it was the turn of World Cup holders Italy. They fought a fierce battle at Highbury in a match which one newspaper reported as 'by our War Correspondent'. Monti, the great Italian centre half, was injured in the second minute. England quickly took the lead and were three up in a quarter of an hour. The Italians retaliated with such viciousness over what they thought was deliberate rough play by England that every England player finished with an injury. Hapgood's nose was broken. In the second half Italy scored twice, but England won an infamous match 3–2.

England had seven Arsenal men in that side, a measure of Arsenal's superiority in the Football League at the time. Having won the Championship with a record sixty-six points in 1931, Arsenal were second in 1932 and then won three times running. The 'magnificent seven' who played for England were Moss, Male, Hapgood, Copping, Bowden, Drake and Bastin. Arsenal also had on their books in this period Alex James, who

1. Zamora, the great Spanish goalkeeper, being challenged by Dean in the England-Spain match at Highbury in 1931.
2. Hughie Gallacher, playing for Chelsea against Arsenal in 1931, gets well above the opposition to win a heading duel. Chelsea won 2–1.
3. The Arsenal team in 1933, at the height of their power. Herbert Chapman, their great manager, is on the left, with Joe Hulme beside him and a young Leslie Compton behind. Beside Tom Whittaker, the trainer, on the right, are Cliff Bastin and Alex James. Eddie Hapgood is second from the right, back row.

1

4

2

3

played for Scotland, and Bob John, who played for Wales, and England internationals Joe Hulme, Jack Crayston and David Jack. Best of all these were Eddie Hapgood, an England full back and captain famed for his goal-line clearances; Ted Drake, a fearless centre forward who established a record in 1935 when he scored all seven goals for Arsenal in a 7–1 first division win at Villa Park; Cliff Bastin, who was known as 'Boy' Bastin when Arsenal bought him from Exeter as a seventeen-year-old and who won every honour in the game by the time he was twenty-one — he scored 157 League goals, including 33 from the wing in 1932–33, Joe Hulme, the only man to have appeared in five Cup Finals at Wembley, and just about the fastest winger in the game; David Jack, a tall inside forward, who appeared in four Wembley Finals, winning two Cup-winners' medals with Bolton Wanderers and a third with Arsenal; and, of course, Alex James.

There were other good performances in the League in the thirties despite Arsenal's dominance. Brentford won all their home games in the third division south in 1929–30, an unbeatable record. Everton, relegated from the first division the same season, won the second division the next, the Championship the next, and the Cup the season after that! Charlton Athletic won promotion from the third division south in 1934–35, from the second division the next year, and finished second in the Championship the following year. West Bromwich won promotion from the second division and the Cup in 1930–31. One of West Brom's best players was centre forward W. G.

Previous page
Cerosoli of Italy saves in the infamous Highbury 'battle' of 1934. England forwards Bowden and Drake are poised in readiness for a mistake.

Three double internationals. England players at both soccer and cricket:
1. **John Arnold, Fulham winger, Hampshire opener and latterly first-class umpire.**
2. **Andy Ducat, Aston Villa captain and Surrey cricketer.**
3. **The great C. B. Fry, of Corinthians, of Sussex, and athlete extraordinary.**
4. **The Moscow Dynamo tour in 1945. 'Tiger' Khomich saves for the Dynamos in the first match, a 3–3 draw with Chelsea.**

1

3

Richardson, who scored four goals in five minutes at West Ham in a first division match in 1931.

A League goal-scoring record was made in 1936 when Joe Payne, a reserve wing half whom Luton had signed from Bolsover Colliery, was asked to try his hand at centre forward during the crowded Easter programme. After starting nervously, Payne found it all so easy. Every time he tried a shot, in it went. To the astonishment of everybody, himself included, he came off at the end of the match with ten goals out of twelve. From then on Joe was always 'Ten-goal' Payne. Unfortunately, he did not enjoy good health, and only two years later, when transferred to Chelsea, he was already in decline. He nevertheless retained the happy knack of usually scoring once in a game.

There was a tragic accident to a goalkeeper in 1931. John Thomson was a heroic figure — young, charming and graceful, he had already demonstrated that he had extraordinary skills that seemed sure to lead to greatness, and at twenty-three he was already an international. In a dull Rangers-Celtic match at Ibrox Park, Sam English, the Rangers forward, was put right through with the chance to open the score. As he shot, Thomson dived to save, there was a sickening collision, and the goalkeeper's skull was fractured. He died that night without regaining consciousness. Several thousand attended his funeral. His name became a legend and his grave a shrine.

The England team had some fine goalkeepers in the thirties. From 1930 to 1936 Harry Hibbs was the automatic choice. He was a small man who needed great anticipation to achieve his supremacy — his handling was superb and he was very safe. Vic Woodley of Chelsea took over from him in 1937 and made his nineteen appearances in consecutive matches. The war spoilt his record. Not far behind was Sam Bartram, 'the best goalkeeper never to win a

1. **Stan Mortensen collides with Derek Ufton of Charlton Athletic at the Valley. Goalkeeper Sam Bartram is caught on the wrong foot and Mortensen scores.**
2. **'Ten-goal' Joe Payne in his Luton days.**
3. **The determination of Ted Drake is seen in this picture as he shoots from the left.**
4. **Celtic's John Thomson tips the ball over the bar. He died in tragic circumstances.**

1

3

4

cap'. He played 583 matches for Charlton Athletic between 1934 and 1956, and it was probably his daring in advancing out of his area when play was at the other end which led the selectors to prefer first Woodley and then others. It made him a favourite with the crowds, however.

In May 1938 an England team went to Berlin to play Germany in front of 110,000 spectators. Before the match the players were required as an act of courtesy to give the Nazi salute. None liked the idea, but they complied, and perhaps it increased their resolution to win. When Germany equalized an early England goal by Bastin, they appeared to get on top but two goals in five minutes by Jackie Robinson and Frank Broome put England 3–1 ahead and Germany from then on were never less than two behind. By the end more goals by Stan Matthews, Robinson again and Len Goulden helped England to a 6—3 victory. England wingers Bastin and Matthews had superb games, one dazzling by his speed, the other by his dribbling.

A player called Willie Hall had a great success later that year. Playing for England against Ireland he scored five consecutive goals in twenty-eight minutes in a 7–0 victory. However, it was the manner of the goals rather than the quantity which was so impressive. Hall was not known as a goalscorer, but on this occasion he combined his great ball-playing skill with perfect shooting. Moreover, he struck up an understanding with Stanley Matthews which looked likely to serve England for years.

Of course, in 1939, football ceased to be of any importance, and before it could get going again after the war Hall was in difficulties with thrombosis. He was forced to retire and eventually both his legs were amputated. Although he remained cheerful, mastered his artificial legs and took a pub, he died quite young.

Many players' careers ended at the outbreak of war, others bestraddled it. Stan Cullis, Wolves captain of the thirties, who played often for England

in 1938 and 1939, took over the Wolves managership after the war, no doubt feeling deprived of twenty or so caps. During the war, Cullis was stationed for some time at Aldershot, a weak third division side who found themselves able to field an England half-back line of Britton, Cullis, Mercer for war-time matches! Cliff Britton, of Everton, did not re-establish himself afterwards, and although his clubmate Joe Mercer went on and on, winning Championship and Cup medals with Arsenal until 1952, all his five international matches were in 1939.

Two of the greatest of all inside forwards, Raich Carter, who led Sunderland to a Cup victory in 1937, and Peter Doherty, who won a Championship medal with Manchester City in the same year, found themselves together at Derby County when football restarted and did much to win the first post-war Cup for Derby. Carter had silver hair, Irishman Doherty red: beneath these distinguished thatches were fine footballing brains.

The great Stanley Matthews played his first game for Stoke City in 1932, and was helping Stoke back to the first division thirty-one years later — the war was but a half-time in his career. Had Tom Finney, England's other outstanding winger, not appeared on the scene immediately after the war and invited comparisons with him, Matthews would have been more generally acknowledged as England's greatest footballer. Both players had the ability to win games on their own and both had peerless dribbling skills. Finney was the more complete footballer, being able to play on either wing or in the centre and possessing a talent for shooting as well as making goals, but Matthews had more mystique and could demoralize defenders by his mere presence. Matthews' individual skill sometimes frightened selectors concerned with teamwork, and he played for England only three times between 1950 and 1953. He was capped fifty-four times altogether.

Tommy Lawton, whose head was the target for many of Matthews' and Finney's centres, played eight times for England just before the war and fifteen times afterwards. He epitomized a type of centre forward much favoured by English selectors — a powerful dashing leader of the line with tremendous heading ability. Dixie Dean set the pattern; Lawton handed it on to Nat Lofthouse.

A great goalkeeper whose career the war divided into two parts was Frank Swift, who won a Cup-winner's medal as early as 1934, but won all his caps after the war. Blessed with

1. **Willie Hall, captaining Spurs, leads his team on to the field in 1936.**
2. **Peter Doherty, one of Ireland's best-ever players, in 1945.**
3. **Stanley Matthews in 1952, in the middle of his Blackpool period.**
4. **Another great winger, Preston's Tom Finney, in his England shirt, 1952.**
5. **Tommy Lawton playing for Arsenal in 1954 against Sheffield United.**

large hands, Swift made amazing saves, yet had the reputation of sometimes conceding easy goals. The best thing, football-wise, the war produced was Swift's successor in the Manchester City goal, Bert Trautmann, a German prisoner of war who didn't go home but stayed to delight crowds with some acrobatic displays.

Outstanding players who developed during the war to make their mark on the game immediately after it included Billy Wright, who had reported to Wolverhampton as a fifteen-year-old in 1939. He quickly established himself as Wolves' captain, then England's, and went on to become the first to play 100 times for his country. Throughout his career as a wing and centre half, Wright retained a schoolboyish enthusiasm for the game and never played far short of his considerable best.

Stan Mortensen of Blackpool first impressed during the war as a guest player for Arsenal, where his fearless diving headers and swashbuckling attacking play made him very exciting to watch. Contrasting with him was Wilf Mannion, a polished, assured ball-player from Middlesbrough. Alf Ramsey made a name with Southampton, and moving to Tottenham in 1949, gave full backs a new image, demonstrating that constructive play could begin in defence. Johnny Carey, of Manchester United and the Republic of Ireland, also demonstrated that cultured football was not out of place at full back.

'The Clown Prince of Football' — that was the title given to Len Shackleton of Sunderland in the late forties. After Matthews, he was the biggest draw in England, yet won only five caps, presumably because his

1. **England v Scotland at Wembley in 1953. George Young and Billy Wright lead out the two teams. England goalie Merrick looks apprehensive, but the score was 2–2.**
2. **A great inside forward before and after the Second World War, Raich Carter, of Sunderland, Derby and England.**
3. **Denis Compton in 1937 with great soccer and cricket fame to come.**
4. **Willie Watson, of Sunderland. Despite winning four English soccer caps, he is best remembered for a magnificent match-saving innings for England against Australia at Lords.**
5. **Martin Buchan, of Manchester United, playing against Spurs at White Hart Lane in 1972.**

dribbling skills were adjudged too great for more orthodox team-mates to cope with. Another Tyneside hero, Jackie Milburn, played only thirteen times for England. He relied on acceleration and played his football on the ground; selectors preferred centre forwards who could head in crosses.

Liverpool won the first post-war Championship, but it was the two teams who finished a point behind them, Manchester United and Wolves, who went on to dominate English football through the fifties. Under Sir Matt Busby, United had two great sides — that which won the 1948 Cup Final, and the completely new young side which was wrecked by the Munich air disaster ten years later. Perhaps Wolves' happiest contribution to English soccer was their demonstration that games with European sides could provide such splendid entertainment. Wolves staged a series of friendlies under floodlights with such teams as Honved of Hungary. They usually won, and produced a national hero in Johnny Hancocks, a tiny winger with just about the most powerful shot in the country. The inch-perfect centres of Hancocks and Mullen and the goalkeeping of international Bert Williams did much to maintain Wolves' challenge over the years.

Portsmouth won their only two Championships in successive seasons, 1948–50, with stalwarts in winger Peter Harris, play-anywhere Jack Froggatt and left half Jimmy Dickinson, who pulled on the royal blue shirt for a record number of 764 League games. Arsenal (twice), Spurs and Chelsea won Championships for London in the first ten post-war seasons. Spurs' success in 1950–51 was welcome in footballing terms, as they played a brand of neat interpassing soccer with fast-raiding wingers in Les Medley and Sonny Walters, a skilful general in Eddie Baily, a dependable goalie in Ted Ditchburn and an inspiring left half and captain in Ron Burgess, who also captained Wales.

1. Bristol Rovers ground at Eastville under 3 feet of water on an FA Cup day in 1951.
2. The Olympic Stadium, Berlin, 1936.
3. The Olympic Stadium, Rome, 1960.
4. Craven Cottage, Fulham, in 1931. The Thames runs swiftly behind the hoardings, which, alas, have now been replaced by a stand.

1

4

2

3

1. Frank Swift saves in Turin. Swift captained England in this magnificent 4–0 victory over Italy in 1948. Neil Franklin is the other England player in the picture, holding off Italian centre forward Gabetto.
2. Trevor Ford, the bustling Welsh centre forward, in his Sunderland days. He won 38 caps.
3. Welsh idol Ivor Allchurch scored 166 goals for Swansea Town (now City) and made 68 appearances for Wales from 1950.
4. Jackie Milburn playing in one of his thirteen games for England. He is shooting past Gyger, of Switzerland, at Highbury in 1948.
5. Jimmy Dickinson leading out the Portsmouth side for which he made a record number of appearances.
6. Danny Blanchflower, captain of Ireland and of Spurs in their double-winning year.

5

6

In Scotland, Rangers won the first post-war Championship, but were strongly challenged for supremacy by Hibernian, who shared equally the first six Championships with them. Celtic took a long time to get into their post-war stride. It was twenty years before they reached a position of dominance. In the meantime Hearts won their first Championship for sixty-one years in 1958, and Aberdeen, Dundee and Kilmarnock registered their only successes in 1955, 1962 and 1965 respectively.

An international flavour was brought to the British soccer scene in 1945 by the tour of Moscow Dynamo. It was the first revelation to home audiences of the humourless and thoroughly disciplined attitude of the Communist countries to sport: several conditions were insisted upon, relating to the opposition, the use of substitutes, practice facilities and social arrangements among others. Nobody took the Russians seriously, but the hunger of the British for entertainment led to the first match, against Chelsea, being gate-crashed by thousands who were locked out. Barriers were pushed over and hundreds got into the ground by crossing the railway line bordering one side. The Dynamos were 'allowed' a 3–3 draw by a generous offside decision in their favour. However, by the time the Russians had defeated Cardiff City 10–1, and an Arsenal side reinforced by England players 4–3, opinions of them had to be revised. The Arsenal match was comic — it was so foggy that from the centre circle neither goal was ever visible. The Russians obviously regarded this match, with the most famous British club, as the climax of their tour, and after the game players told of strange decisions by the Russian referee quite invisible to the spectators. A 2–2 draw with Glasgow Rangers saw Moscow Dynamo depart unbeaten.

In 1947 a Great Britain side beat the Rest of Europe 6–1 at Hampden Park, with an attack which read: Matthews, Mannion, Lawton, Steel, Liddell. The left-wing pair were Scots of great talent whose careers took opposite directions. Billy Steel was transferred from Morton to Derby County for £15,000 in 1947, but his career there was never smooth. Steel

The poise, balance and power of Nat Lofthouse are well demonstrated as he shoots past Belgian defenders Carre and Diricx to score for England in 1952.

1

2

1. Billy Steel chases the ball into the net as he scores Scotland's second goal in a 3–1 defeat of England at Wembley in 1949.
2. Puskas virtuosity. The third Hungarian goal at Wembley in 1953. Johnston is on the goal line, Merrick on the floor, and Wright has just been on the end of a devastating piece of sleight-of-foot by Puskas.
3. The powerful thighs and all-round physique of Duncan Edwards are clearly seen in this picture taken less than a year before the Munich tragedy in which he lost his life.

Next page
The great Manchester United team shattered by the Munich air crash (inset). The team was returning from a European Cup game with Red Star in Belgrade when the plane crashed on take-off after a stop at Munich. Eight players, together with club staff and journalists, died. The team is *left to right, back:* Duncan Edwards, Bill Foulkes, Mark Jones, Ray Wood, Eddie Colman, David Pegg. *Front:* John Berry, Bill Whelan, Roger Byrne (captain), Tommy Taylor, Dennis Viollet.

insisted on training in Scotland and meeting his team-mates only on match days. Three years later he was bought by Dundee for £23,000, more than double the Scottish record transfer fee. In 1954, an automatic choice for Scotland, with 30 caps in six seasons, Steel suddenly decided to go to California. Billy Liddell on the other hand, spent his whole career at Liverpool, turning out over 500 times and winning 28 caps as a powerful goal-scoring winger. He later became a Liverpool J.P.

Scotland had some great defenders in the early fifties. Willie Woodburn of Rangers was dominating at centre half but had one flaw — a fighting nature which led to a series of suspensions and ultimately to a complete ban from football in 1954. George Young of Rangers was right back in many Scottish sides with Woodburn; on Woodburn's suspension he took over at centre half. Young looked awkward and top-heavy, but was a very difficult man to pass. He played fifty-three times for Scotland, usually as captain. Sammy Cox was another Ranger in the Scottish team, usually at left back where he was a fearless tackler. Bobby Evans of Celtic came into the Scottish side in 1949 and played forty-eight times, initially at wing half but later as a successor to Woodburn and Young in the centre.

Until 1950 there was little reason to suspect that England were not still among the soccer masters of the world. In 1947 England arrived in Lisbon on a tour which had seen them lose lackadaisically 1–0 to Switzerland in Zurich. Determined to retrieve their reputation the England team produced a fantastic performance against Portugal, winning 10–0. Tom Finney, a competitor for Stan Matthews's right-wing place, was played on the

1. Alf Ramsey sticking out his chest for Spurs in 1952. Performing the acrobatics is Charlie Wayman of Preston.
2. Rodney Marsh, surrounded by West Bromwich Albion players, scoring his memorable goal in the 1967 League Cup Final. Queens Park Rangers won 3–2.
3. Irish and Welsh greats. Danny Blanchflower of Tottenham fails to stop John Charles of Leeds from crossing the ball in a match at White Hart Lane in 1956.
4. Welsh goalkeeper Jack Kelsey beats England centre forward Bobby Smith to the ball this time, but England won 5–1 at Wembley in 1960.

left wing. It was Finney's first season for England and the first time he and Matthews played on opposite wings. Finney staked his claim to greatness in that match, turning on a dazzling exhibition of all the footballing arts. He rated this the finest England display he'd ever seen, particularly from the point of view of their teamwork.

Another uplifting win came in Italy the following season, in a match played to celebrate the fiftieth anniversary of the Italian FA. Italy expected to win, having prepared carefully, but a superb display by England won them the match 4–0. Matthews and Finney again were outstanding, but pride of place this time went to Stan Mortensen, who had made his début in the massacre of Portugal (scoring four), and by now was an essential member of perhaps England's best-ever forward line.

In 1950 England suffered a humiliating defeat by the USA in the World Cup, and all complacency disappeared. Some muddling results followed, relieved only by a heroic display in Vienna, when, with ten minutes left and the score 2–2, stouthearted Nat Lofthouse set off on a lone dash for the Austrian goal and scored the winner as he collided with the goalkeeper. Carried off, he yet returned for the final minutes and earned himself the proud title 'The Lion of Vienna'. In 1953 and 1954 England's need to rethink her soccer strategy became clear with two crushing defeats by Hungary. Scotland had lost at home for the first time in 1950, 1–0 to Austria, and British football was subjected to a period of re-examination.

This led to a devaluation of the home International tournament, as it was seen that for a time at least the home countries were below top class. England, with a strong attack, and Scotland, with an outstanding defence, won the first five post-war Championships, but Wales shared with England in 1952.

Welsh giants were Alf Sherwood, forty-one times an international at left back; Roy Paul, a polished right half of Manchester City who formed a superb half-back line with Arsenal's Ray Daniel and Spurs' Ron Burgess; Trevor Ford, who played for Swansea, Aston Villa, Sunderland and Cardiff, and for whom Sunderland paid a record £30,000 in 1950, an

The majesty of the Law. The long arm of Blacklaw fails to stop Denis Law from scoring in typical fashion for Manchester United against Burnley in 1965.

intimidating centre forward who frightened goalkeepers with his physical commitment; Jack Kelsey, of Arsenal, first-choice goalkeeper from 1954 to 1962; and Ivor Allchurch, the blond 'golden boy' of Wales, who preferred to play most of his career with struggling second-division Swansea Town. Allchurch was the complete inside forward — fast, exciting, artistic and with a powerful shot. John Charles, the 'Gentle Giant', came into the Welsh side in 1950 aged eighteen, and earned a regular place soon afterwards as an inside forward to Ford and later as centre forward and centre half. His great physique was never used unfairly, even when under great provocation in the 1958 World Cup when the Hungarians cynically fouled him repeatedly. The ball seemed the size of a tennis ball at Charles's feet, and he was like a man playing with boys. Deadly with head or foot, he was attracted to Italy in 1957. Returning in 1962, he was already past his best. Perhaps it is difficult for a man of his size to retain the edge of his form for many years.

Ireland, too, although not having enough good players to win the Championship until all four countries finished with three points each in 1955–56, nevertheless had two or three outstanding ones. Billy Bingham and Danny Blanchflower, who started their careers with Glentoran, each won a record fifty-six caps. Bingham was an orthodox, fast-running, dribbling right winger who played for Sunderland, Luton and Everton, and later managed the Ireland side. Blanchflower was a skilful wing half and captain, thoughtful and articulate,

1. Welsh international Phil Woosnam, who went to America in an attempt to popularize soccer there.
2. Jimmy Greaves scoring for Tottenham against Newcastle in 1969 after a run from half-way. Moncur is the defender.
3. Dave Mackay, a Spurs stalwart when the double was achieved in 1960–61.
4. Spurs manager in 1960–61 was Bill Nicholson, the right half of ten years earlier.
5. Triumphant Tottenham with the League Championship Trophy and FA Cup. *Left to right, back:* Bill Brown, Peter Baker, Ron Henry, Danny Blanchflower (captain), Maurice Norman, Dave Mackay. *Front:* Cliff Jones, John White, Bobby Smith, Les Allen, Terry Dyson.

Captains of England and Ireland. Johnny Haynes has the better of this duel with Danny Blanchflower. Jimmy McIlroy (Ireland) and Bobby Robson (England) watch events.

1

3

56

Great goalkeepers:

1. Jim Standen of West Ham United peers into the floodlit Highbury gloom, a Hammer looking for Gunners.
2. The best goalkeeper in the world? Pat Jennings catches the ball for Ireland as England's Mike Summerbee moves in, Wembley 1972. Jennings remained unbeaten and Ireland won 1–0.
3. Peter Shilton, successor to Gordon Banks in both the Leicester City and England goals.
4. The best goalkeeper in the world until 1972. Gordon Banks watches a shot go past the post in the 1972 League Cup Final. A few months later an eye injury seriously interrupted his career.

who talked a good game and invented the desperate Irish strategy of equalizing before the other side scored. His inside-forward colleague and partner in soccer incisiveness and verbal duets was Jimmy McIlroy, of Burnley, who was adept at shielding the ball with his body and holding it until the best time came to release it. These three helped Ireland to their best recent performance in home matches in 1957 when England were defeated 3–2 at Wembley, and then took Ireland to the quarter-finals of the World Cup in 1958.

In 1955 John Haynes played his first game for England. He was to play fifty-five more, twenty as captain. Haynes was the best passer of the ball English football has had. The rest of his game — shooting, heading, dribbling — was but average, but he earns his place among the greats by virtue of a kind of geometric insight which enabled him to work out angles and find openings which only became apparent when a precisely weighted pass set a colleague free on his way to goal. Haynes' entire career was with Fulham, much of it in the second division. He won no League or Cup honours; only the appreciation of connoisseurs.

The Munich air disaster of 1958 dealt a terrible blow to British soccer and to Manchester United. Eight players died and others were severely injured. Duncan Edwards, England's youngest-ever player, already had eighteen caps when he died aged twenty-one, and the authority of this big strong left half suggested that he would have captained England eventually. Tommy Taylor had nineteen caps, with many more to come, at centre forward. Roger Byrne, left back and captain, was an England regular with thirty-three caps. David Pegg had just gained his first cap, Eddie Colman was surely about to win his. Bill Whelan, a great player for the Republic of Ireland, Geoff Bent and Mark Jones also died.

The young team had won the Championship by large margins in the two seasons before the disaster and seemed set to become the greatest club team of modern times.

A Munich survivor was Bobby Charlton, who became England's best-loved footballer, winning a record number of caps (106) and

The bravery and timing of Bob Wilson. Wilson gets both hands to the ball just as Jimmy Pearce of Tottenham connects. Peter Simpson and Terry Neill are the other Arsenal defenders.

1

2

scoring 49 goals for England, also a record. His greatest assets were speed and directness, a delightful body swerve and a thunderous shot, his best positions being inside or centre forward. He won all the game's important honours, including a European Cup medal, which must have given him great satisfaction. Charlton was one of the game's gentlemen, always chivalrous, never known to commit a bad foul or to retaliate. Like Matthews and Finney and a long line of other great players back to Woodward and Pennington, Charlton played the game as a game and would not allow feuds, fouls or even minor niggling to distract him from the purposes of developing his skills and winning the match.

Manchester United's annual Championship challenge stuttered a little after Munich, until a second place in 1963–64 was followed by a win the following year. Wolves' powers, conversely, reached their peak in the last years of the fifties. Wins in 1958 and 1959 were followed by a season, 1959–60, when Wolves won the Cup and were foiled of the 'double' and a hat-trick of Championships only by Burnley, who had to win their last away match to do it. Wolves then declined and spent two seasons in the second division from 1965 to 1967.

A proud record ended in 1958. Sunderland joined the League in its third season and had been members of the first division ever since, until after sixty-eight years they were relegated on goal average.

Spurs, who were still in the Southern League years after Sunderland had first won the Championship, performed the 'double' in 1960–61, a feat which like the four-minute mile had appeared to have a psychological barrier operating against its achievement in modern times. Blanchflower's silver tongue helped him lead through this barrier such players as barrel-chested Dave Mackay, a Scottish international who still played a good first division game after twice breaking a leg and John White, 'the ghost', who when he wasn't floating through defences

Athletic Charlton:
1. **Bobby Charlton, playing for England against Brazil in Mexico, 1970, stands on one hand.**
2. **An airborne shot for Manchester United against Chelsea in 1966. Eddie McCreadie looks on.**
3. **A man with sad and happy soccer memories.**

1

2

62

floated delightful chips on to the heads of Bobby Smith, England centre forward, or Cliff Jones, flying Welsh winger.

Tommy Harmer had played for Spurs between the Championship years of 1951 and 1961 without ever having a regular place. In tight situations he had the talent of creating openings with inch-perfect chips and clever deflections, but he was extremely small, and looked frail and weak. Manager Bill Nicholson never had the courage to give him an extended run in the first team.

Ipswich Town won the Championship in 1961–62, a remarkable success for a club thought of as typically second division; they had won promotion only the season before. It was a triumph of team spirit, helped by consistent goalscoring by two big attackers, Ray Crawford and Ted Phillips, who between them scored sixty-one of Ipswich's ninety-three goals. Lancashire then took over the Championship and the next six winners were Everton, Liverpool, Manchester United, Liverpool again, Manchester United again and Manchester City.

Manchester United's forward line in these years included two other great players alongside Bobby Charlton — George Best and Denis Law. Winger Best has all the talents. He is a great dribbler who allies strength to finesse making it very difficult for any opponent to take the ball from him, he has a hard and accurate shot, he is a fine header, and he has a fierce competitive spirit. Law's main assets were a quick eye to spot a goalscoring chance, fearlessness in going for it and a tremendous leap which allowed him to produce superb headers from all angles.

Leeds United, who had been consistently just missing League and Cup honours from 1964–65, finally broke the Lancashire monopoly to win the Championship for the first time in 1968–69. They were undoubtedly the best side in England at the time, without a weakness. Cooper and

1. George Best equalizes for Manchester United against Stoke City in a sixth round FA Cup match in 1972. Stoke nevertheless won the replay.
2. Another sixth round match of 1972. Billy Bremner of Leeds United, a notoriously hard tackler, is strongly tackled himself by Cyril Knowles (Spurs).
3. Jack Charlton's giraffe-like neck in evidence as he gets in a header against Mike England.

3

Reaney were fast, attacking full backs, addicted to overlapping their team-mates down the flanks. Cooper, a master of modern full-back play, occasionally played as an orthodox outside left. The tall Jack Charlton at centre half was England's choice for the 1966 World Cup — his giraffe-like neck enabled him not only to nod away countless crosses aimed at his own goal, but also to nod in many vital goals at his opponents' end. Billy Bremner was an extremely combative captain, often, indeed, in his early days too aggressive, earning a reputation as a rough player, but he reformed somewhat and later was as much sinned against as sinning. He would have been in anybody's Great Britain selection of the day, as would his colleague from Eire, Johnny Giles, with whom he ruled so often the mid-field. Giles's play lacked fireworks, but he was always in position and his neat and accurate passing supplied the chances for Mick Jones and, later, Allan Clarke, spearheads for Leeds and England, to score the goals. Utility man was Paul Madeley, good enough to play for England at full back, and good enough to play for Leeds wherever he was required. The outside right, Peter Lorimer, had the hardest shot in Britain. Leeds' supremacy in 1968–69 was reflected in the record number of first division points, sixty-seven.

Celtic took over the Scottish League in 1965–66 beginning a record sequence of wins. Jimmy Johnstone, a small redheaded winger, astonished with some breathtaking dribbling: less spectacular but just as crucial to the all-round consistency of the performances were mid-field man Bobby Murdoch and defender Billy McNeill. Celtic players collected Scottish caps, Cup medals and League medals with a regularity embarrassing to Rangers' supporters in particular, and in 1966–67 added European Cup medals to the collection. It was a time when the idea of a British super-league, in which Celtic could be regularly tested against Leeds and the Manchester, Liverpool and London clubs, was particularly attractive.

In 1960, the Football League Cup was introduced. Many top clubs ignored it at first, seeing it as a minor competition to clutter up still further an already exhausting programme. It

Nine trophies and the men who won them. Glasgow Celtic won all the competitions they entered in 1966–67. The playing staff is photographed with manager Jock Stein and trainers.

1

2

4

5

6

7

has gained some spurious value latterly, as winners are entitled to European competition the following season, but has failed to capture public imagination as the FA Cup has. Few matches are remembered, although exceptions are the 3–2 defeat of West Bromwich Albion by third division Queens Park Rangers in the Final of 1966–67, when Rodney Marsh crowned a scintillating performance with a magnificent individual goal, and the 1971–72 Final, in which George Eastham scored the winner which gave Stoke City a popular if slightly undeserved 2–1 victory over Chelsea — popular because it was Stoke's first trophy.

England were supreme in the Home International Tournament throughout the sixties, scoring nine goals against Scotland in 1961, the highest in a hundred years of matches between the two countries. It was a match in which the great provider, Haynes, played with the great scorer, Greaves; between them Bobby Smith's brawn ensured a wearing time for the Scottish defence.

Jimmy Greaves was British soccer's best marksman. Slight in build, his delicate footwork eased him through tight situations with the grace and artistry of a ballet-dancer, particularly in the penalty area; he shot goals instantly when momentary chances appeared. His dribbling was top-class, but his heading was mediocre and his shooting not explosive. It was his instinctive appreciation of the situation, quick reflexes, utter coolness and accuracy which brought him 491 goals. He never played in any division but the first, and is the only player to score five goals in a match on four occasions.

England celebrated the Centenary of the Football Association in 1963 with a 2–1 win over the Rest of the World and in 1966 celebrated the greatest prize of all — the winning of the World Cup. Several players made or enhanced their reputations in this tournament. Gordon Banks from 1966 till he damaged an eye in a car crash in 1972 was freely called 'the greatest

1. Allan Clarke lets fly for England.
2. Martin Chivers has just scored.
3. Bobby Moore (West Ham) gets the ball away from Chris Garland (Chelsea).
4. Roy McFarland in Derby County strip.
5. Emlyn Hughes of Liverpool.
6. Kevin Keegan, a recent Liverpool favourite.
7. Ron Davies of Southampton leaps high.

Goià

1

3

goalkeeper in the world' and no further words can add to that. George Cohen and Ray Wilson at full back were not only so efficient in defence that not a goal was conceded until the closing minutes of the semi-final, they were also an essential part of the England attack. Geoff Hurst was a powerful spearhead, scoring the quarter-final winner and the first-ever hat-trick in the Final. Bobby Charlton also scored vital goals. Alan Ball did more running and expended more energy than any other man in the competition, nearly always to good effect. Martin Peters, the other main mid-field provider achieved as good results by the opposite means, stealth and positioning. Nobby Stiles and Roger Hunt demonstrated, perhaps, that application could win honours even when natural talent was limited. Jack Charlton sealed the centre and the side was completed by Bobby Moore.

Moore, captain of England, was elected player of the tournament. He played in the 1962 World Cup also and captained England again in the 1970 competition and for many years has been a tower of strength in English soccer. He is a superb defender, with good anticipation and so strong that he rarely loses a tackle. He distributes the ball well, is always in the game and quite unflappable, and is an inspiring captain with an authority that comes from his coolness and the example of his own play.

A change in British football in 1966 of less immediate impact than the World Cup win but of continuing significance, came from the decision to allow substitutes in matches. Reactionaries had fought against this

Previous page
Peter Osgood receives attention from Chelsea trainer Harry Medhurst during a match with Manchester United in 1971. Osgood was on the transfer list at the time for 'not trying', but afterwards settled his differences with the club.

1. **Rodney Marsh of Manchester City attempts to burst between Arsenal defenders Eddie Kelly and Frank McLintock.**
2. **Colin Bell of Manchester City combines determination with grace and balance as he bursts through against Arsenal.**
3. **Arsenal goalkeeper Bob Wilson at the feet of Steve Kindon in a 1969 match against Burnley.**
4. **Francis Lee of Manchester City tries an overhead kick. Spurs' Phil Beal is unimpressed.**

Alan Hudson of Chelsea
has beaten a challenge
by John Pratt of Spurs,
but must untangle his
legs before proceeding.

1

2

5

6

7

innovation for some time, fearing that somehow the 'concession' would be abused, but frequent substitution is now common, and its potential use is part of the manager's strategy when planning match tactics.

Arsenal greeted the seventies with a performance to suggest that the palmy days of the thirties might yet be known again at Highbury. Arsenal finished the 1970–71 season with a tremendous run of success which gained them twenty-seven points from their last fifteen League games and also saw them into the Cup Final. The League run was enough to overhaul by one point Leeds United, who at one time appeared to have the Championship sewn up and, when the Cup Final was won, Arsenal became the fourth side to achieve the 'double'. The feat was performed without a really outstanding player, but with eleven better-than-average ones who understood each other's strengths and weaknesses and played to them with a sound grasp of the needs of the modern game. Frank McLintock was a good example — an inspiring captain who 'read' a match very well and changed the tactics to suit the circumstances with invariable success. Bob Wilson, a Scottish

1. Johnny Giles of Leeds seems to be saying 'I've heard it all before' as he is lectured by referee Dawes of Norwich.
2. Violence from the fans. Twenty-two people went to hospital after disturbances during a Newcastle United v Rangers Fairs Cup semi-final in 1969. Police with dogs cleared the pitch.
3. The same match, as bottles begin to fly.
4. Roy McFarland, Derby County, and Eddie Gray, Leeds United.
5. Italian referee Gouella warns Alan Ball (England) during an international match with Scotland.
6. Ron Harris, Chelsea captain, with the European Cup-winners Cup, 1971.
7. Trevor Francis averaged a goal a game for a long time after his debut for Birmingham City in season 1970–71.
8. Kevin Keegan of Liverpool at full stretch to touch the ball in against Manchester City. Joe Corrigan is as determined to save.
9. Not a strange dance, but West Ham's Bobby Moore and Tommy Taylor attempting to prevent Terry Conroy of Stoke getting in a centre.

1

2

3

international, was consistency itself in goal, risking injury every week with brave dives at the feet of forwards. George Armstrong epitomized the Arsenal spirit. Determination and effort raised him from a routine winger to the brink of a cap. George Graham provided the only finesse, and powerful attackers John Radford and Ray Kennedy provided most of the goals.

The 1971–72 League campaign was unsatisfactory in that the Championship was in a sense won by default, both Liverpool and Leeds failing in their last matches when the title was theirs for the taking. Derby County, with a team in which twin spearheads Kevin Hector and John O'Hare, scoring winger Alan Hinton, schemer Archie Gemmill and polished centre half and captain Roy McFarland were outstanding, was the first side to complete its forty-two matches and ended with fifty-eight points. Liverpool needed a win at Arsenal in their last match to pass Derby on goal average but could only draw 0–0, although claiming that a late disallowed 'goal' by Toshack was legitimate. Leeds United won the Cup Final, and two days later visited Wolves for their last League match needing only a draw to crown several seasons' success with the coveted 'double' which had eluded them for so long. Their crowded programme, however, had produced injuries and tiredness and they surprisingly lost 2–1. Derby County were on a close-season tour abroad when they learned, no doubt with astonishment and gratification, that their rivals had failed and they were the Champions.

Leeds and Liverpool fought out the Championship again in 1972–73, Arsenal also being contenders. Long Cup runs by Leeds and Arsenal perhaps caused their Championship challenges to falter, but Liverpool, too, had a late shaky spell, from which they recovered just in time. Soon after

Easter, victory over Leeds virtually clinched them the title. They deserved to win, but the fact remains that their football was workmanlike rather than inspired. Keegan, Cormack and Heighway provided exhilarating moments, but Liverpool's success was as much based on the more routine strength and honest effort of such as captain Tommy Smith, Emlyn Hughes, Alex Lindsay and Chris Lawler. Clemence was a sound goalkeeper.

Lancashire won all four English leagues, Burnley, Bolton Wanderers and Southport also finishing top of their tables.

Derby County, who had the find of the season, Roger Davies, at centre forward, and who reached the European Cup semi-final, played as well as anybody. Crystal Palace spent a million pounds and appointed Malcolm Allison as manager, but were relegated. Manchester United appointed Tommy Docherty and stayed up. However, they lost the services of George Best, who retired, however temporarily, in ignominy, and Bobby Charlton, who retired more permanently with world-wide tributes. Celtic, for the eighth successive time, won the Scottish Championship, but only by a point from Rangers.

Disturbing trends came to a head in the seventies. Violence by fans had been a problem for some years. Most top clubs were saddled with gangs of vicious, youthful supporters who followed the team around, more interested in the 'bovver' they could cause than in the game itself. The destruction of railway coaches, particularly after a lost away game, became frequent, and shopkeepers in the vicinity of grounds suffered pilfering and smashed windows. Aggravation took place between rival hooligans both on the terraces and outside, and occasionally missiles were thrown on to the pitch. Publicity only served to increase the gangs' notoriety and bravado. Violence by the players was held by some to be an example and a provocation to these louts, and a welcome move by the authorities in season 1971–72 was an instruction to referees to be more severe on players who fouled.

The referee's campaign continued in season 1972–73 and unquestionably has done the game itself much good. It is unedifying and bad publicity when fifty or so players are booked for offences on one Saturday, or when at any given time several players are under suspension, but soccer as an art is improving and players are encouraged to hold the ball and develop the finer skills.

Unfortunately, violence on the terraces has not diminished. Bookings

1. The Big Match. Thames Television cameras filming Spurs v Huddersfield Town in 1972.
2. Britain's worst-ever soccer disaster happened on 2 January 1971 when 66 people died and 140 were injured at Ibrox Stadium, Glasgow. Officials study the buckled crash barriers on the staircase where a dreadful crush occurred at the end of a Rangers-Celtic match.
3. Alan Ball of Champions Arsenal beats John McGovern of about-to-be-Champions Derby County in a 1972 League match. Arsenal won 2–0.

1

4

5

2　　**3**

are provocations in themselves, but basically the vandal element needs no encouragement. Its nastiness is endemic to society at large and football is only a convenient excuse for its expression.

Falling attendances in the 1972–73 season caused concern. It is clear that the altered nature of the soccer crowd itself persuaded many potential followers to keep away. In ten years or so the crowd has changed from being good-natured, basically tolerant, appreciative of 'wags' and largely a reflection of working-class attitudes and humour to being a more parochial, chanting, often bad-mannered and bad-languaged example of the worst aspects of the permissive society. A move to encourage more women spectators in the sixties has foundered.

Meanwhile, soccer itself is as good as ever. The inspiration of Peter Osgood, the goalkeeping of Pat Jennings and Peter Shilton, the power of Martin Chivers, the heading of Ron Davies, the solidity of Mike England, the personality of Derek Dougan, the flick-heading of Alan Gilzean, the goalscoring of Ted MacDougall, the flamboyance of Rodney Marsh — all these graced the sixties as they would have any other decade.

And the stars of the seventies? Some at least can be forecast with confidence. Roy McFarland could become one of England's best-ever centre halves. The young Trevor Francis will develop his precocious knack of scoring goals. Kevin Keegan, who arrived from Scunthorpe United to delight Bill Shankly and the Kop at Anfield will go on to delight all England. Lou Macari, Martin Buchan and David Hay could lead a Scottish revival. Leighton James will remind Welshmen more and more of Ivor Allchurch. These men and their like will never eclipse Steve Bloomer, Vivian Woodward, Billy Meredith or Alan Morton, but they might well one day stand beside them as the greats of British soccer.

1. Cormack scoring for Liverpool against Leeds, Easter, 1973 . . .
2. . . . and being congratulated by Emlyn Hughes.
3. Roger Davies, of Derby County, exciting new player of 1972–73.
4. Arsenal's 'double' dream ends. Hughes (left) scores Sunderland's second goal in the Cup semi-final, April 1973.
5. Leeds also attempting the 'double'. In the other semi-final Richards' shot for Wolves hit the post and Leeds won.

79

FA CUP

In England, to ask the question 'who will win the Cup' is to invite as answer the name of a football team, since to nearly all Englishmen 'the Cup' means the Football Association Challenge Cup.

The Football Association itself was formed in 1863, and is the oldest soccer association in the world. In 1870 C. W. Alcock became Secretary, and it is to him that most credit must go for the institution of the FA Cup. He proposed the idea at a meeting on 20 July 1871, and the first competition was soon under way. Only fifteen teams entered — half the membership of the FA at the time. Alcock himself was the captain of the winners, Wanderers.

Another man at the famous 1871 meeting was M. P. Betts, who, in the first Final, scored the only goal. He played under the pseudonym of A. H. Chequer, an early variation on the 'A. N. Other' theme, since this stood for 'A Harrow Chequer', Harrow Chequers being one of the teams which had entered the competition, but had subsequently scratched in the first round.

It is noteworthy that many of the early FA officials were prominent players of the day. Also at the 1871 meeting was Major Sir Francis Marindin, three years later to be President of the FA. He was the force behind the Royal Engineers, one of the strongest teams in the country, and led them in two Finals. His successor as FA President was Lord Kinnaird, who played in no fewer than nine Cup Finals, winning five winners' medals.

Three other teams joined the Royal Engineers in dominating the early years of the Cup. These were the Wanderers, Oxford University and Old Etonians, and the first eight Cup Finals were between permutations of these four sides.

As Wanderers developed from a club formed by Old Harrovians, it is clear that much of the best Cup

Glidden, with the FA Cup, and West Bromwich Albion players in 1931. It took forty-two years for the next second division victory — Sunderland's in 1973.

football of the times was being played and learnt at the public schools and universities. The two graduates, Heighway and Hall, who played in the Liverpool forward line in the 1971 Cup Final would have provoked no comment, at least by reason of their scholarship, in the 1870s.

Almost everything else about the 1971 Cup Final would have, however. In the early years of the Cup, crowds were much smaller — it was twenty-nine years before a Final was watched by 100,000 people. The style of play was quite different, the emphasis being on dribbling skills. Even the goals were different, tapes being used instead of crossbars, and nets being things of the future. 'Shorts' covered the knees, and the referees used flags instead of whistles.

With the spread of professionalism, legalized in 1885, the clubs whose names are now so well known began to appear in the records. Of the clubs who might have a chance of winning the trophy today, Blackburn Rovers were the first to reach the Final, and they were beaten 1–0 in 1882 by Old Etonians, the last amateur club to win the Cup. Blackburn Rovers recorded the first of their six wins in 1884, and two years later were awarded a special trophy for winning three years in succession. They weren't the first side to do this, the last of the Wanderers' five wins in 1878 being their third in succession. According to the rules in force, this entitled them to keep the Cup, but they returned it to the FA on condition that this rule was changed. No other club has won the Cup three times in succession, and of course it would be a supreme feat were it achieved in these competitive days, but Newcastle United and Tottenham Hotspur have each scored two successive wins since the Second World War.

Great footballing deeds were performed in the fifty years of the Cup before the first Wembley Final in 1923. Perhaps the most remarkable was the performance of 'Proud Preston' in the season 1888–89. They won the Cup without conceding a goal, beating Wolverhampton Wanderers in the Final 3–0. This was also the first year of the Football League, which Preston won without losing a match, becoming the first side to achieve the 'double'. The previous season they had made the record score in an FA Cup tie, beating Hyde 26–0.

Aston Villa became the second side to win Cup and League in the same season in 1897, when they beat Everton 3–2 in the Cup Final. Between 1894 and 1900 Villa won one of the two competitions each season except one.

With Blackburn Rovers, Everton, Bolton and Bury joining Preston as great Cup-fighters from Lancashire, and Derby County, Notts County, West Bromwich Albion and Wolves joining Villa as stalwarts from the Midlands, the Cup traditions of these two areas were well established at the end of the nineteenth century. Bury, in 1903, achieved the biggest Cup Final victory yet, 6–0 against Derby County, and it was a Blackburn Rovers player, W. Townley, who scored the first hat-trick in the Final, in the 6–1 defeat of Sheffield Wednesday in 1890.

In the early 1900s Newcastle United became a force in the game. They won the League three times between 1904 and 1909, and in 1910 began their great Cup record by scoring the first of their six wins, beating Barnsley 2–0 in a replay, after drawing 1–1 in the first match.

Tottenham Hotspur struck an isolated blow for the South and London in 1901, beating Sheffield United 3–1 in a replayed Final at Bolton, after 110,000 people had watched the earlier 2–2 draw at Crystal Palace. Spurs at that time were in the Southern League, and remain the only non-League side to win the Cup. Tottenham won the Cup again in 1921, but it wasn't until 1930 that another southern club, Arsenal, were successful. The six wins scored by southern clubs since 1960 represent nearly half the South's total!

The great Sheffield rivals, Wednesday and United, each won the Cup in the last four years of the nineteenth century, and have now won it seven times between them — the only Yorkshire clubs in the first hundred years of the Cup to win more than once. Barnsley and Bradford City won for Yorkshire in 1911 and 1912, but City's win may have had something to do with Yorkshire 'closeness' since the trophy they won was a new one recently made in Bradford!

This was the third and present trophy, the first having been stolen on a famous occasion in Birmingham in 1895, while it was in the possession of Aston Villa. Taken from a bootmaker's window, the Cup was never recovered, despite huge publicity and the offer of a £10 reward for information. The second trophy was awarded to Lord Kinnaird in 1911 for services to the game.

This then, was the pattern of events in the first fifty years of the FA Cup, leading up to the astonishing scenes before the first Wembley Final in 1923.

Just built, Wembley was confidently expected to hold all who came. Only 53,000 had been present at Stamford

Bridge in 1922, and Wembley's capacity was 127,000, just 1,000 less than the record crowd of 1913. In the event, about 200,000 forced themselves into the stadium, many over the walls, and at the scheduled time for the kick-off the pitch was covered with people. Police desperately worked to clear them. A constable riding a conspicuous white horse did much to urge the crowd back to the touchlines and overnight became the most famous policeman in the country. The match, between Bolton Wanderers and West Ham United, eventually started about forty-five minutes late. Bolton won 2–0, with goals from David Jack and J. R. Smith. Each time the ball went out of play it was likely to rebound from the wall of spectators, but Ted Vizard's story that the best pass he received all afternoon was from the foot of a supporter was no doubt a joke.

Bolton – the 'Trotters' – were much the best Cup-fighters of the twenties. They were back at Wembley in 1926, and again David Jack opened the scoring. This time his goal was the only one of the match against Manchester City. After another three-year interval Bolton took the trophy again, beating Portsmouth 2–0 in the Final, goals coming from Butler and Blackmore. Butler was the only forward to play in all three winning sides, but four defenders were ever-present – Dick Pym, the goalkeeper who did not concede a goal on his three Wembley appearances, Howarth, the right back and two strong half backs, Nuttall and Seddon. Other great Bolton players who played in the first

1. The 'Old Invincibles' – Preston North End of 1885–89. The players are *left to right, back:* Drummond, Howarth, Russell, Holmes, Graham, Mills-Roberts. *Front:* Gordon, Ross (J). Goodall, Dewhurst, Thomson.
2. The 1914 Cup Final at Crystal Palace. Burnley beat Liverpool 1–0.
3. First Wembley Cup winners. The Bolton team of 1923, *from left:* Joe Smith (capt.) Haworth, Butler, J. R. Smith, Nuttall, Finney, Jennings, Vizard, Jack, Pym, Seddon.
4. Tottenham Hotspur won the Cup in 1901 when in the Southern League – the last non-Leaguers to win.
5. The crowd on the pitch before the first Wembley Final of 1923.
6. The rival captains of 1923: George Kay (West Ham) and Joe Smith (Bolton Wanderers).

two Finals were Ted Vizard, the left winger, Joe Smith, who was Blackpool manager in later years, and David Jack, who was back at Wembley twice more in the thirties with Arsenal, getting a third winner's medal.

Cardiff City had their best-ever team in the twenties. In 1925 they were at Wembley to lose narrowly to Sheffield United, and two years later they experienced the greatest moment in their history, taking the Cup out of England for the first and only time. They beat Arsenal 1–0, the goal being credited to Ferguson, but it was more in the nature of an own goal by the Arsenal goalkeeper, Dan Lewis, a Welsh international. Lewis appeared to have the shot well held, but then in a series of fumbles which must have seemed to last an age he contrived to push the ball slowly into his own net. This must be the most publicized goalkeeping error of all time, calculated to haunt Lewis for the rest of his life. Even in 1972 the flickering piece of film was displayed to millions in a special Cup Centenary Year television programme.

This was Arsenal's first Final, and the bitter memory was erased three years later when they won the Cup and began a decade of supremacy in English football which made them the most famous side in the world. Their opponents were Huddersfield Town, who themselves were at the end of a golden period. It would be pleasant to record that goalkeeper Lewis this time

1. The ball entering the net for the only goal of the 1927 Final, fumbled there by Lewis, the Arsenal goalkeeper. Cardiff were winners.
2. Cardiff City: the only side to take the Cup out of England. The players photographed with it are *left to right, back:* Thirlaway, Nelson, Davis (L), Farquharson, Sloan, Watson, Curtis. *Front:* Hardy, Ferguson, Keenor (capt.), Irving, Pirie, McLachlan.
3. Bullock of Huddersfield (left) and Ducat of Aston Villa, the rival captains, shake hands before the 1920 Final at Stamford Bridge. Villa won 1–0.
4. Dixie Dean (white shirt) scores for Everton against Manchester City in the 1933 Final. Everton won 3–0.
5. Two all-time greats. Hughie Gallacher (Chelsea) scores against Elisha Scott (Liverpool) in a sixth-round Cup-tie at Liverpool in 1932. Chelsea won 2–0.

3

won a winner's medal, but injury forced him to be absent. Very much present were men whose names rank with the greatest: Hapgood, John, Hulme, Jack, James and Bastin. Alex James, the short Scot with the centre parting and baggy pants, the archetypal 'schemer', surprised everybody by scoring a goal. He then set up another for Lambert, and Huddersfield were beaten 2–0.

The League superiority of Arsenal in the early thirties under the managership of Herbert Chapman (he died in 1934) was not reflected in their Cup results and back at Wembley in 1932, Arsenal suffered another unhappy experience, losing to Newcastle United, who scored a goal after the ball had been centred from over the deadball line. James wasn't playing this time, but with the introduction since the 1930 game of George Male and 'Policeman' Roberts, who made stopper centre halves fashionable, Arsenal were just about at the peak of their power. Bob John, playing on the left wing, scored an early goal for Arsenal, who seemed to have matters in hand. But Richardson, the Newcastle inside right, got through the defence, centred and Allen headed in the equalizer. Arsenal and their supporters protested that the ball was over the line before Richardson centred, and photographs later proved that it was, but the goal was given, Arsenal lost a little heart, and Allen scored a second which took the Cup to Tyneside.

The cup of Arsenal's Cup woe was full the following season, when they travelled to Walsall, who have spent practically all their existence in the third division, for the formality of progressing to the fourth round. To set the scene for the shock which followed, it should be pointed out that in the five years from 1930 to 1935, Arsenal were League Champions in

1. George Mutch, of Preston, scores the only goal of the 1938 Cup Final with a penalty in the last minute of extra time.
2. Stan Cullis introducing his Wolves team-mates to King George VI before the 1939 Final, which Wolves lost 4–1 to Portsmouth.
3. The broken terracing after the Burnden Park disaster of 1946. Thirty-three were killed in a crush at a sixth-round tie with Stoke City.
4. Shimwell gives Blackpool the lead from a penalty in the 1948 Final against Manchester United.

four seasons and runners-up in the fifth, and that in 1934 they provided seven of the England men who beat Italy in Italy's World Cup-winning year. It is true that Arsenal were slightly weakened by illnesses and injury, but Cliff Bastin, Alex James and David Jack were in the forward line, which failed to score. Playing what came to be known as 'typical third division football', Walsall bustled in a goal, scored a second from a penalty, and made their one and only mark in the history of the game.

Two goals by W. G. Richardson enabled West Bromwich Albion to beat Birmingham City 2–1 in the Final of 1931, the last occasion when a side not from the first division won the Cup. However, in that season Albion finished runners-up in the second division to gain promotion. West Bromwich Albion are great Cup-fighters. Although they have been only once League Champions, no other side has appeared in more Cup Finals and semi-finals, and their five wins are well spaced out between 1888 and 1968.

In the 1938 Final Preston North End beat Huddersfield Town 1–0. The goal was scored in the last minute of extra time from a penalty kick taken by George Mutch, after he had himself been fouled. Strangely enough the previous occasion a penalty had been scored in a Cup Final was in 1922, when Huddersfield registered a 1–0 win over Preston. Huddersfield's goalkeeper in that match was also a Mutch, George's uncle. This had been sixteen years earlier, and sixteen years later, in 1954, Preston made their next Wembley appearance, losing 3–2, one of the goals against them being a penalty.

The last Cup Final before the Second World War produced an upset. Wolverhampton Wanderers were a strong young side master-minded by Major Frank Buckley—a team dedicated to youth like the post-war Manchester United. They were playing Portsmouth, an unremarkable side from the lower half of the first division, and were confidently expected to win comfortably. It was said that Wembley nerves got the better of the young Wolves, and in the event Portsmouth trounced them 4–1, their only Cup win.

The score was 4–1 again in the first Final after the war. Derby County, 'the Rams', with two brilliant inside forwards, Raich Carter and Peter Doherty, beat Charlton Athletic, but only after extra time and two strange happenings. First, the ball deflated,

---

Jack Rowley scores the second equalizer for Manchester United against Blackpool in the 1948 Final.

and then Turner, Charlton's right half, scored for both sides, first putting Derby ahead with an own goal and straightaway equalizing with a free kick! In extra time Derby's great forward line scored three more, two from burly Jack Stamps, who acted as Carter and Doherty's 'battering Ram'. Losing-side Charlton continued a Cup tradition by returning to Wembley next year and winning. Again the match went to extra time before a tremendous shot by Duffy, the left winger, beat Burnley.

The Cup Final of 1948 was a classic between two sides who played attacking football with flair, Manchester United and Blackpool. United had an all-star forward line: Delaney, Morris, Jack Rowley, Pearson and Mitten. Blackpool had the Stanleys, Matthews and Mortensen, and a fine right half in Harry Johnston. Early on Mortensen, who had a good game throughout, was brought down in the penalty area, and Shimwell put Blackpool ahead from the spot. Jack Rowley equalized after a defensive mistake, but Mortensen had Blackpool ahead once more by the interval. In the second half, with Blackpool looking to be likely winners, Jack Rowley scored an equalizer by heading in a free kick. Suddenly United were inspired. Ten minutes from time Pearson scored, and shortly afterwards Anderson added a fourth. United 4 Blackpool 2 — a great match with fine football, changing fortunes and in the end a decisive victory.

Another excellent match was the Final of 1949–50, between Arsenal and Liverpool. Arsenal had a good side, with international full backs and wing halves in Laurie Scott, Wally Barnes, Alex Forbes and Joe Mercer. Denis Compton was outside left, brother Leslie centre half. Liverpool's best player was winger Billy Liddell, a Scottish international. Jimmy Logie, small, Scottish, a latter-day Alex James, controlled the centre of the field for Arsenal, Reg Lewis, a prolific scorer, got a goal in each half and Arsenal won a game of much skills by 2–0.

Newcastle United won the Cup three times in five years from 1951 to 1955, recalling their run of 1905 to 1911, when they appeared in five Finals in seven years, winning once. Their opponents in the 1951 Final were Blackpool, who fielded six of the men who played in the memorable Final three years earlier: Matthews, Mortensen, Johnston, Shimwell, Hayward and Kelly. Newcastle's outstanding players of the period were Jackie Milburn, Bobby Mitchell, Ernie Taylor (who played for Blackpool in the Final two years later), Joe Harvey,

a strong captain, and Frank Brennan, centre half. Blackpool once again played some fine football, but again found opponents playing at the top of their form. Milburn, an exciting centre forward with great speed and a terrific shot, made some electrifying runs, and scored an exhilarating goal after a dash from the half-way line, followed by another with a flashing shot from outside the area after Taylor had back-heeled a pass to him. A local idol, Milburn was known as 'Wor Jackie' all over Tyneside. A popular joke of the time had him visiting Rome and standing alongside the Pope waving from the Vatican balcony to the crowds in St Peter's Square, where two holiday-making Geordies earnestly inquired who that was up there with 'Wor Jackie'.

Newcastle were at Wembley again next year, when their opponents were Arsenal, who at one time had hopes of the 'double'. This match should have been spoiled by an early injury to Barnes, who had to leave the field, giving ammunition to the advocates of substitutes. However, Arsenal fought so well that it was not until six minutes from the end that George Robledo scored the only goal with a gentle header off a post. Newcastle won the Cup again in 1955, beating Manchester City 3–1, with Milburn scoring a rare goal with his head. He, Cowell and Mitchell were the only three players to appear in all three of Newcastle's wins. City, like Arsenal, lost a full back with injury in the first half. Jimmy Meadows, who had recently been capped, sadly never played again.

The year 1953 was notable for many things, including a Coronation and the first ascent of Everest. Sir Gordon Richards after many years won the Derby and Stanley Matthews (later Sir Stanley) after many years won a Cup-winner's medal. Blackpool and Bolton Wanderers in an emotional atmosphere played a match that had a climax which could have been invented for a boys' annual. Shimwell, Johnston and Mortensen, as well as Matthews, had played in Blackpool's two recent Finals. Bolton had a good forward line in Holden, Willie Moir, the captain, Nat Lofthouse, Harold Hassall and Bobby Langton, all internationals. Lofthouse took an early opportunity to test the nerves of Blackpool's goalkeeper with a shot from outside the area. Farm muffed it, and Bolton were ahead after two minutes. Mortensen equalized, but by half-time Moir had restored Bolton's lead. Injury had struck at Wembley again, however, and Bolton's left-half, Bell, was a passenger in the forward line. Bolton had been the better team, but could their weakened

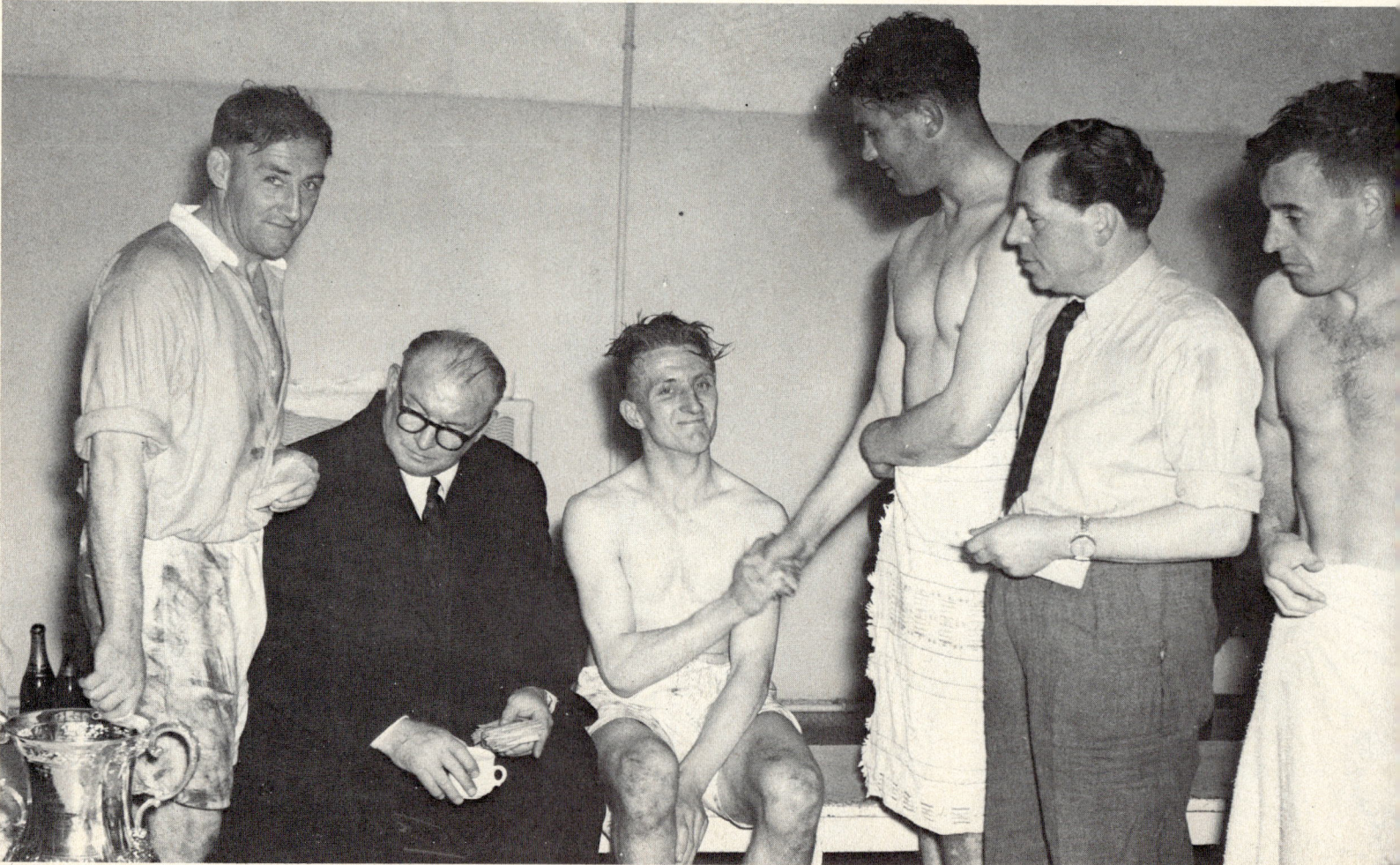

side survive the second half? It seemed so when Bell, not closely marked, soon headed a third goal. Bolton were holding their own, with an injured man, and with the crowd and popular sentiment against them. Nobody could have denied at the time that they deserved the Cup, a fact which has since been forgotten in the light of the excitement which followed. Blackpool at last began feeding Matthews, who sensed that this was his last chance of a winner's medal. Ernie Taylor and Harry Johnston took over the mid-field and poor Harold Hassall, doing the work of two in the reshuffled Bolton side, at last began to find the pressure suddenly overwhelming. One of Matthews' floating centres into a packed goalmouth was forced in at the foot of the far post by Mortensen. With only one goal in it, and the crowd continually shouting for Blackpool, still Bolton held on. Then, with a few minutes left, Blackpool were awarded a free kick just outside the area. Mortensen ran forward and slammed the ball past the wall into the corner for his hat-trick. The result was then inevitable, and the remaining minutes provided a memory of Matthews continually jinking his way down the wing until eventually, almost on time, he ended a dribble with a precise pass

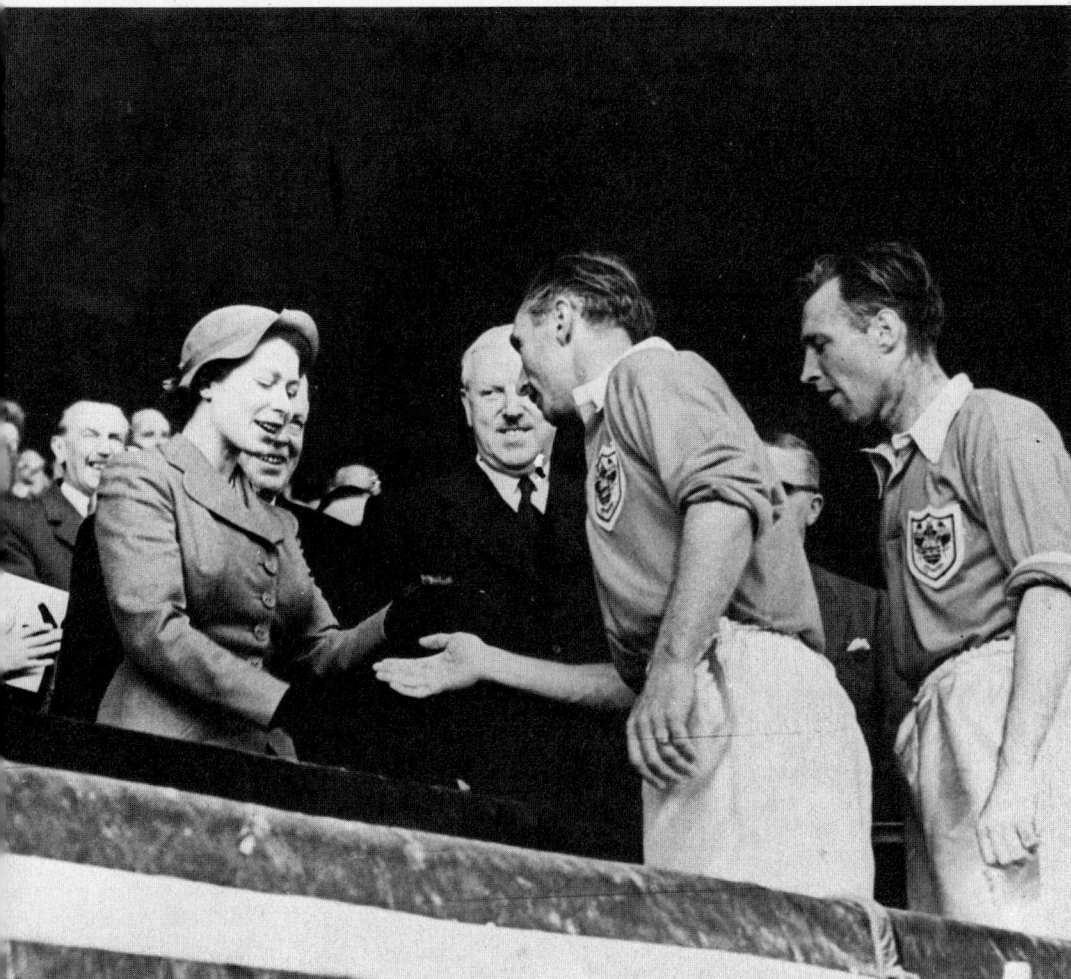

1. Arsenal v Liverpool, the 1950 Final. A long-range view of Reg Lewis (No. 10) scoring the first of his goals.
2. Another view of the 1950 Final. Baron of Liverpool shoots, surrounded by Leslie Compton, Barnes and Mercer of Arsenal.
3. The Arsenal dressing-room after the game. Peter Goring, whose first season it was, is congratulated by Leslie Compton. Manager Tom Whittaker, holding telegrams and tea, looks bored. The FA Cup, Freddy Cox, trainer Grovenor and Reg Lewis complete the picture.
4. Jackie Milburn (not in picture) scores the second of his two goals against Blackpool in the 1951 Final. Farm is the Blackpool goalie.
5. Bill Perry (right) scores the winning goal at the end of the 1953 'Matthews' Cup Final. Mortensen (centre) scored the other three.
6. Stanley Matthews receives his long-delayed medal from the Queen. Sir Stanley Rous looks on.

to Perry who could hardly avoid hitting the winning goal. It was the perfect end to a fantastic match.

After Milburn and Matthews, the 1954 Final seemed, in prospect, to be another opportunity for one of the all-time greats, Tom Finney, to crown a splendid career. But Preston had relied on Finney for so long that they had become too much of a one-man team, and West Bromwich Albion, an all-round side who like others before them and since had forfeited the Championship by attempting the 'double', proved too strong and won a good match 3–2.

Walthamstow Avenue, an amateur club, in 1952–53 provided one of those shocks which enliven the earlier rounds of the Cup. Having disposed of Stockport County in the third round, they were drawn to play Manchester United at Trafford Park in the fourth. The result was an astonishing 1–1 draw, Jim Lewis, the outstanding amateur of the day, who was a regular in the Chelsea side for a season or two, getting the goal. United, however, won the replay, played at Highbury, by 5–2.

Manchester provided one Cup Final side for four consecutive years from 1955 to 1958. City lost 3–1 to Newcastle United in 1955, and the following year won 3–1 against Birmingham City, despite their great German goalkeeper, Bert Trautmann, playing the last fifteen minutes or so with a broken neck. The two Manchester United Finals provide sad memories.

In 1957 the magnificent side nicknamed the 'Busby Babes' won the Championship by a wide margin for the second successive year, reached the European Cup semi-final, and seemed certain to beat Aston Villa in the Cup Final to become the first side in modern times to achieve the 'double'. In retrospect, it seems that

1. Bert Trautmann being led from the field after helping Manchester City beat Birmingham City 3–1 in the 1956 Final. He was found to have been playing with a broken neck.
2. Trautmann in action, turning a shot for a corner.
3. The incident which lost Manchester United the double in 1956–57. Wood lies injured after the collision with McParland in the Cup Final.
4. Sims, the Villa goalkeeper, dives at the feet of Tommy Taylor, Munich victim, in the 1957 Final.

the only thing that could stop them, did. After a few minutes, before the sides had settled down, McParland, the robust Villa left winger, decided to charge Wood, the United goalkeeper, fracturing his cheekbone. Wood went off and United reshuffled their side, with Jackie Blanchflower going in goal. United defended gallantly and successfully for a long time, but mid-way through the second half McParland scored twice. United then threw everything into attack, and Tommy Taylor scored. The match ended with Aston Villa desperately defending. This Manchester United team might well have become the best club side ever, but in 1958, at Munich, many members of it were killed in the plane bringing them back from a European Cup match in Belgrade.

By judicious buying, however, and helped by the FA waiving their rule that players could not play for two clubs in the same Cup competition, Manchester United reached Wembley again that year. Billy Foulkes and Bobby Charlton were the only two players to appear in the pre- and post-Munich finals. One player bought by United was Ernie Taylor, who already owned winners' medals won with Newcastle and Blackpool. United reached the Final with the help of emotional support from the public, and as in 'Matthews' Final' five years earlier the Wembley crowd was unashamedly partisan. The side expected to lie down quietly was poor Bolton Wanderers again, but this time they refused to co-operate in a fairy-tale ending. Lofthouse scored twice, one goal coming when he rudely but fairly shoulder-charged goalkeeper Gregg into the net, injuring him against the post on the way. Bolton won 2–0 with a team that cost nothing in transfer fees.

Tooting and Mitcham United, South London amateurs, provided much excitement in the 1958–59 season by taking a deserved 2–0 lead against first division opponents Nottingham Forest in a third-round match played in the snow. The imminent sensation

1. **Manchester United (dark shirts) scoring their second goal against Walthamstow Avenue in a Cup fourth round replay in 1953 at Highbury. United won 5–2.**
2. **The first of two for Nat Lofthouse in the 1958 Cup Final, as he slides the ball between goalkeeper Gregg and Crowther. Bolton beat the post-Munich Manchester United 2–0.**

failed to materialize when an own goal and a hotly disputed penalty allowed Forest to scramble a draw. They then went on to win the Cup. Norwich City, a third division side, reached the semi-final the same season. Bournemouth, another third division side, had beaten Wolverhampton Wanderers and Tottenham Hotspur in the fourth and fifth rounds of the previous season, 1956–1957, and lost by only 2–1 to Manchester United in the sixth.

The fact that Luton Town beat Manchester City 3–1 in a fourth-round match in 1961 is unremarkable in itself, but consider the feelings of Denis Law. This match was a replay, the first game having been abandoned because of the weather conditions. At the time Law had scored six goals for the eventual losers!

The 'double' which so cruelly evaded Manchester United in 1956–57, and which was being thought of as almost impossible in modern times, was at last achieved by Tottenham Hotspur in 1960–61. Led by Danny Blanchflower, Spurs were a fine all-round side and had won the Championship easily, thus relieving themselves of much strain in the weeks before Wembley. They were also fortunate in their Final opponents. Leicester City have been good Cup-fighters since the war and have reached the Final four times, but they have always lacked the touch of flair necessary to win. Spurs, however, did not beat them with the ease expected, and indeed played lethargically. It was not until late in the game that Bobby Smith and Terry Dyson scored the goals that set the seal on a great season.

Spurs had a harder match in the Final the following season, when they met their old rivals, Burnley. Jimmy Greaves, a new acquisition, scored an early goal, but it was not until Blanchflower scored from a penalty in the second half to make the score 3–1 that Spurs were confident of winning. Burnley's revenge came at the earliest opportunity. They stopped Spurs' hat-trick attempt with a 3–0 third-round win the following year.

Manchester United recorded their long-overdue victory in 1963, with a side quite different from the hastily assembled band who had lost to Bolton five years earlier. Only Foulkes

John Bond (right) looks pleased with his West Ham colleague, Jim Standen, who is punching away from Preston centre forward Dawson in the Final of 1964. West Ham won 3–2.

and Charlton, Munich survivors, remained. Once again Leicester City fulfilled the role of gallant losers. United's outside right was Johnny Giles, strangely sold later to Leeds in one of Matt Busby's rare mistakes. David Herd scored twice in a 3–1 win.

A second division side, Preston North End, reached Wembley in 1964. With the gap between the divisions widening it was no surprise that they could not emulate the win of West Bromwich Albion in 1931. Yet in a match of good football they led twice before a superb header by Boyce in injury time gave West Ham United their first Cup win in their only Final appearance since the famous 1923 match.

As a contrast to the flowing football played, Leeds and Liverpool the following year set the standard for the campaigns of attrition which have characterized some recent Finals. The match, between two of the strongest sides of the time, promised in advance to be a classic, and indeed it was a classic to those who enjoy hard-fought, no-quarter-given contests, but each side was too aware of the other's qualities to play with any freedom. There was no score after ninety minutes, but in extra time Hunt at last scored for Liverpool. Bremner, who never gives up, equalized, but St John, with a thrilling header, won Liverpool the Cup. It is surprising, in view of Liverpool's footballing tradition, that this was their first Cup win. Leeds waited until 1972 to register a first victory.

Everton, who have been a more consistent and successful Cup side than arch-rivals Liverpool, made a great come-back to beat Sheffield Wednesday in the Final of 1966. Two down in the second half they equalized with two goals from Trebilcock, a surprise choice for the side, who came from the obscurity of Plymouth Argyle, played eleven games for Everton, had his two moments of glory in the Cup Final and returned to comparative obscurity with Portsmouth. Everton's winning goal came when Wednesday's Young failed to control a hopeful kick down the centre. Temple raced past him, dribbled on at speed and hit a tremendous shot past Springett.

Chelsea had many Cup frustrations in the fifties and sixties, several times reaching the semi-final without appearing at Wembley. In their third consecutive semi-final in 1967 they were playing bitter rivals Leeds, and were a goal up. Lorimer then 'equalized' from a free kick, but the kick was ordered to be retaken because Chelsea players were not ten yards from the ball. Leeds couldn't

equalize again and Chelsea were in their second Final, their first at Wembley. It was also the first all-London Wembley Final, opponents being Tottenham Hotspur. Spurs do not lose Cup Finals — five appearances, five wins is their record — and Chelsea became their third victims of the sixties, rather more emphatically than the score of 2–1 suggests. Dave Mackay was the only player who was in all three Spurs' sides, although Cliff Jones was substitute in 1967.

Attrition set in with a vengeance in the 1968 Final when Everton and West Bromwich Albion fought a niggly battle. The only goal was scored for Albion in extra time by Jeff Astle. An instinctive shot with his left foot, after the ball rebounded to him, flashed into the net. Astle's left foot was less effective than either his right or his head, and it is regrettable that two years later, against Brazil in a vital World Cup match, he had time to deliberate before putting a much easier left-foot chance past the post.

It was time for another Leicester City performance in 1969. Relegated to the second division that year, they nevertheless reached the Cup Final once again and demonstrated some improvement by losing only by one goal, scored by Manchester City's Young.

Leeds United were the strongest club in England at the end of the sixties, and were attempting the 'double' again in 1969–70. Their route to Wembley took in the Borough Sports Ground, Gander Green Lane, Sutton, where they were drawn in the fourth round to play amateurs Sutton United. The programme summed up the aspirations of all the small teams which battle out the preliminary Cup rounds in the hope of a day's fame and glory sharing a pitch with the greats:

. . . Our team have earned, by sheer effort over a long period the right to meet, on equal terms, the team which many consider to be the finest in the world. Suffice it to say that it is at times like these that we know that the years of effort have been worthwhile, and whatever today's result, no one can now take this great moment from us.

'This great moment' — the eighty-nine-year-old Sutton president, born in the year that Old Carthusians beat Old Etonians in the Final, and present as a seventeen-year-old at the formation of the club in 1898, waited seventy-two years for it.

The match was played in a festival atmosphere, and nobody minded that Leeds' superior fitness and skill enabled them to win 6–0. Sutton had

1

2

their moments and actually made the first shot at goal. The Sutton centre half, Faulkner, dominated England international Mick Jones and was signed as a professional by Leeds immediately afterwards. Alas, after a few games for the first team, injuries checked his career, and he was transferred.

Leeds' Final opponents were old rivals Chelsea. The match, or rather two, for there was a replay, had everything — tension, skill, effort, soft goals, good goals, and in keeping with modern standards and the feeling between the two teams, not a little 'needle'. There was even something of a Chaplinesque comic-who-becomes-a-hero figure in David Webb. Eddie Gray, the Leeds outside left, had a superb game at Wembley, leaving Webb lunging at air as he beat him first this way and then that, time after time. After some excitements at each end, Jack Charlton went upfield for Gray's corner, got his head to the ball as he rose with a crowd of players and sent it slowly towards the goal. Harris and McCreadie were on the line and perhaps if either had been alone he would have cleared easily. As it was Harris seemed more interested in appealing for a foul on Bonetti, and McCreadie, as if mesmerized, aimed a slow-motion kick at the ball as it trickled past him. Perhaps the appalling state of the Wembley pitch, blamed on a show-jumping event held there earlier, had something to do with it. Just before half-time Leeds returned the gift when Houseman's long-range drive to the far corner passed under Sprake's body as he dived too late.

There was no slackening of the pace in the second half — these were two supremely fit teams. Hutchinson and Osgood had three shots blocked in one thrilling assault on the Leeds goal; Gray shivered the bar at the other end. Late in the second half Clarke hit the foot of Bonetti's left-hand post with a header, Dempsey and Lorimer collided as the rebound came past them and Jones shot into the opposite corner. It seemed Leeds might have won, but a free kick on the left was taken by

1. Peter Bonetti punches clear from the head of Mick Jones in the Chelsea-Leeds Final of 1970. Eddie McCreadie and Peter Osgood watch for slips.
2. David Webb (Chelsea), Eddie Gray and Terry Cooper (Leeds) clash in the same match.
3. The Final of 1970 was long and hard-fought. Peter Osgood of Chelsea helps Terry Cooper of Leeds get over cramp.

3

99

Harris, who pulled the ball back to Hollins, and his centre to the near post was headed in by Hutchinson. In extra time a tremendous shot by Chelsea centre half Dempsey was pushed over by Sprake, and Bonetti, who played magnificently in both matches, was forced to make several good saves. The final thrust was with Leeds, when Giles volleyed hard a Gray centre. Webb threw himself across the goal, foot first, and the ball struck it and flew over the bar.

The replay at Old Trafford was as hard-fought and exciting. Bonetti was injured in a collision with Jones, and Jones soon afterwards scored with a good shot after Clarke had beaten two men in a run from half-way and given him a perfect pass. Cooke had a splendid game for Chelsea, and in the second half chipped over a cross which Osgood headed past Harvey, who was deputizing for Sprake. Extra time came again, Hutchinson made a long throw-in to the near post, and Jack Charlton's attempted clearance sent the ball further across goal. Webb, who was playing left half instead of right back for Chelsea, to relieve him of the job of marking Gray, led a charge of Chelsea players to head the winner. For the last five minutes Chelsea brought on a defender, Hinton, for Osgood, and held on to the lead it had taken nearly four hours to obtain.

The following season Leeds were the victims in the fifth round of a tremendous giant-killing performance by fourth-division Colchester United. Colchester had had their Cup moments before. In 1947–48, as a non-League club, they were not eliminated till the fifth round, when finalists Blackpool beat them, and they beat first-division Huddersfield on the way. Against Leeds, they took the lead in the eighteenth minute when Crawford, an ex-England centre forward headed a fine goal, and increased it six minutes later when Crawford scored again. Ten minutes into the second half,

1. **Billy Bremner, captain of Leeds against Chelsea in the 1970 Final, stares at the muddy pitch in exhaustion.**
2. **Liverpool's Peter Thompson (No. 12) goes to congratulate Steve Heighway who has just put Liverpool ahead 1–0 in extra time in the 1971 Final.**
3. **Most people, himself included thought George Graham (centre) had equalized for Arsenal in the 1971 Final, but the goal was later given to Eddie Kelly (left).**

1

2

Colchester's Simmons headed a third. With half an hour left Hunter headed a goal for Leeds, who at last began to play to their best form. With fifteen minutes to go Giles scored again, and the rest of the match was a bombardment of the Colchester goal. In the dying minutes, Smith, the Colchester goalkeeper, who had an inspired game, made a fabulous save from Lorimer, and Colchester had performed the impossible.

Leeds later that season were pipped for the Championship by a fantastic final run-in by Arsenal, who scored twenty-seven points out of a possible thirty, and then became only the fourth side in ninety-nine years to perform the 'double'. Arsenal survived the semi-final against Stoke with a last-minute penalty equalizer. Their Final opponents were Liverpool, and the match followed the modern cautious tradition with neither side taking a chance, and both sides missing in haste the openings which nevertheless appeared. The match went to extra time, and Heighway gave Liverpool the lead by shooting in from an acute angle when a centre looked more likely, particularly to Arsenal goalkeeper Bob Wilson. Kelly equalized for Arsenal, his prod deceiving Clemence, the Liverpool keeper, by evading the legs of friend and foe alike. Arsenal deservedly won the match with the best goal of the three, when after an interchange of passes with Radford, Charlie George scored with a fine drive.

Hereford United, a Southern League side, provided the early excitement of the Centenary Year competition when they drew a third-round match at Newcastle. In the replay Macdonald scored a late goal for Newcastle, but not late enough, for in the remaining minutes Ron Radford scored the goal of a lifetime for Hereford. Winning a hard tackle near the half-way line, he stumbled on, took a return pass, and from well outside the area fired in a tremendous shot which found the top corner of the net. Hereford gained new

Two giant-killing acts:
1. The goal which put Newcastle out of the Cup in 1972. Ricky George beats Iam McFaul to give non-League Hereford United a 2–1 win.
2. Ray Crawford, of Colchester United, pushes the ball past goalkeeper Gary Sprake of Leeds while lying on the floor. Reaney and Charlton look on helplessly. This was Crawford's and Colchester's second goal in a 3–2 fifth-round upset.

life, and Ricky George scored the winner in extra time. Hereford went out in the next round to West Ham, but once again forced a replay before finally succumbing. Their performances helped to win them a place in the Football League the following year.

Leeds, once more chasing the elusive 'double' (they lost the Championship by a point) were at Wembley to play Arsenal, attempting a second consecutive win. To celebrate the centenary of the Cup there was a parade before the match of men dressed in the strips of all the clubs who had won the trophy from the Wanderers onwards. The game itself, like the previous year's Final, was cautious, yet hard and skilful, with defences generally on top and only split-second openings coming. Leeds showed more flair in their attempts to beat the close marking and solid tackling, but Arsenal nearly took the lead when a hard shot by Ball aimed at the corner of the net was kicked away at full stretch by Reaney. In the second half Lorimer put Jones away on the right, and McNab, on the edge of the penalty area near the by-line, made the sort of committed, smothering tackle which had succeeded all afternoon. This time, however, he missed, the ball remained in play and Jones just kept his feet. A precision centre followed, and Clarke scored the only goal with a perfect header. Leeds, at last, had won the Cup.

The Cup competition of 1972–73 will always be remembered for the performance of one team: Sunderland. If one man had to be singled out it would be their manager, Bob Stokoe, who joined them when the season was well advanced and Sunderland were struggling in the second division. When the season was over Sunderland were near the top of the table and had the Cup on their sideboard.

Sunderland's best performances on their way to the Final were the defeat of first division Manchester City after forcing an away draw, and a semi-final victory over Arsenal, who were making a strong attempt at the

1. **This shot from Peter Lorimer in the 1972 Final beat Arsenal goalkeeper Geoff Barnett but hit the post.**
2. **Allan Clarke's header was more fortunate, finding the corner of the net for the only goal. Players from the left are Simpson, goalkeeper Barnett, Lorimer, scorer Clarke, Storey, McLintock, Rice, Gray and Bremner (No. 4). Mick Jones crossed the ball from the right.**

1

2

League-FA Cup double. Sunderland beat them 2–1 at Villa Park, and were worth their win. Wearsiders had turned up at the semi-final in thousands, and from then to the Final the town of Sunderland was as soccer-crazy as any town has ever been. A Cup win in 1937 had been Sunderland's only Wembley appearance, a dismal record for the home of the nineteenth-century 'Team of All the Talents'.

Sunderland's Final opponents were Leeds United, attempting to emulate Newcastle United and Spurs with two successive post-war wins. The scene was set, then, for one of soccer's most dramatic stories: the second division club of faded glory versus the most consistent and professional team in England.

The match did not start auspiciously. An ugly foul on Allan Clarke in the first minute, soon followed by another, was not the way for fairy-tale heroes to begin. However, the mood was shrugged off, and both teams settled down to bright football, Leeds having shots blocked and Horswill going close for Sunderland. After half an hour Sunderland's Hughes was seen to be limping, but in the 31st minute he was quick enough to rush in on Harvey, Leeds' goalkeeper, when Sunderland's captain, Bobby Kerr, had apparently wasted a good position with a speculative long shot. Harvey was forced to touch the ball over the bar for a corner. Hughes took it, the Sunderland centre half, Dave Watson, jumped for it with two Leeds defenders, all missed, the ball struck Halom's knee and bounced up for Porterfield to smash home a fine right-foot volley. Leeds' reaction was to go for a quick equalizer, but Sunderland bodies and the fists of Jim Montgomery blocked every shot. Clarke was once through from a fine pass by Madeley, but a superb tackle by Dave Watson put the ball behind for a corner. Montgomery parried a Lorimer effort, and Sunderland's right back Malone, whose impassive expression throughout contrasted with the hysteria all round the ground, just managed to head away a cross with two Leeds attackers waiting to nod it in.

Leeds attacked at the start of the second half, and Cherry soon had the ball in the net, but Clarke had knocked it from Montgomery's hands unfairly. Shortly afterwards Leeds were denied a penalty when Bremner seemed to be tripped in the area; it was certainly not Leeds' day. Twenty minutes into the half came the game's most memorable moment. A cross from Reaney on the right was met beautifully by Cherry stealing up on the left. He

headed hard for the far corner: a copy of the header with which Boyce of West Ham had beaten Preston, the last second division side to reach the Final, in 1964. Montgomery beat it down, but it went to Lorimer, who with all the goal to aim at hit it first time hard and true. But Montgomery was getting up even as he hit the ground. He threw himself across the goal and diverted the ball on to the underside of the bar. The TV commentators on both channels said 'Goal', but the ball bounced down the right side of the line for Sunderland and was scrambled away.

Leeds did not despair, and flowed forward with constant attacks, often leaving only Madeley back to return clearances to the Sunderland end. But Sunderland defended doggedly, if at times a little fortunately, with centre half Dave Watson outstanding. With most of the Sunderland players looking weary, it seemed Leeds' fitter-looking side must score, but Sunderland held out, and contrived enough attacks to keep Leeds stretched. Indeed the last real effort fell to them, when Halom had a shot blocked and from the rebound brought a flying save from Harvey. Near the end, thousands of whistles from the crowd anticipated the referee's, and the excitement was tremendous.

Many saw Sunderland's triumph as a victory for old-fashioned team spirit and determination over the modern ideal of slick professionalism and the well-drilled squad. Perhaps this is unjust to Leeds.

What is certain is that the result was good for soccer interest in North-east England, where success has been rare of late, and it was good for the FA Cup, where results, in the later rounds at least, had become predictable. Who but Leeds men, then, would have wished it otherwise?

1. **The 1973 Cup Final. Ian Porterfield (left), of Sunderland, hits a right-foot volley past team-mate Vic Halom and Norman Hunter and Allan Clarke of Leeds United. David Harvey just touches the ball . . .**
2. **. . . but cannot stop it finishing in the net. Dave Watson, Denis Tueart and Porterfield (arms raised) turn towards Mike Horswill (No. 4) to celebrate the only goal of the match.**
3. **Sunderland manager Bob Stokoe hugged by two of his heroes. The hat, despite his efforts, was soon lost.**

SCOTTISH CUP

The first competition for the Scottish Cup was held in season 1873–74, two years after the Football Association Challenge Cup got under way. Scottish teams were already taking part in the FA Cup tournament, and the Scottish Cup initially was a secondary competition. Its early years were marred by bitter disputes between the clubs.

Queens Park were instrumental in the inception of the Cup and fittingly they were the first winners. Of the fifteen other entrants, only Dumbarton, Kilmarnock and Third Lanark still operate in the Scottish League. Queens Park went on to win the first three Cups. Their strongest challengers were Vale of Leven, who were the first side to score against them, and then the first to beat them. This occurred in the semi-final of 1876–77, and caused a long coolness between the clubs, as Queens Park claimed that marks found afterwards on the pitch indicated that Vale used illegal studs. Vale of Leven went on to win the Cup, and emulated Queens Park by winning three times in succession. The third victory came after a dispute with Rangers. The Final was drawn 1–1, but Rangers protested that the referee had refused them a legitimate winning goal. A spectator swore that the ball rebounded into play when it struck him after crossing the line. Rangers refused to replay and the Scottish FA gave Vale the Cup.

After this Queens Park again won three times consecutively, but the second of these wins produced another controversy. Dumbarton were beaten 2–1 in the Final, but immediately protested that spectators had interfered with the play when Queens Park scored their winner. The Scottish FA this time agreed with the protest and ordered a replay. Queens Park, naturally, objected to this decision, but the replay took place and Queens Park won 3–1. The same two sides met in the Final the following year, and again there was a row, this time over Dumbarton's equalizing goal

Dixie Deans jumps for joy after scoring for Celtic against Hibernian in the 1972 Scottish Cup Final. Jim Herriott is the disgusted-looking Hibs goalie.

in a 2–2 draw. Queens Park again won the replay, 4–1. Dumbarton registered their only win in the next season, 1883, beating Vale of Leven, once more after a draw.

In 1884, by which time hardly a leading Scottish club was on good terms with another, Queens Park were due to play Vale of Leven in the Final. Vale simply did not turn up, and Queens Park won by default.

To prove that there was some uninhibited football as well as wrangling taking place in the Scottish Cup, Arbroath in 1885 made the highest score in British soccer when they beat Bon Accord 36–0, Petrie scoring thirteen times.

Scottish clubs were still entering the FA Cup competition, to the discomfort of the Scottish FA. In 1886–87 seven teams took part, and Queens Park reached the semi-final. There was a bitter match with Preston, who won 3–0, allegedly with the help of some very rough play. The Scottish FA took the opportunity of ruling that henceforth no members of the Scottish Association could enter the English competition.

The Scottish Cup thereby grew in stature, but undignified arguments continued. In 1889 Third Lanark recorded their first win, but had to beat Celtic twice in the Final to do so. The pitch for the first match was declared unfit because of snow, but the teams were ordered to play anyway, Third Lanark winning 3–0 and claiming the Cup. Celtic's view that the match was a friendly was upheld, and the teams had to play again, Third Lanark this time winning 2–1.

Celtic won the Cup for the first time three years later. Both sides protested about the conditions in the Final and Queens Park, who lost 1–0, were awarded a replay. Once again it made no difference for Celtic won the second match 5–0.

Two years after Celtic's first win Rangers won for the first time. Their Final opponents were Celtic. A crowd of 30,000 highly partisan supporters saw Rangers' 3–1 victory in the first of many stirring Cup Final encounters between the clubs.

Strangely enough the following Final, in 1895, was between two teams called St Bernards and Renton, who have since faded from the top-class soccer scene. St Bernards, an Edinburgh side, won 2–1. This was the last occasion when a team not currently in the Scottish League won.

Queens Park made their last appearance in the Final in 1900, losing 4–3 to Celtic. The turn of the century was a fitting time for Queens Park to take their bow. They were

giants of nineteenth-century soccer, and can claim that no club has done more to shape the modern game. Original participants in both the FA and Scottish Cup, they arranged the first international match between Scotland and England and supplied the whole Scottish team. They instigated the modern passing style of play. Because they remained amateur, they slid from eminence in the twentieth century, and today, with a huge stadium at Hampden Park for a scattering of spectators, are a splendid anachronism.

There were ugly scenes at the replayed Final of 1909, between Celtic and Rangers. Celtic were attempting a hat-trick of League and Cup 'doubles'. Rangers fans were incensed in the first match which Celtic drew when the ball was adjudged to have crossed the line after Quinn, their aggressive centre forward, had forced Rennie, the Rangers goalkeeper, to spin round to avoid a head-on charge. The fans expected extra time in the replay when the ninety-minute score was 1–1. This was contrary to the rules, but the crowd had been misled by incorrect newspaper stories. The Rangers players left the field, but some Celtic players, themselves deceived, momentarily remained. When it was announced that there would be no more play, some Celtic supporters invaded the pitch in protest. In minutes a full-scale riot was taking place, with rival factions fighting each other and the police, throwing bottles and stones, tearing up fences and goalposts, starting fires, and even knocking down and clubbing the police horses. When the Fire Brigade arrived, the firemen were beaten up and their equipment wrecked. At the end hardly a part of the ground or its surroundings had escaped damage and over a hundred badly injured people were in hospital, including fifty-eight policemen. Both the Celtic and Rangers clubs petitioned the Scottish FA to abandon the tie, and the Cup for 1909 was withheld. The scenes at this match cemented the foundations of the aggression which some supporters of Catholic Celtic and Protestant Rangers have shown to each other ever since.

Rangers had a very lean spell in the Cup, failing to win for twenty-five years between 1903 and 1928, despite five Final appearances and ten Championships. Celtic meanwhile carried off the trophy nine times. In 1928 the two teams met in the Final for the first time since the 1909 hooliganism. Eighteen internationals were on parade and 118,000 spectators turned up to watch. The great Alan Morton was on the wing for Rangers, and Celtic had the

prolific Jimmy McGrory at centre forward and the tragic John Thomson in goal. Facing the wind Rangers kept the score-sheet blank till half-time, and then early in the second half were awarded a penalty. Skipper David Meiklejohn was forced to take it as no other Ranger would accept the responsibility. He scored, and set Rangers on the way to a 4–0 win. He also started eleven great years for Rangers, as from 1928 to 1939, when war started, they won the Cup six times and the Championship nine times.

An unfortunate mistake by Motherwell's international centre half, Alan Craig, in the 1931 Final put back Motherwell's first victory by twenty-one years. Playing their first Final against the mighty Celtic, outsiders Motherwell were two up in twenty minutes. They held on fairly comfortably until with eight minutes left Jimmy McGrory headed a goal for Celtic. In the last minute Bertie Thomson, the Celtic outside right, was juggling with the ball on the touchline. One report suggested that as he could not win a Cup medal he intended to keep the ball when the whistle blew. Instead he booted it towards the Motherwell goal. The goalkeeper had it well covered, but Craig went up for a header and the ball spun off his head into the goal. Celtic won the replay 4–2.

In 1937 a record crowd for a British club match, 147,000, saw Celtic play Aberdeen in the Final. It was a classic game, which Celtic won 3–1. The Celtic outside right was Jimmy Delaney, who thus won his first Cup-winner's medal. He ended his career with a unique collection of four: for Celtic in Scotland, Manchester United in England, Derry City in Northern Ireland and Cork in Eire. Not bad for a man whose brittle bones were famous for the ease with which they snapped.

The only second division club to win the Cup triumphed in 1938. East

1. Prolific goal scorer Jimmy McGrory, of Celtic, challenging a goalkeeper in a 1931 Cup tie.
2. Jimmy Delaney, who won Cup medals in four countries, in his Falkirk days.
3. The Rangers-Celtic Final in 1966, which Rangers won 1–0 in a replay. Celtic goalkeeper Ronnie Simpson jumps to save from Forrest.
4. An attack at the other end. Celtic's McBride heads for goal but Rangers' goalkeeper Ritchie palms away.

1

2

Fife, from the small port of Methil, had never won a major honour. Their opponents were Kilmarnock, and remarkably not one of the twenty-two players was an international. McKerrall, the Fifers outside left, earned a peculiar place in the history books by getting a winner's medal in his only Cup-tie. East Fife won after two exciting matches, a 4–2 victory following a 1–1 draw.

After the Second World War, Aberdeen won their first Cup, but then Rangers, with most of the Scottish national team's defence, won three times running. Motherwell, in 1952, beat Dundee 4–0 in the Final with a team heading for relegation and generally considered inferior to the side that had lost so unfortunately to Celtic in 1931.

Two Glasgow sides fought the Final of 1955, but this time Celtic faced Clyde instead of the old enemy, Rangers. Jock Stein, later their manager, was Celtic's centre half. Confidently expected to win, Celtic conceded an equalizer three minutes from the end of the first match, and over-reacted by changing the forward line for the replay, with full back Fallon at centre forward. Clyde won 1–0.

Hearts won the Cup after fifty years in 1956, beating Celtic 3–1 in the Final. Their manager was their popular pre-war player Tommy Walker, and their strength was a 'Terrible Trio' of attackers, Alfie Conn, Willie Bauld and Jimmy Wadhaugh. Dave Mackay, who later won fame with Spurs, was right half.

Hearts' success was followed by others for clubs whose Cup wins have been rare. Falkirk won in 1957, Clyde again in 1958, St Mirren in 1959 and Dunfermline Athletic, for the first time ever, in 1961.

Normal service was resumed in 1962 when Rangers scored the first of another hat-trick of wins — the third

1. **Dunfermline centre forward Pat Gardner thumps the ball past Hearts 'keeper Jim Cruickshank to help his team to a 3–1 Cup win in 1968.**
2. **Celtic beat Rangers easily in the 1969 Final. Steve Chalmers beats McKinnon and goalkeeper Martin to score the fourth and final goal.**
3. **A shock for Celtic in the 1970 Scottish Cup Final. Derek McKay (No. 7) puts Aberdeen two up.**
4. **Aberdeen goalkeeper Bobby Clark beats Celtic's Jimmy Johnstone to the ball in the same match.**

2

and last time they performed this feat. The second and third wins accompanied easy victories in the Championship, Rangers last period of domination in Scottish football. They beat Celtic in the Finals of 1963 and 1966, each time after a replay. But in 1966 Celtic began their record run of Championship victories. Seven consecutive Championships and four Cup wins between 1966 and 1972 not only eclipsed Rangers and proved them by far the strongest side in Scotland, they were arguably also the best in all Britain.

In 1969 Celtic played Rangers in the Cup Final. Easy victories, by 4–1 for Celtic and 6–1 for Rangers, in the semi-finals promised a great match and a large crowd turned out to watch. It proved to be almost a no-contest. Despite being without their match-winning winger, Jimmy Johnstone, Celtic were a goal up in two minutes, by Billy McNeill, who had a splendid match; were three up by half-time, Lennox and Connelly scoring; and ran out easy 4–0 winners, Chalmers getting the final goal.

In view of their great superiority in Scottish circles, it was astounding that Celtic should come such a cropper in the Cup Final of 1970. Their opponents, Aberdeen, were rated 6–1 outsiders, but 108,000 spectators nevertheless came to see the slaughter. Aberdeen first saw prospects of victory when in the twenty-seventh minute they were awarded a penalty. A cross struck a defender's hand, and although Celtic protested about the decision, there could be no arguments about the goal, Joe Harper shooting cleanly into the corner of the net. As the minutes ticked by, and a Celtic 'goal' was disallowed, Aberdeen's chances improved, but even their most optimistic supporters could hardly believe in the imminent triumph until seven minutes from the end, when the young winger Derek McKay scored a second. There were even then a few anxious moments as Lennox reduced Celtic's arrears with two minutes left, but McKay scored again and Aberdeen supporters made a joyous trip home.

1. Celtic's Lou Macari appears to be standing on the hair of Hibernian goalie Jim Herriott in the 1972 Final. Macari was transferred to Manchester United in 1973.
2. The Rangers-Celtic Final of 1971. Celtic goalkeeper Evan Williams challenged by Rangers centre forward Colin Stein (now with Coventry).

Celtic were back in the groove again in 1971. Perhaps they felt more comfortable facing old rivals Rangers in the Final than upstarts Aberdeen. It would be the fortieth time that either Celtic or Rangers had won the Cup. A crowd of 120,000 saw Lennox give Celtic the lead. In the second half seventeen-year-old Derek Johnstone came on as a substitute for Rangers, and three minutes from time he headed the goal which earned Rangers a replay. It was his first Cup-tie. The second match was a spectacular triumph for Celtic's Jimmy Johnstone. With mazy dribbles which took him to all corners of the Rangers half, he kept the defenders in a dither all afternoon. After twenty-four minutes Lou Macari scored a simple goal for Celtic and almost immediately Johnstone was sent crashing in the penalty area. Harry Hood scored. Derek Johnstone came on for Rangers in the second half, as he had in the first match, and straightaway his shot was helped in by Jim Craig. But he and Rangers could do no more and Celtic won 2–1.

Hibernian reached the Final in 1972, with a good 2–0 victory over Rangers in the semi-final. Their opponents were, almost inevitably, Celtic, and if Hibs had any thoughts of emulating Aberdeen's performance two years earlier they were rudely shattered. Celtic played their two outstanding young strikers, Lou Macari and Kenny Dalglish, but it was veteran centre half Billy McNeill who opened the scoring, as he had in the Final with Rangers in 1969. 'Dixie' Deans then scored three and Lou Macari two more, and Celtic were easy 6–1 winners. This equalled the highest score made in the Cup Final eighty-four years earlier, and with ten points to spare in the Championship, Celtic were emphatic masters of Scottish soccer.

Celtic were beaten in an exciting Final in 1972–73 by Rangers, who fittingly celebrated their centenary and gained revenge for a one-point defeat in the Championship. Dalglish put Celtic ahead with a superb goal after defence-splitting passes by Jimmy Johnstone and Deans. Parlane equalized with a good header, and Conn put Rangers ahead in the first minute of the second half. Connelly equalized from a penalty, but Rangers deservedly won when Derek Johnstone headed a free kick on to the post, from whence the ball ran along the goal line to hit the other post before Forsyth tapped it in unchallenged.

Parlane (No. 9), Rangers, heads past Hunter in the 1973 Final.

THE WORLD CUP

A last-minute equalizer in a World Cup Final. Wolfgang Weber, of West Germany, beats the lunging Ray Wilson and diving Gordon Banks to make the score 2–2 in 1966. Other players are Martin Peters (behind Weber), Uwe Seeler, George Cohen (on ground), Bobby Moore, Karl-Heinz Schnellinger and Jack Charlton. England won 4–2 after extra time.

THE WORLD CUP

There can be little argument now that the World Cup is one of the pinnacles of the sporting calendar. It has reached a peak alongside that of the Olympic Games; in terms of prestige, build-up, kudos, national excitement and international interest they are probably equals. Both take place every four years, both are plums of great wealth falling into the laps of the host country, and both, coincidentally, have recently followed each other to the same city. Only in the scope of its multi-national embrace, and arguably in the variety of its events, does the Olympic Games take precedence. Perhaps not yet as many countries compete for the glory of clasping the World Cup, but soccer's influence is ever-widening and even if the participants in the last sixteen of the competition regularly involve permutations of a hard core of nations, with the added unpredictable spice of a few newcomers each time, the public appeal of the finals reaches into the furthest corners of the globe. More or less wherever a television aerial can be mustered the viewers will be in at the kill, supporting the team that either politically or emotionally responds to their needs, or simply, and for football's sake hopefully, the team that plays the more exciting game.

Victory in the World Cup can be interpreted in many different ways — as a triumph of attacking football or defensive football, of spontaneity or strategy, of flair or science, ball-playing or physical vigour, and sometimes even of talent. The victorious nations themselves will see in their success a vindication of a national style, and not just a national style of football but also of a way of life. When England won in 1966 it was not merely a victory for their measured skills on the Wembley turf but, by implication, a recognition of the English character — sound, reasonable, phlegmatic under fire, resolutely understated. It was appropriate at Wembley. When Brazil ran out the winners four years later in Mexico City, their victory was no less appropriate. In the fiery kettle of the Aztec Stadium,

under the glare of the noonday sun, it would have been a travesty if their brilliant, elastic and highly sophisticated form of advanced beach-football had not carried the day.

Meanwhile, in the intervening years between finals the defeated soccer nations furrow their brows and wonder what style to adopt to be victorious the next time. Club managers, too, take note and come home inspired to turn their own pedestrian forward lines into imitation Peles, Tostaos, Jairzinhos. . . . Should they use wingers or shouldn't they? Is 4–4–2, 4–2–4, 4–3–3, or even 2–3–5 the answer? The truth in these matters is of course only relative — a team can only play to the limits of its ability. England will never play like Brazil simply because the English are not Brazilians, but having seen Brazil play they can perhaps play more like them. Thus the World Cup has come to be the fulcrum around which the soccer public balances its judgments of the evolving game.

In some ways the World Cup is inequitable. The bias is bound to be towards the host nation, and to the other countries suited to those conditions. It is as hard for the Brazilians to play in English mud as it is for the English to play in breathless Mexico. But by and large it is not unlikely that the team playing the finest football in the world at that time will win, or at least reach the Final. The knock-out system means that they may not be faced in the Final by the second-best team, but they are unlikely to be faced by one of the 'rabbits'. What is inequitable in terms of pure footballing ability is the qualifying system, which ordains that sixteen finalists are produced from sixteen groups, some of them extravagantly inferior in quality to the others. No detached observer could seriously contend that El Salvador, competitors in Mexico 1970, were a superior side to Portugal or Hungary, for example, neither of whom qualified for the trip. Yet it would be entirely wrong to say that El Salvador had no right to be in Mexico. People talk long and hard after World Cups about the 'good of the game', and undoubtedly one of the features that contribute to this semi-mythical state is the knowledge that football is being played at every corner of the globe and that the national team of El Salvador, for instance, has the opportunity of qualifying to play alongside the giants of Brazil. Undoubtedly that is a great boost for El Salvador and an even greater boost for the game of football in El Salvador. (The fact that they had to fight a war on their way to the finals is, for the purposes of this argument, immaterial.)

If there is a wide discrepancy between the standards of the best and worst teams in the World Cup finals, there is almost certainly no fairer way of organizing the qualifying rounds. A World Cup has to mean what it says, and while the absence of, say, Portugal and Hungary can mean that some formidable individual talents are denied our view, the presence of El Salvador and Morocco can be, in a different sense, an equally enlightening experience. From them we may learn how the general standard of the game has progressed in their continents; from them we may rudely learn that to patronize is to invite a kick in the teeth. Who for example, would have set the chances of the North Koreans in 1966 at a pin's fee? Yet tiny and underrated, they came to Middlesbrough, lost to Russia, drew with Chile, eliminated Italy, qualified for the quarter-finals and led Portugal by three goals before the scythe of Eusebio finally cut them down. In the meantime they had shown what dedication and a ruthlessly practical approach to the game can do, and had set the stadiums of the North on a roar, not to mention having handed out a humiliation to the Italians as punishing as England's defeat by the United States in 1950.

The scrupulous military preparations of the North Koreans for the 1966 World Cup were not as atypical as some observers seemed to think. Nations prepare for World Cups now as if for war. Nothing can be left to chance. The important thing is the elimination of any kind of eventuality, on the field or off it, that might jeopardize ultimate victory. Practices vary from country to country, but a cross-section of reports on the build-ups to recent World Cups might reveal similar basic patterns. Dossiers are compiled on each player; like a beauty queen his vital statistics are recorded; his eating, sleeping and drinking habits are noted; his hobbies and interests outside football, if any, chalked down — presumably sometimes his sexual proclivities. Weaknesses may in some cases be indulged so that the strengths remain unimpaired. The player is cocooned from harmful influences so that he is perfectly free from extraneous pressures when he steps out into that hostile bowl of a packed stadium in a foreign country. At the crucial hour his genius must be seen at its best; like a prize stallion he must be groomed to the minute.

The feeling of being an object in an international market-place is a familiar one to the modern international player. He is conditioned from an early

The Jules Rimet trophy that belongs to Brazil, who won it for the third time in 1970.

age to adapt himself to the idea of having a price on his head, to the possibility that he may be horse-traded by his employers without so much as a whinny from him (in Britain a cool five per cent of his price stifles that). Even so, the fact that so many of the highest-paid performers can still play marvellous football when it matters must be a tribute to some kind of creative resilience that rises above the sordid financial pressures, and indeed above the prize stallion treatment. It may be because it is what the player knows best. It may be all he does know, but there it is, in his feet, and he must use it or go under. With all the staggering factors at stake in a World Cup — money, fame, prestige, not to mention the small matter of the joy or dejection of a whole nation — we may perhaps wonder at the truly remarkable amount of gifted football that has been played during the World Cup competitions. We must at least be grateful for it, and for the fact that all the molly-coddling preparations and the grooming for the market-place has not totally emasculated the talent before it has been displayed. A footballer's life is a short one, and it looks like getting shorter. We must hope to catch a glimpse of a player at his peak, before the pelvic muscles are worn thin — and the four years between World Cups can make the crucial difference.

1930
URUGUAY

Once upon a time, when the World Cup began, the story was rather different. Not much in the way of money or glamour attended the stars who took part in that first footballing concourse of nations. To begin with, there were only a handful who did take part. Several of the major European footballing countries were absent as was any side from Britain, the four British associations having unwisely withdrawn from FIFA. It was probably considered of little consequence at the time, for to most of the British footballing public, the World Cup, like Czechoslovakia in another context in 1938, was an event taking place in a far-away country of which they knew little – Uruguay.

In fact the Uruguayans had made a considerable impression on the international scene, winning the Olympic title in 1924 and in 1928 before large crowds of enthusiastic Europeans. Thus they were obvious candidates for hosts when the FIFA congress of 1928 voted to stage a World Cup tournament. The reasoning behind the resolution to inaugurate a World Cup was the fact that professionalism had taken a hold in many countries and debarred them from being represented at the Olympic Games by their best players. The trophy to be played for was named after the Frenchman Jules Rimet, president of FIFA, and five countries applied to stage the first competition – Italy, Spain, Sweden, Holland and Uruguay. The last named had the strongest case, for in addition to their already proven footballing qualifications, the year decreed, 1930, was the centenary of their independence. They planned to build a vast commemorative stadium (a feat they achieved in eight months), and as a proffered carrot, guaranteed to pay the expenses of each team that participated. They were duly awarded the first tournament, but alas their carrot was not succulent enough for most of the Europeans. Air travel was only in its infancy and one by one, Germany, Austria, Hungary, Italy, Spain, Switzerland and Czechoslovakia balked at the length of time involved in travelling to and from Uruguay, and at the fact that they would have to pay their players over that period. The Uruguayans were furious.

It was certainly an inauspicious start. The Uruguayans had come to two successive Olympics in Europe; why could the European nations not return the compliment, and compete for an even higher honour? On reflection it is very sad that the first World Cup was limited in the way that it was. Only thirteen countries took part and of those only five were not South American.

From Europe, France, Yugoslavia, Rumania and Belgium braved the ocean to Montevideo and, at that time, they were, so to speak, second division sides of the Continent: the fifth team came from the United States, large men of great stamina and tremendous enthusiasm. It was slightly ironic that several of the American team were ex-British professionals, mostly Scots lured from meagre wages in Glasgow to richer pastures across the Atlantic. What is sad also is that if British sides had participated in the Uruguay World Cup they might have had their eyes opened. It was all very well to sit back in the knowledge that they had fathered the game; what wasn't seriously realized, not for another twenty-three years in fact, was that the child had already come of age in several parts of the world and in a different image to the parents. It took the Hungarians to rub that one in in 1953, and there are some who think that the lesson still hasn't been learned.

If the Uruguayans were slighted by the poor entry for their World Cup, they nevertheless approached the competition with undiminished zeal, determined to prove that their Olympic titles had not been hollowly won, that indisputably they were the finest team of that era. Already in those Olympic tournaments they had shown a professionalism in their approach to training, and to winning on the field, which had paid handsome dividends. In Paris in 1924, for example, while some other teams enjoyed the traditionally amateur combination of a night life on the boulevards and a cavalier generosity on the field, the Uruguayans had spurned the bright lights and devoted themselves exclusively to the science of their game. The results were predictable – their opponents ran out of steam in the second half, the Uruguayans ran out the winners.

Now, in Montevideo, they showed themselves years ahead of their time by preparing with monastic dedication. For two months their squad of players was locked away in a hotel, and when their star goalkeeper Mazzali was caught stealthily crossing the entrance hall in the early hours of the morning he was sent home and the reserve goalkeeper Ballesteros took his place. Uruguay survived, however, the banishment of Mazzali. Ballesteros acquitted himself with honour, and the home nation lived up to its reputation, though observers who had seen them win their Olympic golds claimed that by now their best was behind them.

For the competition, the thirteen teams were divided into four groups: Argentina, France, Chile, Mexico; Brazil, Yugoslavia, Bolivia; Uruguay, Rumania, Peru; USA, Paraguay, Belgium. One team from each group was to qualify for the semi-finals. The early games had their quota of drama, particularly where the French were concerned. Opening the proceedings against Mexico (though not in the

Centenary Stadium which was not quite completed), they lost their splendid goalkeeper, Alex Thépot after only ten minutes with concussion from a kick in the face. In spite of this they cantered through to a comfortable 4–1 victory, and Thépot returned the next day, fit in body but bemused in memory, to play a blinder against the mighty Argentinians. Thépot might have been forgiven for thinking his brain had been permanently damaged when the referee blew the whistle for time some five minutes early; by then the Argentinians were leading by a solitary goal scored by their formidable centre half Monti, but the French were launching a late and vigorous assault on the Argentine goal. Angrily they protested to the referee and had retired to their dressing-room when the hapless official discovered his error. In confused circumstances he restarted the game and they played out the remaining five minutes, but the Gallic impetus had gone. They subsequently lost to humbler Chile, and their interest in the tournament was over.

The Argentinians however continued the sequence of high comedy. In their next match, against Mexico, which they won 6–3, five of the nine goals were from penalties, lavishly awarded by the Bolivian referee, Mr Ulysses Saucedo. Impartial observers reckoned that this was at least three too many. Then, when they played Chile, a brawl on the field just before half-time had to be quelled by police. But the high point was reached when they met the United States in the semi-final. At one point during the second half, as the USA bowed before a tide of

Argentine goals, the American trainer ran on to the field to make feverish protests about a refereeing decision. In his frenzy he cast the contents of his medical bag about the field, one of which was a bottle of chloroform, which broke. The fumes rose up and engulfed him, and he was led meekly from the scene. Chaplin would have been proud of it.

Up to that match the United States had done splendidly, reaching the semi-finals without conceding a goal. Their 3–0 win over Belgium had been straight-forward, though played at a furious pace, but their victory by an identical margin over Paraguay raised considerable interest. The Paraguayans had defeated Uruguay in their last international before the World Cup, and against them the Americans deployed subtleties not previously expected of such huge men. They showed deft ball control and used the short-passing game to great effect. As a result they came to the semi-finals as a favoured side; but the Argentinians were ultimately in a different class and, inspired by the belligerence of Monti, went through to the Final by 6–1.

In the other groups, the Yugoslavs sprang a surprise by defeating Brazil and then easily disposed of Bolivia. Uruguay inaugurated the Centenary Stadium on the appropriate day, 18 July, with a somewhat scrambled victory over Peru, and later defeated Rumania 4–0. The Rumanians (personally picked, it was said, and keenly supported by King Carol himself) had opened their programme with an inflammatory match against Peru, another of the many games characterized by eccentric refereeing, in which their right back broke a leg and the Peruvian captain was sent off. Rumania had won 3–1, but the Uruguayans qualified for the semi-final. In the latter the strange refereeing continued. Yugoslavia scored in the fourth minute, Uruguay replied with two goals, one of them clearly offside, the Yugoslavs had a 'good' goal disallowed, then Uruguay scored doubtfully again after the ball had plainly gone out of play. The second half, however, belonged legitimately to the home team, and they played close to their best form to win by a 6–1 margin.

The Final was an affair worthy of the occasion. It was the third time in less than three years that the two sides had met, their last Olympic Final having gone to a replay. The task of refereeing it was awarded to the Belgian John Langenus, resplendent in cap and plus-fours. Knowing the little love lost between the two countries he requested guarantees of safety for himself and the linesmen, and soldiers ringed the stadium. In the event his fears were unfounded, the major problem coming before the kick-off over the choice of ball. Both teams insisted on playing with a ball of their own manufacture; Langenus appeared on the field with one under each

arm, the captains tossed, and it was agreed to play one half with each. The Argentine ball was used first and they came off the better with it after Dorado, the Uruguayan winger, had scored an early goal. Peucelle equalized, and in the thirty-seventh minute a shot by Stabile (later a manager of the Argentine team) put the visitors ahead. The Uruguayans protested for offside, but the goal stood and was received with surprising equanimity by the mainly Uruguayan crowd. If this reflected a quiet confidence in their team, it was rewarded. Iriarte and Dorado began to dazzle on the wings and ten minutes into the second half Pedro Cea equalized after a superb solo run. Ten minutes later Iriarte had given Uruguay the lead, but there were anxious moments as the Argentinians counter-attacked and a searing shot by Stabile struck the cross-bar. It wasn't until the closing seconds that the result was sealed, Castro, who had replaced the injured Anselmo at centre forward, making it 4–2. Thus Nasazzi, the Uruguayan captain, held the World Cup aloft for the first time. Montevideo rejoiced, a national holiday was declared, and the Uruguayan Consulate in Buenos Aires was stoned.

The first World Cup Final had seen plenty of good football, free

and fast-moving, not yet shackled by the restrictive practices of the third-back system which was being adopted in Britain. Both sides played well; the Argentinians were perhaps let down by uncertain goalkeeping, but they had in Stabile the highest scorer of the competition and in Monti the most combative centre half. Ultimately the overall team strength of the Uruguayans triumphed — Nasazzi at right back was outstanding and the half-back line of Andrade, Fernandez and Gestido was a dominating force both in attack and defence. With these behind them the forwards had the fuel to drive towards goal. Today, on the basis of their recent World Cup performances, it is perhaps hard to imagine Uruguay and Argentina playing enterprising open football, and it is a comment on how the game has changed to record that they did. It was unlucky for them that they did not have the opportunity to defeat a more representative selection of the world's teams on their way to the Final. Uruguay had at least the satisfaction of inaugurating the competition successfully, they had a new stadium to hold 100,000 spectators and they had brought off a hat-trick of victories in the world arena. And the other competing nations went home richer by far.

1. **Jules Rimet presenting the trophy named after him to the President of the Uruguayan Football Association after Uruguay's victory in 1930.**
2. **The Uruguayan team which defeated Argentina 4–2 to win the first World Cup in 1930: Gestido, Nasazzi, Ballesteros, Mascheroni, Andrade, Fernandez, Dorado, Scarone, Castro, Cea, Iriarte.**

2

1934

ITALY

The 1934 World Cup was an unreal affair. The shadow of political propaganda hung over it, the current of political expediency ran through it, and may have won it. Italy were the hosts, more particularly, as the gaseous publicity proclaimed, the Duce himself. 'Every one of our guests felt the throbbing of the masculine energies of a bursting vitality, in this our Mussolini's Italy', said Giovanni Mauro, the Italian delegate to FIFA. The official report of the competition tendentiously recorded that 'the Duce conceded to every one of the matches played in Rome the privilege of his presence which, more than any other factor, galvanized the two teams on the field'. Probably the only players galvanized were the Italians who played a muscular aggressive game, much in the style of the Fascist image. The Germans were also present, playing bludgeoning, methodical football, cheered by massed ranks of swastika-waving supporters. It was too early for the clouds to be really black, but the retrospect is uncomfortable and there is a feeling that the repercussions might have been unpleasant for some if Italy had not won.

Italy fought hard for the right to stage the World Cup. It was only after eight FIFA congresses that they were awarded it. The clamour for the competition was such that thirty-two nations lined up to participate. Uruguay had led the way; now, where fools had feared to tread in 1930, all rushed in. It was plain from the size of the entry that the tournament could not be confined to one city, and Italy claimed that they had the required centres. They were even prepared to run the competition at a loss (in the hope that Italy would win it and the world take note of Mussolini's new-born land). They needn't have worried on any score — financial and footballing success attended them, and the world took note.

A qualifying competition was held to reduce the entries to sixteen for the finals, and thereafter it was played as a straight knock-out tournament. Uruguay stayed indignantly at home, still smarting over the poor European response in 1930. Argentina deliberately fielded a team made up of reserves, Italy having poached three of their star players, including Monti, on the grounds of their Italian ancestry. The Argentinians feared they would poach more if they sent their best players. In the event the Italians made only one conquest and that at the hands of the Americans; the player was their centre forward Donelli who had been born in Naples, and that club captured him after the competition.

When the final sixteen had qualified, the Italians, fearful of small gates if the giants met each other in the early rounds, decided upon a somewhat arbitrary method of seeding. They selected their considered eight best — Italy, Czechoslovakia, Hungary, Argentina, Austria, Germany, Brazil and the Netherlands — which was somewhat hard on Spain and Switzerland. No matter, in the first round the Spanish beat the Brazilians in Genoa and the Swiss defeated the Dutch in Milan. It is strange to read of Brazil being dispatched in the opening rounds of these first two World Cups, but though naturally gifted ball-players, they were not yet an organized force, and were further handicapped by the absence of their two full backs in Italy. Spain *were* organized, a distinct dark horse, led from the back by the redoubtable Zamora.

In the opening match in Rome, the Italians were much too good for the United States, though it was no doubt comforting to Donelli to score his naturalized country's only goal. The Italians replied with seven, and sadly it seemed that the American success in Montevideo had failed to ignite the necessary spark across that huge land. In Bologna the weakened Argentinians went down 3–2 to the Swedes, though both the goals they scored were absolute dazzlers and, as in 1930, they were handicapped by shaky goalkeeping. In Florence the Germans uninterestingly disposed of the Belgians 5–2, the centre forward Conen scoring three goals in a one-sided second half. In Trieste the highly rated Czechs were extremely fortunate to come through against a promising Rumanian side that led them by a goal to nothing at half-time. Goals by Puc and Nejedly in the second half won it for Czechoslovakia, but they had to thank the splendid Planicka (another goalkeeping captain) for keeping the Rumanians at bay. Meanwhile, far away in Naples, the Hungarians at last took a healthy revenge over the Egyptians who had astonishingly beaten them at the Olympic Games ten years earlier. For those with a phonetic sense of humour it is perhaps worth noting that the Egyptian goalkeeper was Moustafa Kamel, which may well have been his sentiments by the time Hungary's fourth goal whistled past him.

Undoubtedly the match of the first round took place in Turin where the French put up a tenacious struggle against the renowned Austrians. As in Uruguay, France were underrated at peril. Unlucky with an injury to Nicolas, their centre forward, who was a passenger for most of the game, they were still the dominant side; after ninety minutes the score was 1–1, both teams scored again in extra time and then the Austrians, through their inside left Schall, were awarded the decisive goal — 'awarded' because there was not much doubt he was offside. It was tough luck on the French, but

perhaps there was some poetic justice in the progress of Meisl's *Wunderteam*. It was naturally assumed that they would be the chief threat to Pozzo's Italy, but Meisl knew their best was behind them and this first match confirmed it. Still playing with the Vienna School elegance and finesse that had delighted Europe, they seemed battle-weary after a long season and the lively French had opened the scars in their spirit.

Their quarter-final with Hungary almost certainly scarred their bodies, an ugly brawling scrap between old rivals in which Markos, the Hungarian winger, was sent off. An exhibition of football was expected; what was served up was a mess, with only flashes of what might have been. A new recruit to the Austrian team, Horwarth, scored after seven minutes, Zischek made it 2–0. Dr George Sarosi scored for Hungary from the penalty spot and his nine compatriots fought ferociously for the equalizer. But the Austrians held out and in a way it was a tribute to their more measured talents.

The Germans methodically, and again uninterestingly, disposed of Sweden on a wet day in Milan, and the Czechs defeated the Swiss by the odd goal in five, scored by Nejedly just seven minutes from time. This was an exciting match, in which the Swiss played with great *élan* and once again the Czechs had to thank Planicka in goal for their survival. As for the other quarter-final, between the home nation and the ageing Spaniards, it was a stain on Florence's canvas. Over-tolerant refereeing allowed both sides physical liberties they should never have had, the more so when Spain took the lead through Regueiro in the first half and the Italians found themselves pounding fruitlessly against a defence in which the old hero Zamora played a game of legendary resilience and the full back Quincoces proved himself the finest defender in the competition. Italy equalized in the second half, but the match went to extra time, inconclusively except for the damage bodily inflicted on the players. The Spaniards came off worse — seven of their side, including the much-battered Zamora, were unable to turn out for the replay the next day. Italy introduced four new players, and this match left an even nastier taste than the first because it was even more spinelessly refereed. Bosch, the Spanish outside left, was crippled after five minutes and the visitors had two goals disallowed, one of them inexplicably. To add to their difficulties their two full backs knocked each other out as they raced to intercept the same forward, missed and collided. The gifted Meazza scored the only goal of the game for Italy, heading in from a corner, but there were many who felt that the fully fit Spanish eleven were the better side and might well have won the Cup. Mercet, the Swiss referee, was suspended by his own association.

Two days later the Italians

deservedly won their semi-final. The Austrians were beaten as Meisl had gloomily predicted they would be, because the Italians, especially their Argentine imports, were beefier players and better able to play on a mud patch. The delicate Austrian game floundered in the morass, and the game was decided by a single goal, scored by Guaita. The Italian victory was a tribute to their stamina so soon after the two punishing games with the Spaniards; at the same time it was a somewhat melancholy farewell to the Austrians. Zischek 'The Ghost' missed an open goal in the closing minutes and the great Mathias Sindelar, their tall and graceful centre forward, was policed out of the game by Monti's iron tackling.

In Rome the Czechs qualified for the Final by cheerfully outplaying the ponderous Germans 3–1. Their only lapse was a mistake by the hitherto faultless Planicka which gave Germany a soft consolation goal. Before the Final itself the third-place match had to be got out of the way, a doubtful inauguration which even today holds comparatively little for either side. The Austrians went down to the Germans 3–2, and nobody was much surprised — apart from a period in the second half when they played as though inspired by memory, their *weltschmerz* seemed absolute.

The Final was played in Rome before 55,000 spectators, with gate receipts of more than 750,000 lire. The captains, Combi and Planicka, tossed and retired between their respective goalposts. Both were to hold out until twenty minutes from the end — then Puc took a corner, the ball was played back to him, and he drove it fiercely past Combi. The Czechs almost sealed the match shortly afterwards, a shot from Svoboda hitting the post, and Sobotka fluffed a simple chance. Eight minutes from the end the clouds lifted for Italy, and it was like some divine intervention so curious was the goal. A shot by Orsi seemed well covered by Planicka when it inexplicably swerved in mid-flight and left him groping the air. So once more the Italians played extra time; urged on by the frenzied crowd, their superior strength and determination wore down the enthusiasm of the Czechs, whose subtle short-passing game lost its edge as their stamina waned. Schiavio scored the decisive goal which tighter, less tired Czech marking would earlier have prevented. Once again the host nation had won the Cup and in this case it was probably the deciding factor. But credit should not be taken away from Vittorio Pozzo whose achievement it was to integrate a collection of temperamental individuals into a team and invest them with the single-mindedness of winning.

1938

FRANCE

France were hosts for the 1938 World Cup, chosen to honour the guiding efforts of Jules Rimet. This time there were thirty-six entries, but before the competition got under way Argentina surprisingly withdrew and later the *Anschluss* meant that Austria were removed from the lists. The Germans took the opportunity to strengthen their team with Austrian players. Uruguay again declined to participate and the Spanish were absent, fighting a different kind of war. Britain, though not members of FIFA, were invited to fill a gap but refused. For the first time the holders and the hosts had automatic byes to the final rounds, again to be played on a knock-out basis. Once again the first round of the tournament proper was subject to seedings.

Of the first-round matches only two were decided within the ninety minutes of normal time, France beating their neighbours Belgium

3–1, and Hungary dispatching without difficulty the qualifiers from the Asian group, the Dutch East Indies. The other unknown quantity in the last sixteen, however, Cuba, performed with great panache against the Rumanians. Somewhat in the manner of Peru in the 1970 World Cup, they played with inventive zest, equalizing a first-half Rumanian goal shortly before full time, then leading 3–2 in extra time before the Rumanians forced a replay at the last gasp. For the replay the Cubans made an eccentric team change, dropping their goalkeeper Carvajales, who had been the star of the first match, and playing Ayra in his place. As it turned out, it was not such a dumb decision – Ayra reached even greater heights of excellence and Cuba won, scoring two goals within five minutes in the second half in reply to the Rumanian one. The winning goal looked suspiciously offside, but was given and it was no injustice on the run of play. The other match to go to a replay was between the Germans and the Swiss. The Germans were favourites, particularly with their Austrian reinforcements, but the Swiss had recently defeated England in Zurich, and the Germans, on the same English tour, had been

beaten 6–3 on their home ground. An evenly balanced game ended in a 1–1 draw; for the replay Sepp Herberger, the new German manager, formidable predecessor of Helmut Schoen, brought back Szepan who had been their outstanding centre half in the 1934 competition, and played him at inside left. At half-time Germany led 2–0; Switzerland pulled one back, then lost their winger Aebi, injured. The Germans failed to capitalize on his absence and when he returned the Swiss equalized through Bickel. Then the fine Swiss inside forward Abegglen set his seal on the match by scoring two splendid goals.

In Le Havre a weakened Dutch team held out for ninety minutes against the Czechs, but conceded three goals in extra time, while the holders found themselves equally pressed to get past staunch Norwegian opposition in Marseilles. Leading by a goal after only two minutes, the Italians then underwent a torrid examination by the Norwegian forwards, in particular by the fearsome Brunyldsen, leading the line like the prow of some Viking ship. The woodwork was struck at least three times and Olivieri frequently brought to full stretch in goal before the

Norwegians were justly on level terms. In extra time, however, Piola, the bright new light in Italy's forward line, escaped the rigid marking of Eriksen just once to score the goal that mattered.

From a spectator's point of view, the match to have seen was in Strasbourg where, on a muddy pitch, the Brazilians and the Poles went on a mad goalscoring spree. Each side was blessed with a really talented striker – Poland by Willimowski, and Brazil by Leonidas, the Black Diamond. The latter, amazingly, tried to play on the mud without his boots, was ordered by the referee to put them on, and scored three times in the first half. Willimowski scored only once, but added two more in the second half. A goal for each side by lesser mortals meant that full time came with a scoreline of 4–4. In extra time Leonidas and Willimowski both added to their tally; finally the eleventh and decisive goal was achieved by Romeo for Brazil. It was a pity that one of these two sides had to be eliminated so early – however the Brazilians had served notice for the first time of their immense potential.

The glittering promise was somewhat tarnished in their next match. In fact the contest at

Bordeaux between the Brazilians and the Czechs must go down as one of the nastiest encounters of all time, not far behind the notorious 'Battle of Berne' in 1954. For no particular reason the match became a complete bloodbath, two Brazilians and one Czech were sent off, two Czechs were wheeled off to hospital and the game ended at 1–1 with only seventeen players on the field. Leonidas had scored for Brazil and Nejedly, elegant survivor of the 1934 team, had levelled the match from the penalty spot. Alas he was to be later hospitalized with a broken leg, along with their other veteran hero Planicka, who broke his arm. As so often happens, the memory of this match was intimidating and the replay was conducted with equanimity – though Brazil had made nine changes and Czechoslovakia six. The Czechs led through Kopecky, who was subsequently injured and had to go off; Leonidas equalized and then Roberto volleyed in the winner for Brazil.

In the most interesting quarter-final, a large crowd in Paris were dismayed to see their national heroes bow out to the Italians. Pozzo's *azzurri*, garbed here in Fascist black, capitalized on mistaken French tactics which gave Piola the opportunity to turn on a superb display, which he crowned with two goals in the second half. The French goalkeeper had already given the Italians a gift goal in the first half, and though Heisserer had pulled it back for France, there was only one team in it for most of the match. In Lille the Swiss, who had performed so well against the Germans, put up only tepid resistance to the Hungarians and lost 2–0, and in the fourth match Sweden (through to this round because of Austria's absence) walked all over the Cubans. Wetterstroem became another four-goal hero, and even that was only half of his team's tally. Thus the Cubans, having shown a brief bright spark, were rudely extinguished and, to date, have not since rekindled it. As a footnote it is perhaps interesting that the Swedes were managed in this competition by a Hungarian, and that the Brazilians also owed much of their new-found strength to a Hungarian coach.

In Sweden's semi-final their Hungarian manager's native knowledge of the opposition was useful to them for maybe thirty-five seconds in which time they scored a goal. After that Hungary scored five times, Dr Sarosi and Szengeller, who scored a hat-trick, carving up the Swedish defence at will. It is said that play was so concentrated in Sweden's half that a blackbird settled on the pitch at the Hungarian end and enjoyed the worms at leisure. In Marseilles, the Brazilians committed an astonishing act of *hubris*. Blithely announcing that they were saving Leonidas and Tim for the Final, they took the field without them and paid the penalty – literally, for Domingas Da Guia stupidly scythed down Piola in the box and Meazza scored the decisive second goal from the spot. Colaussi had netted first for Italy; Romeo's goal in the second half merely made the scoreline more respectable for Brazil. It was a tragic waste, a travesty of what might have been a luminous confrontation of two highly talented teams. How would Leonidas and Tim have coped with Italy's formidable full backs? Would Da Guia, normally a most unphysical player, have conceded so foolish a penalty if not frustrated by the handicaps so wilfully imposed by the Brazilian management? Alas the war precluded the possibility of a second chance to match these teams.

For all this, the Final was no disappointment. As in 1934, the dialectic matched ruthless Italian logic with sinuous East European subtlety. In the sixth minute Italy scored a goal of devastating directness through Colaussi; within a minute Titkos had neutralized it. But gradually as the game developed Italy's superb attacking trio of Meazza, Piola and Ferrari acquired the freedom they sought. Before half-time Piola and Colaussi again had given Italy a 3–1 lead; all these goals had been laid on by Meazza. The Hungarians came back strongly after the interval, and Sarosi reduced the deficit with a somewhat scrappy goal from a goalmouth shambles. Pozzo, however, had trained his team too well for them to feel downcast, or even threatened, by Hungarian resistance: they were possessed of a dedication that sought victory without frivolity, and they had the players to accomplish it. Ten minutes from time Piola fittingly scored the fourth and final goal. It was the culmination of four triumphant years in which they had won two World Cups and the Olympic Gold, and their team in Paris was their finest of those years. Foni and Rava excelled at full back, the forward line as a whole was swift and incisive, and Piola the outstanding player of the tournament. His only rival for that garland was Leonidas; down in Bordeaux Brazil had defeated Sweden 4–2 for third place, and the Black Diamond had scored twice.

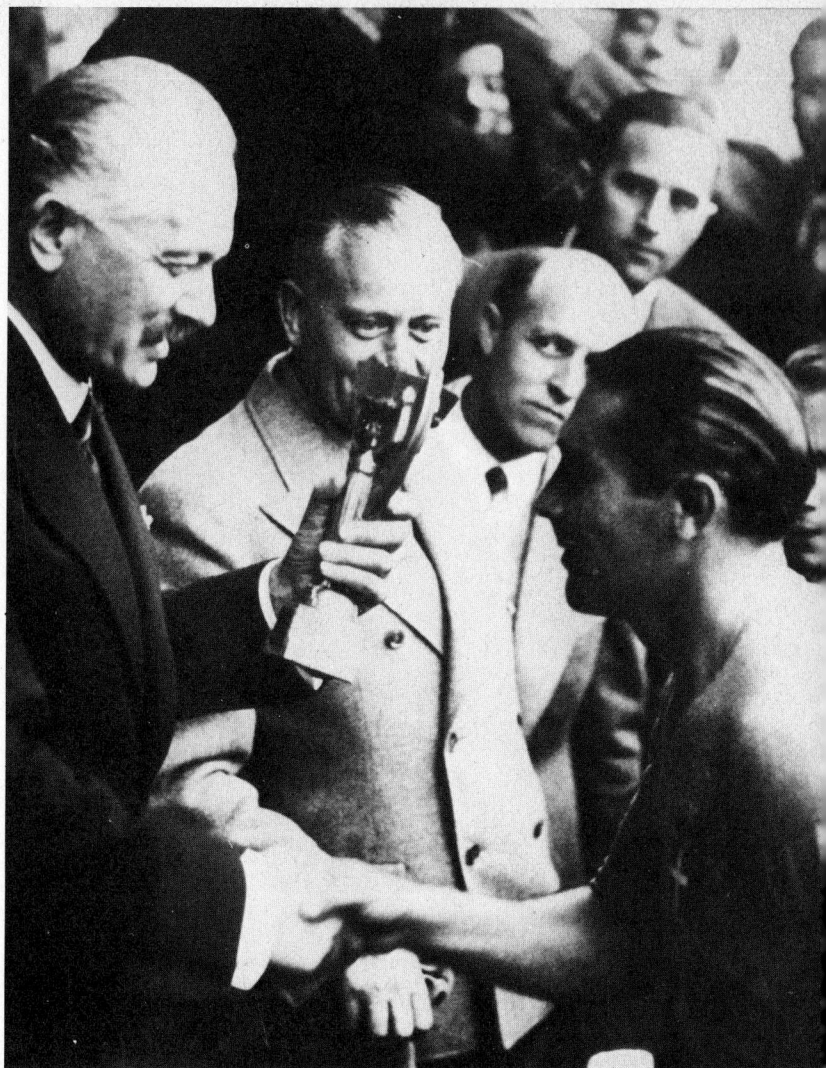

1. **Italian captain Meazza receives the World Cup after the 1938 victory in Paris.**
2. **Vittorio Pozzo victorious. The Italian manager, surrounded by his team, clasps the Jules Rimet trophy for the second time after Hungary had been beaten 4–2.**
3. **With the Italian defence, for once, split wide open the Hungarians score their first goal to level the scores in the 1938 Final.**

1950

BRAZIL

For twelve years the World Cup was in abeyance. The Germans had hunted for the trophy itself during their occupation of Rome, but the Italians had diligently salted it away in a Swiss bank. When the Brazilians were selected as hosts they, like the Uruguayans twenty-years before, embarked upon the building of a great stadium — the Maracana in Rio. Another parallel with that first World Cup was the thinness of the entry — eventually only thirteen nations competed. Many of the potentially powerful countries were absent — Russia, Hungary, Czechoslovakia, Austria, Germany (still excluded from FIFA) and, stupidly, Argentina and Scotland. The Argentinians had quarrelled with the Brazilian footballing authorities and decided to sulk. Scotland, incredibly, announced that if they did not win the Home International Championship (from which two teams qualified for Rio) outright, they would not go. England beat them 1–0 at Hampden Park, and though there were Brazilian spies at this game, expecting the strongest opposition to come from these two teams in the World Cup, the Scottish FA stuck Lear-like to their insane decision. They must surely have later regretted it, given England's bizarre failure.

There were some delightful oddities in the rulings laid down for the tournament — it was decreed that all the goalposts would have to be square and that competitors would have to wear boots. The competition was organized round four qualifying groups, played on a league basis, from which the four winners would go into a final group, also to be played on a league basis. The last-minute withdrawals of India and France meant an imbalance in the groups, the principal beneficiary being Uruguay who had only to play Bolivia. In the other groups were Brazil, Yugoslavia, Mexico and Switzerland; England, Spain, USA and Chile; Italy, Sweden and Paraguay.

In the scarcely finished Maracana Stadium Brazil opened the ball against Mexico, with a team on which some £50,000 had been spent in secluded preparation for this assault on the trophy and which was greeted with guns and fireworks on its entry into the ground. The game itself was without spark, however, and Brazil strolled to a 4–0 victory which was nothing less than expected, though their forward line showed vital promise of things to come and Ademir notched two of the goals. On the same day and in the same stadium, England defeated Chile (who had Robledo of Newcastle

playing for them) with a similar lack of excitement, and needed oxygen to do so. It was in Group III that the first rabbit was produced out of the hat, for in Sao Paulo the Swedes defeated the favoured Italians 3–2 and were applauded from the field by the largely Italian immigrant crowd for their skills. Shorn of the principal luminaries of their Olympic victory, who were playing for foreign clubs, the Swedish team had nevertheless been superbly rebuilt and coached by a Yorkshireman, George Raynor, principally fashioned around a highly gifted attacking trio of Palmer, Jeppson and Skoglund. Jeppson scored twice, and the cleverly applied directness of his team was too much for the more flowery Italians. The latter were, of course, no longer driven from within by the crazed nationalism that had secured their pre-war victories, and the recent Torino air disaster had further weakened their resources and perhaps affected their spirit. Nevertheless, not to be outdone, Italian clubs signed up most of the Swedish players at once.

The subsequent two matches in Group III were less distinguished — Sweden were held to a 2–2 draw by a lively Paraguayan team, not lively enough subsequently to contain a much-remoulded Italian side who won 2–0. But Sweden's point from the draw carried them through, and the holders were out. Back in Group I it did not seem there would be many threats in store for the Brazilians when the Yugoslavs comfortably outplayed the Swiss to the tune of 3–0 on the bumpy ground of Belo Horizonte, later the graveyard of English football. But maybe Flavio Costa, the Brazilian manager, who watched the match, was more concerned with politics than with the Swiss methods of defence, for when the two teams met in São Paulo he indulged local favours by selecting local players and the gesture was nearly ruinous. The Swiss deployed their celebrated bolt formation at the back, bewildering the free-moving Brazilian forwards, and although the host nation controlled the majority of the play their two somewhat fortunate goals were equalized, and almost on the whistle the Swiss missed an open goal which would have given them a remarkable victory. As it was, political indulgencies went for nothing and the Brazilians needed a police escort from the stadium. Their hopes began to look less than rosy when the Yugoslavs rubbed out the Mexicans 4–1, and then the Swiss defeated the Mexicans 2–1. Brazil's encounter with Yugoslavia was therefore to be decisive — a draw for the latter would be enough.

Before this, however, the whole football world had been turned topsy-turvy by the events in Group II. The English might have been warned that the shades of Bunker Hill were to be reborn when the curious potpourri of players who made up the United States eleven led Spain by a goal to nothing until

ten minutes from the end. Only then did their defence collapse and allow the Spaniards three generous goals. But it still seemed like a charity game when the two lined up to do battle in Belo Horizonte, and it must still seem like a nightmare to those who played for England on that day — no mean eleven: Williams; Ramsey, Aston; Wright, Hughes, Dickinson; Finney, Mannion, Bentley, Mortensen, Mullen. The Americans were captained by McIlvenny, recently granted a free transfer by third division Wrexham, and on the sidelines sat Stanley Matthews, unselected for his country. The mockery of the occasion was further heightened by the fact that many of the American team had enjoyed a night on the town with a typically careless abandon. The ground certainly favoured the less skilful team, but the English made the mistake of playing too intricately, as though they were at Wembley, and time and again their attacks fizzled into nothing. Shots struck the post, sailed over the bar, or flew wide of the mark, and then, at the other end, the unbelievable happened. Bahr crossed a ball that Williams had covered when the Haitian centre forward, Gaetjens, rushed in and touched it past the goalkeeper with his head. Instead of rousing the English to their combative best, the goal merely befuddled them further. Desperation crept into their play, complicated manœuvres were employed in situations that demanded simplicity, and the Americans were able to defend their lead with unfussy strength and growing confidence. It is argued that Mullen's header from a Ramsey free kick crossed the line before being hacked away for a corner, but it was only one of a multitude of chances that went begging, and the Americans were chaired from the field. It was certainly a triumph of huge proportions; alas it was ultimately meaningless in that it made no dent in the American public's disinterest in football, and then they were properly thrashed 5–2 by Chile.

Spain had earlier defeated Chile by the same margin as England had done, so England had to beat Spain to have a chance of entering the final pool. They lost 1–0 with a side that had Matthews and Milburn

restored to it, the latter mysteriously having a goal disallowed for offside. So England went home empty-handed and their only possible excuse might have been Neil Franklin's absence — shortly before the tournament he had left England to play club football in Colombia. The accusation that could be levelled against them was that their preparation for the World Cup had been inadequate.

Spain and Sweden were thus through to the final group; so were Uruguay who predictably trampled on Bolivia 8–0 in the only game that they played. Brazil and Yugoslavia contested the final place, an encounter that was marred by a curious incident before play began. On the way out from the dressing-room the star Yugoslav forward, Mitic, crashed his head against a steel girder and cut it badly. The referee, Mervyn Griffiths, refused to delay the start until Mitic had been repaired, and Brazil took advantage of the reduced opposition to score in the opening minutes. Mitic later appeared, heroically swathed in bandages, and played heroically too, but Brazil had their lead, and then sealed it with a second.

There were those who thought Brazil fortunate to reach the finals; they would instantly rue such an opinion, and fortune had nothing to do with it. Against Sweden, and then against Spain, the Brazilians played as though saying, to paraphrase Al Jolson, 'You ain't seen nothing yet.' People hadn't, nobody had, least of all the Swedish and Spanish, both of proven talents. It is possible that there have never been finer exhibitions of sustained inventive football than Brazil provided in these two matches. Their spontaneity seemed inexhaustible, their skills were certainly insurmountable. Sweden missed an early chance, and scored late in the game from a penalty, a

Bert Williams (left) and Ted Ditchburn, the two goalkeepers in the England party who made the ill-starred trip to Brazil for the 1950 World Cup.

gesture on the score sheet. Brazil scored seven times, and four of them went to Ademir, who with Zizinho and Jair made up possibly the most devastating attacking trio of all time. Their play was electric in its skills, and their understanding, backed up by Bauer behind them, was quite extraordinary. When Spain came to face them it was the same story. Rashly the Spaniards, cock-a-hoop after their defeat of England and after holding Uruguay to a 2–2 draw, pronounced that they would crush Brazil into their native dust. Instead they were beaten 6–1, more outclassed even than Sweden had been, and the score might have been doubled – the Brazilians gave up looking for goals towards the end and played exhibition football that, naturally, sent the crowd into ecstasies. It made the dreary iron-clad defensive systems of Europe seem more meaningless than ever; it was as though the Brazilians had not lost the state of footballing innocence, and yet had never known other than the most sophisticated of its arts.

Uruguay, by comparison, had seemed thus far no more than rather bad-tempered mortals. Their match with Spain was abrasive; against Sweden they were fortunate to overcome a team who led early on and only lost by the odd goal in five through inferior stamina. Sweden would, however, salvage some deserved honour by defeating Spain and ensuring themselves of third place. Thus though played on a league basis, the World Cup had a 'Final' ready made, and not many of the 200,000 crammed into the Maracana Stadium would have given a cruzeiro for Uruguay's chances. Brazil needed only to draw. They had only to play as they had played against Sweden and Spain and justice would be done. And so they did play, for the duration of the first half, brilliantly, ever on the attack, conjurors of football. But no goals came. The Uruguayans, aware of the massive over-confidence of the people of Rio, had calmly accepted the position of underdogs and planned their strategy with quiet intelligence. They organized a defence from which the great Brazilian forward line could not disentangle themselves, and when they did, Maspoli in goal excelled himself. Two minutes into the second half Brazil finally breached the wall, Friaca scoring. Uruguay were not shaken; they turned organized defence into organized attack, Brazil failed to reinforce their back line and twenty minutes later the ever-dangerous Ghiggia swept down the wing, crossed to Schiaffino, who scored with precision. The *élan* went out of Brazil's football, while Uruguay found new strength in the knowledge that they could not only keep out Brazil but penetrate them, too. It was they who were the aggressors now, and ten minutes from the end Ghiggia scored the decisive goal, cutting in from the wing and shooting between the

hesitant Barbosa and the near post. At the end a nation mourned, too shattered to riot, finding dignity in applause for the Uruguayans. The expectations had been so high that several people had died, listening to the radio commentary, and at the ground some sixty had fainted from the shock. It was like a Greek tragedy, and if the Brazilians had not won the victory their talents deserved, they could only point to the retributive wrath of the gods at their presumption. Uruguay for their part, magnificently led by Varela at centre half, had played with abundant intelligence and could boast Andrade (nephew of the pre-war star), Ghiggia and the delicate Schiaffino as being equal in stature to anyone on the opposite side. All the same it is still hard to believe, a story, like England's defeat by America, to be read again and again in the impossible hope that history was sleeping and it was all a mistake.

1954

SWITZERLAND

Memories of the 1954 World Cup are very mixed. Held in diminutive Switzerland, who thus bulged at the seams with invading foreigners, it was in a way the high-water mark of a particular kind of attacking football that thereafter began to decline as more and more countries tediously adopted safety-first defensive tactics. But in that soccer tournament at least half a dozen of the teams on show were excellent by any standards, and played football of a type that is now only to be seen in rare glimpses of joy. It was also, for those who bleat today that rough play is getting worse, probably the dirtiest World Cup of all, with the infamous 'Battle of Berne' topping the bill. Finally, as in 1950, the greatest team of the time was robbed of the trophy it plainly merited and for a similar reason – complacency.

Sixteen teams, in four groups, contested the finals, with an odd system within each group whereby two of the teams were seeded not to meet each other. There was also a foolish rule which decreed that all games should go to extra time if the scores were level. This meant that some teams were subjected to unnecessary stamina-sapping marathons. Two teams from each group qualified for the quarter-finals, to be played on a knock-out basis. England and Scotland were both participants, the British Home International Championship still being allowed as a qualifying hurdle, and Scotland were to discover on their first entry into this tournament the folly of their ways in not going to Brazil in 1950. Spain

were absent, losing the right to take part on the toss of a coin after only drawing with Turkey, a strange failure. The Argentinians still had their faces turned to the wall, for no good reason. Favourites were of course the mighty Hungarians, Olympic Champions in 1952, scourge of England at Wembley in November 1953, and even more comprehensively, in Budapest the following spring. Playing the deep-lying centre-forward game, which Hidegkuti commanded with such strength, they had also of course the superb talents of Czibor, Kocsis, Boszik, Grosics and Puskas still at their disposal. It is strange that the last named, instrument of so many victories, should perhaps have been a cause of their ultimate downfall.

In the early matches Western European eyes were opened, firstly by Yugoslavia's unexpected defeat of the French, whom many had thought would do well, and, secondly, by the inexhaustible well of talent from which the Brazilians seemed able to draw. Their great central attacking trio of 1950, along with most of that team, were gone, but in their opening game, in which they put five goals past the Mexicans, they proudly displayed their new ones, notably Djalma Santos and Nilton Santos at full back, Didi at inside right, and the formidable Julinho outside him. Bauer and Baltazar were the survivors from Rio, and the mixture looked almost as compulsive. The precise Swiss were very likely amazed at the way Didi defied science by 'bending' his free kicks in their clear mountain air.

The matches in Group II were distinguished by an embarrassment of goals, a total of forty-one being scored in five matches. Hungary began it by beating the hapless South Koreans 9–0, and then Germany easily disposed of Turkey 4–1. The Koreans had qualified by defeating Japan twice, both matches being played in Tokyo because no suitable ground existed in Korea. Their journey to Switzerland must have seemed very long and expensive when the Turks scored a further seven against them. The supreme irony of the tournament came in the first encounter between Hungary and Germany. The latter were cunningly managed by Herberger who realized that even if beaten by Hungary his team would be sure to reconquer Turkey in a play-off for a place in the quarter-finals. He thus decided to field a team consisting largely of reserves, thereby revealing nothing of his own strengths and probing the weaknesses of the opposition. Hungary, playing at full strength, won easily by 8–3, Kocsis scoring four times, but in doing so they suffered two serious blows. The only obvious one at the time was the injury to Puskas, who had to leave the field after being kicked by Liebrich, and did not fully recover before the end of the tournament. The other blow, which would only be realized too late, was the assumption that, having beaten the Germans so easily, they could do it

again, even if faced by the first-choice eleven. Herberger was vilified by the several thousand Germans who had flocked to the tournament for what they thought was an act of utter stupidity. Later, of course, he would be their greatest hero; for the moment he had to salvage some reputation in the public eye by reaching the quarter-finals, and his prophecy came true when his team thrashed the Turks a second time, 7–2.

Meanwhile in Group III Scotland had made a not undistinguished World Cup début against Austria and their defence had done particularly well. But failure to convert promising moves into profitable ones lost them the match, by the single first-half goal scored by Probst. England, for their part, had in Group IV drawn a match they should have won. The star of the game was Stanley Matthews who had not only played far too well for the Belgians but also for the more earth-bound talents of his own side. The other forwards had failed to capitalize on the profusion of openings that he created for them. In spite of this England led by 3–1 with only a quarter of an hour to go, with two goals by Broadis and one by Lofthouse; within the space of five minutes this lead was obliterated by Anoul and Coppens, and, absurdly, the match went to extra time. Again England went in front with another goal by Lofthouse, again England generously allowed Belgium to equalize, this time thanks to Dickinson who headed a free kick smartly past his own goalkeeper, and there it finished. Their chances of reaching the quarter-finals looked doubtful when the home nation astonishingly defeated the Italians. This was the first of the 'rough houses', for which in this case the Brazilian referee was in part responsible. Switzerland scored an early goal, and from then on the game degenerated into a contest in which the ball was possibly kicked less often than the players. Italy equalized through Boniperti, and in the last quarter Switzerland scored what proved to be the winner through Hugi. But the real trouble occurred when the referee strangely disallowed what would have been Italy's equalizer, and he was chased off the field by the Italians.

England, however, mastered the Swiss without undue stress when they met, a match without much spectacle. Mullen and Wilshaw scored for England, McGarry made a promising début at right half, and Wright played for the first time at centre half with notable success. They were thus assured of a quarter-final place, which meant that after Italy had recovered their composure and beaten the Belgians 4–1, they had once again to play the Swiss to decide the other qualifier. In the event the bloodbath was not repeated, but Italy played abysmally badly and allowed the previously uncelebrated Swiss to run rings round them. Switzerland won 4–1.

Elsewhere British hopes were

rudely dented when Scotland came face to face with the holders. Uruguay, playing for the first time in a European World Cup, had several of their 1950 Cup-winning team still playing, including Maspoli in goal, Varela, Andrade and the elegant Schiaffino. In their opening match they had been untroubled by an uninteresting Czech side, and won through goals by Miguez and Schiaffino. Now they faced a Scottish team, broken apart by internal dissension and by the resignation of its manager. More to the point they faced a Scottish team who, through insularity or arrogance, had failed to go to Brazil in 1950 and had thus learned nothing of that kind of football. Uruguay took them apart 7–0, five of the goals being scored by the two wingers, Abbadie and Borges, who made the Scottish defence seem as rooted as Glasgow statuary. Admittedly the temperature was about 100 degrees, but this further underlined the Scottish deficiencies — they were garbed in thick shorts and shirts, while the South Americans were equipped with the streamlined lightweight kit which is commonplace today. The other qualifier from this group was Austria, who produced sparkling form to defeat Czechoslovakia 5–0.

Back in Group I another match took place in which the referee was attacked. France were awarded a penalty late in the game, which was to give them a decisive 3–2 lead, and the Mexicans vented their wrath on Mr Asensi. It is perhaps worth noting that officials are much less likely to suffer this kind of physical assault today. They almost certainly suffer the same abuse, but for different, economic, reasons. In this particular match the result had no meaning, for Brazil and Yugoslavia were both assured of qualifying by their 1–1 draw which, again ludicrously, they were compelled to pursue into extra time. This was certainly the finest of the group matches, the Yugoslavs controlling the first half and scoring immediately after half-time through Zebec, the Brazilians supreme after that, hitting the woodwork twice and equalizing with a magnificent shot by Didi. Extra time made no difference to the scoreline. The referee was a Mr Faultless of Scotland. He was not attacked.

Thus in the quarter-finals Germany were matched with Yugoslavia, Hungary with Brazil, Austria with Switzerland, and Uruguay with England. All but the first of these were to provide yet more goal-harvests, though the Hungary-Brazil match became notable for something quite different. The Germans were very fortunate to beat the Yugoslavs who controlled the game for two-thirds of its length, unluckily conceded an early own goal through their centre half Horvat and were dispatched from the competition by a second German goal, scored by Rahn almost at the end. In a way it was a pity, because the Yugoslavs were an attractive and talented side, and in Zebec, Vukas, Boskov, Beara

and Cjaicowski they possessed real world stars. Beara in particular, a fine ballet-dancer, was always a delight to watch in goal with his acrobatic leaps and dives. The Germans were skilful but somehow dull.

There was nothing remotely dull about the derby between Switzerland and Austria. On a blazing hot day the host nation quickly went into a three-goal lead which deterred the Austrians not at all. Cleverly realizing that they could not break the verrou formation of the Swiss defence, they decided on a policy of shooting at any and every opportunity, whenever they saw the whites of the posts. They scored three goals in three minutes, surely a record, and then a further two, which Switzerland answered with another, giving a half-time tally of 5–4. In spite of the heat (perhaps because of it — the Austrian goalkeeper suffered from sunstroke) the goal glut continued in the second half — Austria led 6–4, Switzerland closed it to 6–5, and finally Austria sealed it at 7–5. The renowned Ocwirk, now playing at wing half for Austria, played an immensely polished game, as did Vonlanthen for Switzerland, but the heaviest scorer was the appropriately named Wagner who finished with three to his name.

In Basle England and Uruguay met in a match which was unfortunately decided by weak goalkeeping. Merrick, for England, had one of those nightmare afternoons which sadly obliterated the good account the English gave of themselves elsewhere. Again Wright and Matthews played magnificently, the crowd revelling in the skills of the latter and chanting his name delightedly. Uruguay scored after five minutes, Lofthouse equalized, and the Uruguayans were subjected to a period of sustained English attack. Then Uruguay took a scarcely merited lead when Merrick allowed a speculative long shot from Varela to elude him. In the second half Uruguay were discomfited by having three virtual passengers — Varela, Andrade and Abbadie, all limping — but Schiaffino was given room to score early on and England were faced with a two-goal deficit. Finney reduced it in the sixty-eighth minute, the English forwards missed several more chances, Matthews hit a post, and then Uruguay scored a further 'soft' goal through Ambrois which made their victory certain. Probably it was not an injustice.

The fourth quarter-final was the match which, came to be known as the 'Battle of Berne'. Brazil and Hungary might have provided not just the match of the tournament but the match of the decade. Instead they were both smitten with nerves, fearful of the outcome. The match was contested in teeming rain and was refereed by the Englishman, Arthur Ellis — there are those who say he saved an explosive situation from getting worse, there are others who say one of his decisions was crucial. The

tone was set early on when Lorant of Hungary was cautioned for a bad foul, but laughed in the referee's face. Then Hidegkuti scored in the fourth minute, and had his shorts removed, which is nothing if not provocative. Four minutes later Kocsis headed a second goal. So Brazil were trailing and, firmly interested in restoring their position, stopped at nothing to do so. The Hungarians were no innocents in the struggle and, almost predictably, gave away a penalty which Djalma Santos converted. At half-time 2–1, and Hungary resumed with Toth a passenger on the wing. Then came the crucial decision — a mix-up in the Brazilian penalty area in which Kocsis collided with Djalma Santos, another Brazilian defender fell to the ground (and possibly touched the ball with his arm), and the mêlée ended with a penalty being awarded to Hungary. Santos had placed the ball as though to take a free kick for Brazil, and the Hungarians had fallen back as if expecting the same when the referee gave his decision the other way. The penalty put Brazil behind 3–1 and all hopes of a peaceful settlement were from then on obliterated. Julinho scored a wonderful individual goal to reduce the arrears, but Boszik and Nilton Santos swapped punches and were sent off (requiring police to calm the situation). Humberto Tozzi hit the post, Didi hit the cross-bar, Humberto Tozzi perpetrated a foul which resulted in his being sent off, and to rub salt in the Brazilian wounds, Kocsis immediately headed in one of his 'specials'. The final score on the field was 4–2, but off it the fight raged in the dressing-rooms with fists, bottles, bad language and several casualties. The Brazilians claimed they had been robbed; the public certainly had — of a football match.

Fortunately the semi-final between Hungary and Uruguay restored some of the balance, a great performance by two contrasting teams at their best. Puskas was still injured, but the Hungarian attack remained lethal. Uruguay were without Varela and Abbadie, but found a stunning forward replacement in Hohberg. Czibor scored after thirteen minutes, and then Hidegkuti added another immediately after half-time. Once again, however, the Uruguayans showed their resilience. Prompted by Andrade, they launched attack after attack on the Hungarian goal, but it was not until the seventy-sixth minute that they scored their first, Schiaffino combining with Hohberg who scored with a cleverly delayed shot. The Hungarians played for time, lost popularity with the crowd and, three minutes from time, lost their lead, Hohberg again being the scorer. Overcome with emotion, or congratulations, or whatever, he had to leave the field, but came back as extra time began. However the Hungarian stamina was the greater and while Andrade was recovering from cramp, Kocsis headed a goal, and soon after headed another to make it 4–2 in Hungary's favour. It

was the first defeat that Uruguay had ever suffered in a World Cup; it was also on a par with their finest performances.

In the other semi-final Germany destroyed Austria 6–1, a margin made more flattering by the poor form of Zeman in the Austrian goal. The Austrians recovered to beat a demoralized Uruguay 3–1 in the match for third place, while Hungary and Germany set about each other for the second time. As in Rio four years previously, the favoured side were swollen with over-confidence; as in Rio they took a lead which ought to have proved decisive. In fact Hungary led by two goals, through Puskas (a gift) and Czibor, after only eight minutes. But the Germans countered at once, scoring when Morlock slotted home a cross, and eight minutes later were level when Rahn drove home a loose ball after a corner kick. Both sides now began to play at their best and Hungary's superior talents ought to have been rewarded. But they were faced by Turek in the German goal who made save after save of superhuman proportions; Hidegkuti hit the post, Kocsis the cross-bar, Kohlmeyer kicked off the line. Thus it continued, Hungary attacking, Germany counter-attacking, until six minutes from time when a sad mistake by Boszik allowed Schaefer to pounce on a weak pass and set Fritz Walter free. His centre was fiercely converted by Rahn. Almost at once Puskas scored at the other end, but it was given offside. Then Czibor forced Turek to make his most remarkable save yet, diving full length to clutch the ball just inside the upright. It was too late — Germany had won 3–2, and Hungary could have few complaints. Herberger and Fritz Walter between them had fashioned a sound policy and had produced football which, if less illuminating than the Hungarians at their peak, was solid and skilful. Puskas should probably not have played for he was only three-quarters fit and unable to make much impression on the play; his presence meant that Budai was excluded, another mistake.

Two years later the Hungarian Revolution put a definitive end to that great football team, driving some of its members overseas and Puskas, of course, to new heights with Real Madrid.

1. **Uruguay on the way to their first World Cup defeat. Hidegkuti scores Hungary's second goal in their 1954 semi-final.**
2. **Hungary on the point of scoring their first goal in the 'Battle of Berne'. Hidegkuti, with arms raised, waits to receive the ball while Castilho is stranded out of the Brazilian goal.**

1. 1954 World Cup Final. Confusion in the Hungarian goalmouth and a German attack is somewhat fortunately scrambled away.
2. In the same match Morlock, Germany's inside right, eludes Grosics's dive and slides home his country's first goal.

1958

SWEDEN

The build-up to the 1958 World Cup was the biggest yet — fifty-three nations entered and the qualifying matches around the world aroused immense interest. When the entrants had finally sifted down to the sixteen who would go to Sweden there were some surprises and a good many unknown quantities. Uruguay were absent, astonishingly eliminated by Paraguay; Spain and Switzerland were also out, in a group from which Scotland emerged the winner. The four home countries were all in fact present in Sweden, having each qualified in different groups, though Wales slipped in at the last minute through a withdrawal. Northern Ireland had achieved the final stages at the expense of Italy, and would demonstrate that their presence was by no means a fluke. By the time the competition began there were no clear favourites, though Brazil, who had a new manager and several unknown cards in their pack, were obviously feared; the Swedes had the advantage of home territory and the fact that their expatriate stars had been returned to them; the Germans and the Hungarians had declined since Switzerland; Russia were competing for the first time and Argentina were back at last. England's strength had been severely cut by the tragic loss of Duncan Edwards, Roger Byrne and Tommy Taylor in the Munich air disaster. They, too, had a new card up their sleeve, sadly not dealt during the tournament — the eighteen-year-old Bobby Charlton. It is strange to look back and realize that when England played Brazil in their group both Charlton and Pele were confined to the sidelines. The Brazilian was in fact injured but he at least would later be allowed to make his mark in the competition.

When Sweden began the proceedings against Mexico it was for the home crowd more an occasion of nostalgia than of expectation. In their ranks were Liedholm and Gren, who had been part of the 1948 Olympic side,

Skoglund and Mellberg from their 1950 World Cup side, and Hamrin and Gustavsson, returned from Italy. Grace and skill were there but so were the shades of middle age; but as the game progressed there were no signs of debility and the hosts strolled out easy 3–0 winners. In the other groups the Germans impressively defeated Argentina 3–1, with an attack cleverly arranged to accommodate the diverse talents of Helmut Rahn (who scored two of the goals), the ageing Fritz Walter and the newcomer Uwe Seeler. France, about whom nobody had thought twice, demolished Paraguay 7–3, and showed that they had a formidable attacking spearhead in Piantoni, Fontaine and the superb Kopa, back from Real Madrid. Fontaine scored a hat-trick. Meanwhile England struggled to hold the Russians to a 2–2 draw, after trailing 2–0. An authoritative Soviet defence and the long agile arms of Yachin kept them out until Kevan headed a splendid goal from a free kick and, finally, Finney levelled the scores from a penalty. It was poetic justice of a kind for he had been crippled by some graceless Russian tackling, and would in fact take no further part in the World Cup.

In Group I the Irish made a magnificent début, defeating the Czechs by a goal scored by Wilbur Cush, and in Group III Wales were equally impressive in holding the Hungarians to a 1–1 draw. Boszik had scored after only five minutes, but the massive John Charles, though much abused by the rough treatment of the Hungarians, rose above their defence to head an equalizer. Boszik, Grosics and Hidegkuti were all that were left of that invincible side of the early fifties, and Hidegkuti was now thirty-eight. But that was no rarity in this tournament. Scotland, in Group II, also played solidly to hold Yugoslavia to a 1–1 draw — it was the first point won by Scotland in a World Cup and, to date, it is the only one, a depressing reflection on a country which provides so many gifted individuals and so seldom the team for the occasion. In Sweden they never played badly, but they subsequently lost by the odd goal in five to Paraguay, and the odd goal in three to France. It is perhaps significant that Bill Brown in goal was the recipient of the highest accolades.

The Brazilians opened their programme with a somewhat unsatisfactory win over Austria. Though they scored three goals without reply, two going to José Altafini (nicknamed Mazzola because of a likeness to the late Italian star), the performance was vaguely unsettled. The team chosen was a strange one: Pele was injured, but Garrincha was unselected, as were Zito, Vava, and Djalma Santos. The Austrians were ponderous, regretting perhaps their omission of Ocwirk, now playing in Italy, but Brazil failed to exploit, as they would later have done, the opportunities. What did emerge was the basis of the 4–2–4 system

which Vicente Feola had impressed upon them, and with which they would subsequently dazzle all comers when they exhibited the true colours of their play. These were still not on show when they came to face England, not by any means the dull match which a goalless draw might suggest but a remarkably even one, in which Colin McDonald in the English goal played very well and the defence as a whole shrewdly dampened the fires of the Brazilian forward line. England might even have won if they had been awarded a deserved penalty, and it was felt that Finney's presence could have troubled the Brazilian defence. As it was, the English forward line looked merely pedestrian, with Haynes below his best.

Germany, coming from behind, scored two goals through Helmut Rahn (again) to share a draw with Czechoslovakia, but in the same group, Northern Ireland, who had promised so much in their first match, were sharply rebuffed by Argentina. The South American champions were the two veterans, Nestor Rossi and the forty-year-old Angel Labruna. Ignoring a third-minute goal by McParland they prompted their team to play delightful football and the Irish, foolishly relying on defence, conceded three goals. Thus Argentina and Germany looked the likely candidates from this group for quarter-final places, but an astonishing upset and a completely inexplicable one gave Irish hopes a lift. The Argentinians were routed by Czechoslovakia 6–1, and it is difficult to say which was the greater anomaly — the brilliant way the Czechs played or the abysmal performance of the Argentinians. In a way the Czechs are to blame for the consequences, for the Argentinians, having been given a predictable reception on their return to Buenos Aires, never again returned to the elegant, free-moving, virtuoso game. Instead they adopted the miserly bone-crushing tactics, based on survival at all costs, which have governed their game ever since.

The Irish, for their part, raised their game heroically to hold the Germans to a 2–2 draw, a thrilling match in which Rahn neutralized an early goal by McParland, McParland scored again and Seeler equalized that. The Germans had more of the play, but Gregg played a wonderfully brave game in goal and was, more than anyone, the instrument of Irish survival. They thus had to play off against Czechoslovakia. In Group III Wales should perhaps have beaten the undistinguished Mexicans; instead they let in a last-minute goal which equalized Ivor Allchurch's earlier effort. In the same group the Swedes assured themselves of first place by defeating Hungary 2–1, but it was a scrappy match. The Hungarians were miserably at odds with themselves, having dropped Hidegkuti and put Boszik in his place, who was quite unfitted for the role, there were some

controversial refereeing decisions and only Skoglund and Hamrin on the Swedish wings and Tichy at inside-forward for Hungary brought novelty to the proceedings. Subsequently, secure of their progress, the Swedes played a largely reserve team against the Welsh, which resulted in a goalless draw, and because the Hungarians easily beat the Mexicans 4–0, Wales and Hungary were also faced with the prospect of a play-off.

Meanwhile in Group IV more interesting things had been happening. Russia had been untroubled by the battle-weary Austrians, winning 2–0, but now they faced a Brazilian side into which had been drafted Zito, Pele and, at the players' instigation, Garrincha, 'The Little Bird' with the twisted knee and the incredible speed. The whistle for the kick-off must have seemed to the Russians like the signal for a fireworks display. In the first minute Garrincha hit the post, in the second minute Pele hit the post, in the third minute Vava scored. The exhibition continued with relentless brilliance. Igor Netto was quite unable to mark Didi, as instructed, and the latter set his forwards free as if on long strings of superbly controlled puppetry. That Brazil only scored once more, through Vava late in the second half, is neither here nor there. They had found the level to which they had continually aspired, and which would make them world-beaters. How depressing beside this to record that England left their team unchanged and could only manage a 2–2 draw with Austria. This meant a play-off against the Russians for a place in the quarter-finals, the third British side to be in this position. Only Group II had been decided on a clear-cut basis, with France and Yugoslavia sharing the honours. The meeting between these two had provided a vivid seesaw game, which the Yugoslavs, against the run of the play, had won by the odd goal in five from a French defensive error. Fontaine scored both the French goals. Yugoslavia subsequently drew 3–3 with Paraguay.

In the play-offs Ireland and Wales achieved extraordinary successes, the former once again mastering the Czech forward line where Argentina had failed (and where they themselves had failed against Argentina) — this despite the fact that Gregg was injured and unable to play, and Uprichard, his deputy, was injured in the course of the match. So, too, was Peacock but the ever-dangerous McParland added to his impressive goal tally to equalize the Czech lead, and when the match went into extra time coolly executed the winner from Blanchflower's free kick. Wales did no less well against Hungary in a match which was scarred by uncharitable tackling. Poor John Charles was viciously policed and quite unable to display his true gifts, unprotected by a disinterested Russian referee. Hungary scored first, but Allchurch

133

struck a thunderous volley to equalize and then Grosics gave away the decider, Medwin nipping in to intercept a short goal kick directed at the full back. For the Magyars it was an undistinguished departure from the world arena; for the Welsh a triumphant début.

England made changes to their attack for the play-off against Russia, introducing Brabrook and Broadbent but not, alas, Bobby Charlton. They were perhaps unlucky to lose on the run of the play, and in the relative number of chances created, to a goal by Ilyin that went in off a post, but in this kind of competition they were still handicapped by a reluctance to plan a professional campaign, by management that may have been competent but was hardly inspirational, and by players who were plainly exhausted after a long domestic season. This particularly was evident in the play of Haynes and Douglas. *Plus ça change.* What is perhaps unforgivable is that England only took to Sweden twenty players out of the permitted maximum of twenty-two. If Finney had not been injured they might have done better. But their approach was too peripheral ever to have won it.

The quarter-finals were somewhat reduced in quality by the fact that three of the teams had undergone

1. Giant among forwards, John Charles tussles for the ball with Budai. In this play-off for a place in the 1958 quarter-finals Wales achieved a remarkable victory over the Hungarians.
2. Pele and Svensson, the Swedish goalkeeper, compete for the ball in the 1958 World Cup Final.
3. Derek Kevan of West Bromwich Albion who led England's attack in the 1958 World Cup.
4. In their play-off for a quarter-final place England did less well than Wales, succumbing to the Russians. Here Johnny Haynes and Yachin go up for a ball together.

exhausting play-offs. Only the Germany-Yugoslavia contest featured two fresh teams, an unattractively physical performance earning the Germans a place in the semi-final with a single goal scored by the inevitable Rahn. There was likewise a certain inevitability in the stardom of Hamrin in Sweden's 2–0 defeat of the Russians. Playing with a sustained brilliance on the wing he scored one goal, made the other, and finally gave the enigmatic Swedes the glimmerings of enthusiasm for their team's successes. In the other two matches British hopes evaporated. The Irish really were unlucky for they had to play after an eight-hour coach journey. Gregg, still hobbling, was drafted back into the side because Uprichard was even more crippled, and Casey, too, had to play with a badly cut leg. The French were altogether too lively and scored four goals without the Irish even getting in a shot worthy of the name. But theirs had been a truly spirited World Cup performance; Peter Doherty had proved an enlightened manager, and the team owed much to the generalship of Danny Blanchflower at the back and of Jimmy McIlroy at the front, not to mention the finishing skills of McParland. Wales's defeat at the hands of Brazil was highly honourable, because they were without John Charles who might have taken one or two of the chances that were offered. As it was, they defended with tremendous energy, confusing the Brazilian attackers, and only a somewhat fortunate goal by Pele, from a shot either deflected or mishit past Kelsey, separated the teams at the end.

For the first time the Swedes had excited vociferous support when they met the Germans in their semi-final at Gothenburg. It may have made the difference in a game that was patchy but rarely dull. Germany led through a brilliantly executed goal by Schaefer which was equalized by Skoglund in slightly doubtful circumstances. The Germans protested that Liedholm, who made the final pass, had brought the ball down with his hand, but the Hungarian referee ignored their pleas. The second half saw a crop of unpleasant fouls, one of which led to Juskowiak being sent off after he had retaliated on Hamrin. Germany were further handicapped by an injury inflicted on Fritz Walter, and this paved the way for Sweden's winning goals, one scored by the veteran Gren, the other, one of the most dazzling of the tournament, by Hamrin after a virtuoso dribble. Perhaps, in the end, it was his talent which, more than any other factor, took the Cup away from the Champions.

France, who had been the revelation of the finals, lost 5–2 to Brazil. Vava had scored first, and then Fontaine had the honour of being the first in the competition to find the Brazilian net. The match was evenly poised until Jonquet, the French centre half, was injured — far too great a handicap against

the Brazilian attack. Didi struck their second goal and then Pele gave the Stockholm crowd a taste of his potential with a wonderful hat-trick. A late goal by Piantoni for France was of no importance. It is, however, to France's great credit that they were quite unbroken by their experience, for in the match for third place they destroyed Germany 6–3, Fontaine and Kopa combining superbly, the former scoring four goals which gave him a grand total of thirteen for the competition, a figure that is unlikely to be overtaken.

Aware perhaps of Brazil's anxiety to grasp the World Cup at last, the Swedes, still under the astute managership of George Raynor, applied some psychological pressures before the Final, and might reasonably have felt confident of success after Liedholm had scored a carefully individual goal in the first five minutes. But their dreams were chimerical. Brazil were not disturbed, building their assault with method, and above all, deploying their talents on a disciplined rein. The two Santos, Djalma and Nilton, quickly snuffed out the threats of Skoglund and Hamrin while at the other end Garrincha and Zagalo proved quite unstoppable. Garrincha was individually the architect of their first two goals, twice in the first half leaving the Swedish defence rooted to turn the ball into Vava's path. With a 2–1 scoreline at half-time there was still, theoretically, hope for the Swedes; in the second half the new Black Diamond of Brazil expunged it when he scored one of the most spectacular goals of all time. Receiving a high cross in the penalty area Pele juggled the ball on his thigh, flicked it over the head of a Swedish defender, caught it on his thigh, repeated the performance with another defender, and then smashed the ball on the volley into the net. The poor Swedes must have felt they were spectators at a variety show. Brazil were dominant now, defending in depth, attacking in depth, ever fluid, ever unpredictable. Zagalo added to the total, Sweden bravely retaliated with one by Simonsson, but the Brazilian cup was full when Pele rose like a salmon to head his country's fifth. At seventeen years of age he had only just embarked on his remarkable career, and Brazil had only just achieved what they had so often seemed to merit. In Sweden, wisely governed by Feola and Dr Hilton Gosling, they had exercised their natural brilliance and effervescence, but contained it within a system, without the recklessness or the ruthlessness that had marred their earlier World Cup performances. At their best they played with a continuous bubbling rhythm as though saying, 'Let me borrow the ball for just a few seconds and I'll show you what I can do.' Individually they excelled, collectively they delighted, and the colour they brought to those sombre Swedish skies is inextinguishable.

135

1. World Cup Ballet 1958. Sweden's Skoglund manages to pass just in time to escape the desperate lunge of Brazil's Zito.
2. Their Cup at last. The Brazilians joyously partake of the lap of honour after their great victory in Stockholm.
3. Vava scores the first of Brazil's five goals in the Final, from a pass by Garrincha who had completely bemused the Swedish defence.
4. The young Pele weeps on Didi's shoulder after Brazil's 5–2 defeat of Sweden in the 1958 World Cup.

VÅR FEMTE SVENSK GÅR I OSCARIA SKOR M

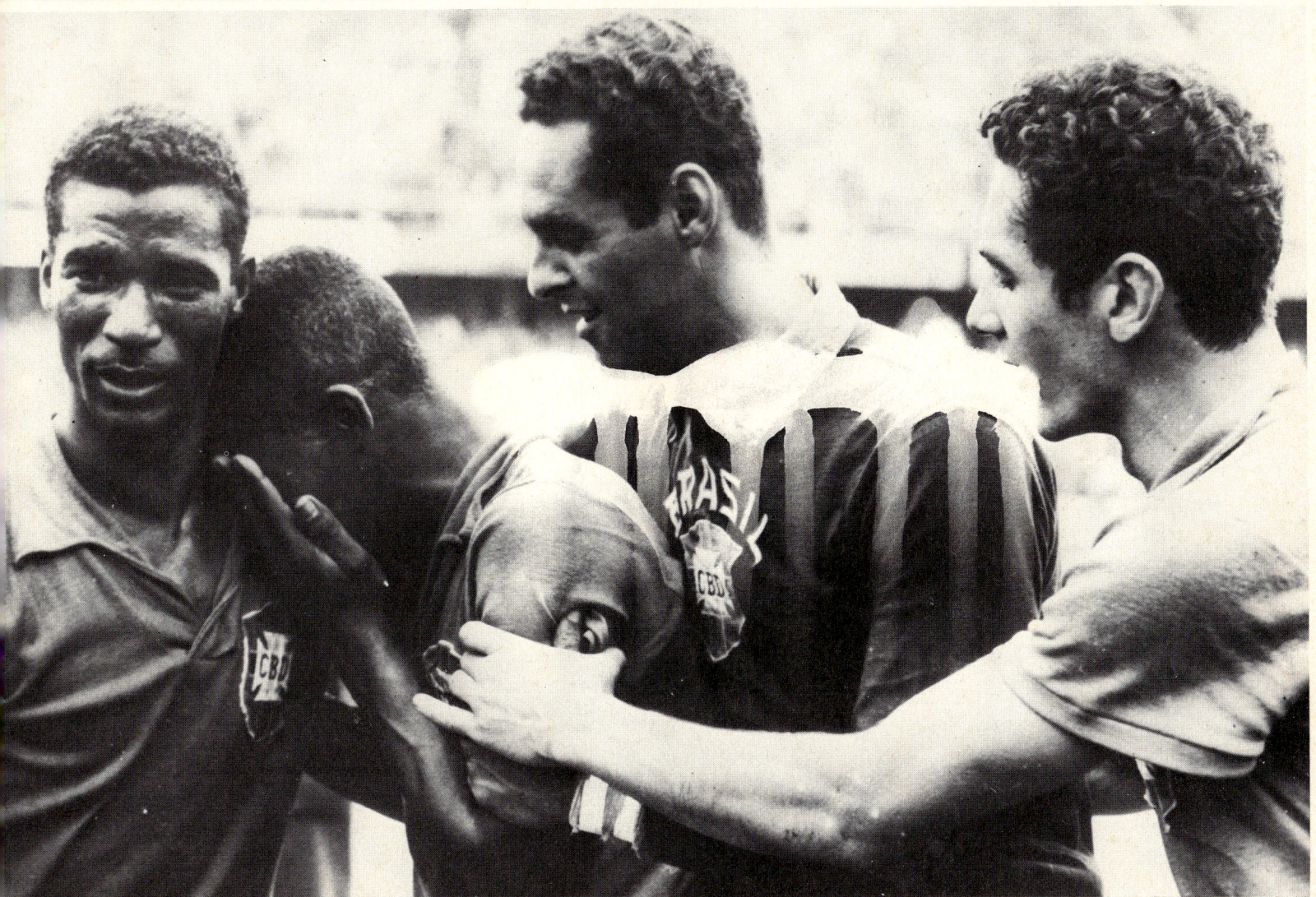

1962

CHILE

There is something about the 1962 World Cup which forbids enthusiasm. It is not merely that, from an English point of view, it took place far away on the further shores of South America, in poor beleaguered Chile, decimated yet again by a violent earthquake and more or less granted the World Cup as a gesture of public sympathy. Rather the temperature of the interest remains below feverish because of the somehow unsensational nature of the whole tournament. Apart from the Chileans themselves, local heroes to the last, there were no great upsetters of reputations, and no matches that seemed to embed themselves naturally into the memory. Perhaps it was simply that the best teams present were either not as good as they had been or as good as they were going to be. If they were, then some strange alchemy in the Andean air must have worked on their gifts, inhibiting talent, bridling the spontaneous and encouraging the tentative. It was not dull, nor was it supremely thrilling. World football seemed cast into a limbo that was somewhere between free-flowing attack and vice-like defence, in which scores would always remain low. No more the lavish totals of Berne – ever after it would seem, scorelines of 7–5, 6–4, 5–3 and so forth would indicate charity matches or eccentricity. (There were a few high totals in Chile but on the whole they belonged to one-sided contests.) At least Brazil were again the winners and, thus far in the annals of soccer history, that has always been a good thing.

The South American nations were well represented. Together with the hosts and the holders, Uruguay, Colombia and Argentina were qualified; from Eastern Europe came Russia, Hungary, Czechoslovakia, Bulgaria and Yugoslavia; Germany, Italy, Switzerland, Spain and England were the flagbearers for the rest of Europe; and Mexico for the Americas. After the rash of British names in the previous World Cup, England's solitary challenge looked thin. And was. Once again, under the amiable managership of Walter Winterbottom, they seemed to approach the World Cup without single-mindedness, without appearing to expect success, the tournament still regarded perhaps like some bizarre circus that trundled by every four years in distant capitals. They would change their attitude quick enough when the circus was posted to their own back lot.

Chile, frenetically supported by the populace, performed convincingly enough in the opening match, Sanchez scoring twice in their 3–1 victory over the Swiss. Maybe the Chilean public over-rejoiced because they feared their team's success would be short-lived – the other teams drawn in the group were Germany and Italy. But these two fought a thoroughly uninspired battle, graceless and goalless. Germany, still under Herberger, maintained their hefty indifference to the physical legalities of the game, Szymaniak demonstrating, as he would continue to do, that he was one of the most destructive wing-halves of his time. They were more popular than Italy, however, who were disliked for their habit of poaching South American players of Italian extraction. Thus here they had Altafini from the 1958 Brazilian team, and Sivori from the Argentine in their line-up. But not those two in the one forward line nor Seeler, Schaefer and Helmut Haller in the other would make any dent in the defensive walls.

Nor, for those who had come expecting to see a fiesta of football, was there much joy to be had from Brazil's opening match. Their team, with marginal differences, was the one that had set Sweden on fire four years back, but the flame seemed reluctant to catch, and Mexico put up a sturdy resistance. Only Pele rose to his full magisterial height, laying on a goal for Zagalo, converting a memorable one himself in which he more or less danced a samba round the entire Mexican defence. Perhaps it was that some of the team had been playing in Spanish league football and were unsettled by the experience. Spain, like Italy, was another country to poach extensively from abroad – witness the rise of Real – and here in Chile their national ranks contained the great Puskas himself, Santamaria from the Uruguayan World Cup side of 1954, and, theoretically, Argentina's greatest export, Di Stefano, who never played, protesting injury. It was rumoured that he and Herrera, the manager – yet another expatriate – were temperamentally incompatible, which may have been the real reason for his absence. Even so, with the sinuous gifts of Del Sol, Suarez and Gento and the ageless left foot of Puskas Spain should have done better. But they were beaten by a determined Czech side, the only goal being scored by Stibranyi.

In Group I, held in one of the more distant corners of Chile, there was some excitement, not all of it related to the finer arts of football. Uruguay barely scraped through against Colombia, by the odd goal in three, and then Russia and Yugoslavia contested a blood-curdling match in which the most remarkable feature was that nobody was sent off, not even Jerkovic who aimed a blow at the referee. Dubinski, the Russian full back, was carried off with a broken leg, the direct result of a foul, and the offender, Mujic, was not allowed to play for the rest of the tournament by order of his manager. It was perhaps not surprising that

Yugoslav passions were roused – they were the more positive side and only Yachin had stood between them and a certain lead. As so often happens on these occasions, the chances at the other end had been snapped up, and the Russians won 2–0. The Yugoslavs continued on a tide of high passion when they met Uruguay, but this time they won by 3–1. However, each side had a player sent off, and though, as in the Russian match, there was much good football, the undercurrent of violence was always uncomfortably present.

The first game in Group IV matched Argentina and Bulgaria, both as heavily cloaked in defensive plating as an armadillo. Somewhere along the line the Bulgarians must have made a mistake for they let in Facundo to score and provide Argentina with two points. Then England faced their former tormentors from Hungary, who turned out to be tormentors still. It was as if nine years had taught nothing – still the English played their bland straightforward game, honest and predictable; still the Hungarians danced and jigged their way across the field as if every move was novelty. Grosics, survivor between the goalposts, must have watched it all with a knowing air. Tichy, whose formidable shooting had made its mark in Sweden, deceived Springett with a long-range effort and though Flowers equalized through a penalty, Hungary were deserving winners when their new recruit at centre forward, Florian Albert, scored a wonderful individual goal. Fortunately England were nettled into life and in their next game they stormed the Argentinian defence. Peacock replaced Hitchens at centre forward and took much of the pressure off the other attackers, among whom Charlton was outstanding on the wing. He and Greaves both scored and Flowers repeated his performance from the penalty spot; Sanfilippo netted a consolation goal for the South Americans.

The only major surprises of the tournament happened in the next batch of games which saw the Russians almost undone by Colombia and Italy hysterically dispatched by Chile. The first of these was one of those freak matches in which a side seems to be so in control it could win with its eyes shut, and then proceeds to throw it away with its eyes wide open. Half-way through the first half Russia led by 3–0. Colombia had pulled one back by half-time, but a further Soviet goal in the second half seemed to put the issue beyond doubt. It was then to be observed, possibly for the first time, that the great Yachin might have feet of clay, and very heavy clay. He let in a second Colombian goal direct from a corner kick, then two further goals, and if he had not shed his clay boots in time and brought off some spectacular saves in his accustomed manner the Colombians might easily have won. The Chile-Italy affair was, by contrast, an

unpleasant semi-political episode. An Italian journalist had written some articles that seemed to cast every kind of slur on the Chilean people, and the latter had been rightly indignant, so that when the Italian footballers came face to face with their beloved team it was in an atmosphere of undisguised opprobrium. The two goals by which Chile officially won the match are scarcely remembered; what every observer recalls is the tremendous left hook with which Sanchez broke Maschio's nose, seen by millions of eyes around the world on the television screen, unseen and unpunished by Ken Aston the referee. Two Italians were later sent off for lesser offences, and the match never rose above the level of a publicized street brawl.

Brazil continued in their comparatively unremarkable vein with a goalless draw against Czechoslovakia, a game saddened by the premature departure of Pele who pulled a muscle and was not seen again in the tournament. Spain somewhat restored their fortunes with a last-minute win over Mexico, but they needed to beat Brazil to have a chance of qualifying, and, with several team changes and a first-half goal by Adelardo, they almost did so. But yet another Brazilian 'discovery', Amarildo, playing instead of the injured Pele, scored two goals later in the game, and this meant that Brazil and Czechoslovakia went through to the quarter-finals. The latter were already certain of their place when they faced Mexico, which may explain their 3–1 defeat. There were those, however, who considered the Mexican side of this World Cup hard done by, drawn in a difficult group, by no means outclassed by Brazil and unlucky to lose to Spain.

Germany, continuing to play over-physically, sunk the inept Swiss 2–1, though their win was assisted by the fact that the Swiss forward, Eschmann, had his leg broken by Szymaniak. They then faced Chile, who were certain of qualifying, and the Germans made sure of their quarter-final place by a 2–0 victory, unattractively achieved. Thus Italy were out, and an easy 3–0 win over the Swiss in their last game made no difference to anybody, probably not even to them.

In Group I Russia, again performing erratically, managed to come out top of the table by a 2–1 defeat of Uruguay, another game marred by a decisive injury on the losing side. With eleven men Uruguay might have won; Russia only clinched it in the final minute. Meanwhile their earlier opponents, Colombia, as if exhausted by the excitement of that game, foundered 5–0 to the Yugoslavs, Jerkovic scoring a hat-trick. Another hat-trick was recorded in Group IV against the name of Albert when Hungary completely routed the Bulgarians 6–1, though their collective brilliance was slightly dissipated by a featureless 0–0 draw with Argentina. Worse still was England's game with Bulgaria, likewise goalless. Bulgaria were out of the competition, but they concentrated solely on defence and England, as so often, lacked the necessary flair to break it. However, they qualified on goal average, over Argentina.

The quarter-finals certainly threw up three results that would not confidently have been predicted. Firstly the Chileans, to the unconfined joy of the nation, won a gallant victory over the Russians, who had probably played too inconsistently to deserve to go further. Surprisingly the finger of accusation could again be pointed at Yachin, one of the greatest goalkeepers of modern times, but here in South America strangely beset with ill-judgment. He might on a normal day have saved both Chilean goals without extending himself. Russia scored a single goal through Chislenko. An even greater shock was the Czech victory over the Hungarians. Czechoslovakia's manner of advancement to this stage had been patchy to say the least, and their performance in the quarter-final gave no reason to think that it should have been otherwise. Hungary, attacking with their usual verve, were in complete control of the play, but were the victims of a freakish breakaway goal. The Hungarians did everything but score, and it was ironic that the only time they did get the ball into the net it should be disallowed for a doubtful offside decision. Czechoslovakia were deeply indebted to Schroiff, their goalkeeper.

It was also something of a surprise, though no injustice, when Yugoslavia defeated Germany. The Germans, for all their tactical astuteness and the efficiency of their play, had won few friends in Chile. They played, as indeed did so many teams, as though not prepared to lose and unmindful of the means by which they would achieve that end. The Yugoslavs fortunately played as though prepared to win, and when Radakovic scored in the closing minutes it was the reward for flair over competence. As for England they didn't have quite enough of either, and Brazil had a good deal too much. Garrincha had one of those days when he could have danced his way through a minefield, scoring two of Brazil's three goals. He headed in from a corner in the first half, England equalized through Hitchens, playing again in place of the injured Peacock, and then in the second half two of Garrincha's 'banana' kicks were the undoing of Springett. The first he stopped but Vava snapped up the rebound, and the second boomeranged inside the right-hand post. So England once more packed their bags early and departed. With a forward line that included Douglas, Greaves, Haynes and Charlton they might have been expected to present a more potent threat, but somehow frailty of purpose overcame them once again. Haynes seemed unable to impose the beautiful brush-strokes of his game upon the whole picture,

Greaves was generally marked too heavily, but as a bright hope for the future England had at least unearthed a commanding new half-back in one R. Moore.

In Sweden Brazil had started . . . . slowly and only got into their stride in the last two matches; the pattern was repeated in Chile, and it was fortunate for them that their motor was really humming by the time they met the host nation in the semi-final, for they had to overcome not only a team riding high on the tide of its own surprising success

Garrincha, the 'Little Bird', was a star on the right wing in two of Brazil's World Cup wins: 1958 and 1962.

but an intensely partisan crowd, howling for their blood. They won a little of it when Landa and Garrincha were sent off the field and the Brazilian's head was cut open by a bottle. Prior to that, however, he had left his indelible mark on Chile, scoring twice in the first half. Chile pulled one back before half-time, then in the second half Brazil went 3–1 ahead when Vava nodded in from a corner. The match came to a boil when Chile reduced the lead through a penalty, but Brazil, despite physical buffetings and the torrid partisanship of the Chilean spectators, gathered their multiple talents together and Vava's second headed goal from Zagalo's centre was the final blow.

As for Czechoslovakia, they once more confounded the prophets, beating the more obviously gifted Yugoslavs by three goals to one. Yet again Schroiff was the Czech saviour, only Jerkovic beating him in the second half after a goalless first period. Kadraba had earlier scored for Czechoslovakia, and then Scherer put in a couple, one from a penalty. The Yugoslavs had generally played well and attractively throughout the tournament, and it was small wonder that they felt deflated, subsequently surrendering third place to Chile. Rojas scored the only goal of the match.

Thus to a Final for which Brazil were obviously favourites, though no one dared now underestimate the Czechs, and they had, after all, held Brazil to a goalless draw in their group match. In the event they played better than they had done throughout the tournament, while Brazil were below the exciting form of their semi-final. For this reason it was not a fiesta of a match, governed by a surprising caution on the part of the Champions. Perhaps the ghosts of 1950 had not yet been truly laid. Czechoslovakia played coolly and maturely, and scored first through the clever Masopust. But, alas for them, Schroiff seemed to have expended his brilliance in the earlier struggles and he allowed Amarildo to score from a narrow angle which he should have covered. It was 1–1 at half-time, and for most of the second half there was nothing to choose between the teams. Pele would probably have made the vital difference: without him Brazil lacked a certain dynamism, because Garrincha was heavily policed on the wing and Didi not the orchestrator he had been in Stockholm. It was probably Zagalo, who never seemed to tire, working both in defence and attack, who most helped them to their victory. Zito scored the second goal twenty minutes from time, and Vava made it 3–1 after another goalkeeping mishap by poor Schroiff. Altogether it was faintly disappointing, and although Brazil were still the best ambassadors of football in the world it was plain that age was beginning to rust their hinges, that a great team was poised on the brink of the melancholy slope of decline.

1. Luis Suarez, inside left for Inter Milan, and for Spain in the World Cup, Chile 1962.
2. Hungarian stars of different eras: Josef Bozsik of the 1954 World Cup side and, in the background, Florian Albert of the 1966 team.
3. World Cup Final, 1962. Schroiff and Vava go down, Pluskal towers above them as a Brazilian attack founders in the Czech goalmouth.
4. Schroiff, the Czechoslovakian goalkeeper, whose heroics between the posts had much to do with his country reaching the 1962 Final.
5. Zito leaps for joy after scoring Brazil's second goal to give them the lead in the Final in Santiago.
6. Pele, unable to play in the Final, embraces Amarildo after Brazil have beaten Czechoslovakia 3–1 and captured the trophy for the second time.

1966

ENGLAND

For England at least the 1966 World Cup was unquestionably a watershed — for several reasons. Firstly they were the hosts, secondly they won it, thirdly the importance of the event assumed massive proportions, fourthly millions of people previously unreceptive to the game, became enraptured with the tournament, and for a good many the flavour must have lingered, because a new football public was, temporarily, born. All these things happened for the first time. How far they were true of the rest of the world, in terms of public interest, is debatable. For Chile, for example, no doubt the watershed had been 1962; it may have been just coincidental that England's World Cup was the one that first rivalled the Olympics for a global audience, crowned by a *Boy's Own* Final played out before a watching audience of 400,000,000 and a further listening audience of 200,000,000.

Until it actually happened the British public took some convincing, even complaining beforehand of the proposed saturation TV coverage. When it was over the World Cup was installed in their minds as the most important event in football, the Home International Championship was toppled from its sacred bovine pedestal, and a great new public who had previously associated football with muddy contests fought out in dingy surroundings were awakened to the prospect of a game that contained drama and poetry and the absorbing irregularities of human conflict. The World Cup gave them characters to identify with as readily as those of *Coronation Street*, their television screens showed blithe summer and not drab winter, and (for the English) their team was winning. What more could you want?

If you were a purist you would very likely have wanted better football, fewer crushing tackles and a winning team worthy of assuming the mantle of Brazil. Not that England were at all unworthy on the run of the play; they just played a different game from Brazil. A new age had been born, rationalized, self-contained, the collective defences and the careful build-up to attacks aimed at minimizing risk. Possession was three parts of the law, a method that proved sound and successful but was inevitably prosaic. Their football scarcely ever took wing — it could not for it was literally wingless and, to the hypercritical, trussed as well. At least it would seem so in subsequent years: then it was all heady with the wine of victory and the English fervour in the stands with its

nationalistic clap-clap chanting must even have raised a German eyebrow or two. But at least the British had discovered the World Cup was important; they had appointed a manager after Chile to achieve its victory, a man who said England would win it and when they did was knighted for his pains. Two years later the man who first won the European Cup for an English club was knighted also. Thus in 1966 football in Britain had come to life and had had bestowed on it the patronage of respectability.

At the outset it was a wide-open Cup. England, like every host nation before them, had been accorded that degree of favouritism, but their new resolution under Alf Ramsey had also led observers to believe it was their best chance yet in playing terms. England were also drawn in the easiest group, for France and Mexico were not reckoned to be among the serious threats. Uruguay also in Group I were an uncertain quantity. Elsewhere the West Germans were an obvious danger — they had never been less than efficient in any World Cup and their record in the competition was good; Argentina, like Uruguay, might prove impenetrable; Bulgaria and Russia could be heavily competent; Portugal, Hungary and Brazil were locked in a confusion of talent in Group III — all touched at some point with genius. Spain generally had too many disparate individual talents; the Swiss and the Chileans would probably prove unexceptional; Italy, as always, were a fine team but a bad risk away from home; and, soya sauce to the mixture, there were the North Koreans, quoted at vastly long odds but to prove a delightful addition to the blend. It was particularly sad that none of the other home countries had qualified on this occasion — Scotland, the best bet, had been eliminated by Italy and that would have its ironies.

Public interest could hardly have been quickened by the now traditionally uninteresting opening game, in which England and Uruguay built as large a monument to unimagination as Wembley can have seen. There were no goals, the Uruguayans were not interested in scoring any, the English incapable of scoring any. Ramsay played one orthodox winger in Connelly, but the mixture of Ball, Greaves, Charlton and Hunt looked unfruitful. Behind them Norbert Stiles made his unforgettable presence known to the British public at large; those who could take their eyes off his vampiric exhortations may have been troubled by the fact that his gifts as a linkman looked to be more destructive than constructive.

It was fitting after this that the first goal of the competition should be scored by Pele; it would also be his last, for some unforgiveable Bulgarian tackling would cripple him and virtually put him out of the tournament. More protective refereeing might have saved him; as it was, the Goodison crowd had but a glimpse of his genius, an

astonishingly powerful free kick that tore through a crowd of defenders and into the net. Garrincha scored Brazil's second goal with another free kick, his special gift — the banana shot. For Brazil 2–0 had been satisfactory enough, but they looked short of rhythm in midfield, Edilson and Lima not worthy replacements for Didi and Zagalo. In Sheffield the West Germans signalled their strength by striking five goals past the Swiss, though the latter were without two star players, excluded for disciplinary reasons; in Middlesbrough the Russians won 3–0 against the North Koreans, and that was no surprise either. The North Koreans looked so small it was tempting to feel protective about them and to find their determination endearing — the friendly souls of the North-east would, in fact, quickly take them to their hearts.

Group I continued unexcitingly when France and Mexico drew 1–1 at Wembley, two poor teams playing poorly. Then at the White City France went down 2–1 to Uruguay, scoring their only goal from a penalty and faced by a Uruguayan team more interested in two points than they had been against England. Equally unremarkable were the Group II matches in which Argentina beat Spain 2–1, and then Spain beat Switzerland by the same margin. The Spanish played much better in the latter game, but they were essentially a disappointment, as they had been in Chile. Individual talents — Del Sol, Suarez, Gento, Peiro, Amancio — promised more than their sum was able to produce. Argentina for their part commanded respect — for their play if not for their tackling. Artime scored both goals, and the forward line was cleverly generalled by Onega.

All the good things were happening in the North-west. At Old Trafford two of the dark horses — Portugal and Hungary — played excitingly, the Hungarians as ever delighting with their *élan*. Portugal matched them in attacking flair, but the result was a little unjust, for Hungary did not deserve to go down by a 3–1 margin. They did not really deserve to go down at all, but uncertain goalkeeping cost them two goals. Augusto scored twice for Portugal, the towering Torres once, and Bene scored Hungary's goal. He would score again, after three minutes, in their next match, against Brazil, a far cry from the 'Battle of Berne', but the first time Brazil had been defeated in a World Cup match since that day. The gods favoured Hungary — the Liverpool rain fell unremittingly, Pele was unable to play, the Hungarians were quick and energetic, the Brazilians ponderous by comparison with their halcyon days. Some of them were plainly too old, others not yet experienced, but a new centre forward, Tostao, showed promise and scored their only goal. It was 1–1 at half-time, in the second half the Hungarians took control sweeping forward in

fast raking attacks, one of which was crowned by the most memorable goal of the tournament. Albert, who played superbly, combined with Bene down the right wing, the ball was chipped back inside and Farkas, thundering forward, met it on the volley with lethal power. Later a penalty by Meszoly would depress Brazil even further.

In physical terms, the 'Battle of Berne' had not been repeated; nor, thankfully, was the 'Battle of Santiago' when Italy met Chile in Sunderland — not that Roker Park is exactly the setting for a display of Latin flamboyance. It was an unimpressive game, and the Italians were unimpressive in victory. A goal apiece by Mazzola and Barison could not obscure the team's inability to impose itself on moderate opposition, consisting for much of the game of ten men. All the same it was still presumed that Russia and Italy would be the certainties to qualify from the group, and mild amusement was the order of the day when North Korea held Chile to a 1–1 draw. It perhaps went unnoticed how ruthlessly practical the Koreans were in approach, how they were therefore learning every minute; by these means they finished on level terms with a side that had threatened to dominate them, by these means they would puncture the great Italian balloon.

At last at Wembley, a goal was scored worthy of the name, one of the most nostalgic memories of the tournament. Bobby Charlton collected the ball, accelerated forward with that famous swerving stride, the Mexican defence fell back like the Red Sea, from outside the penalty box the shot was unleashed and thunderously it found the target. The Mexicans for some reason had decided only to defend against England, so the goal was nothing less than they deserved, and Hunt added another in the second half. Peters and Paine had replaced Ball and Connelly, but the lack of Mexican involvement made it difficult to judge whether this was a more satisfactory England attack. Their final match in the group against France, with Callaghan replacing Paine, did nothing more to resolve it. France were handicapped by an injury to Herbin, the game was speckled with bad-tempered fouls, and Roger Hunt's two workmanlike goals merely provided the statistic that England were top of their group. Earlier Uruguay had made sure of their place by indulging in another goalless draw, this time with Mexico. Wembley had certainly had its share of cynical, uninteresting football.

In Group II an equally charmless and goalless encounter between Argentina and West Germany gave them each a point, which was patently all they sought. Albrecht of the Argentine was sent off. Argentina, without Albrecht, then beat Switzerland 2–0 at Villa Park, an uninspiring game though the spearhead of Artime and Onega was again conspicuous and they shared the goals. West Germany, however, came out top of the group on goal average when they beat Spain 2–1, but it was a close thing and the Spaniards, with an almost completely changed forward line, rose above their previously indifferent form to give the Germans a scare. If they had lost this game, they would not have qualified.

But this was all dully predictable compared with the events in the northern capitals. On the Saturday the Russians had beaten Italy 1–0, a result in itself not considered significant because Italy only had to draw with North Korea to be almost certain of qualifying. The manner of their defeat was depressing, however, in that it was without spirit and without even the briefest glimpse of their true form. The Russians scarcely dazzled, but the political importance of victory to them makes their machinery continue to work when talent has failed. They could recover from bad form: Italy could not. Smitten as if by a mortal sickness to their self-esteem, they faced the North Koreans with infinite weariness, predictably missed their chances, lost Bulgarelli with an injury and the game by Pak Doo Ik's goal scored just before half-time. The Koreans, growing ever more daring, swarmed like flies round the decaying Italian carcass. Poor Italy — their post-war record in the World Cup had been lamentable, they had now suffered the upset of the decade, and they flew home to be predictably pelted with rotten fruit. No doubt their mothers would console them.

Russia's final match with Chile was therefore a formality; they won 2–1 to head the group with North Korea in second place. Meanwhile Group III had witnessed the eclipse of Brazil. Portugal, lively and persistent and helped by their opponents' creaking defence, had beaten Bulgaria 3–0 at Old Trafford, the name Eusebio appearing on the score-sheet for the first time. Thus, to have even a chance of survival, Brazil had to master Portugal, a nice political irony. It was hardly the moment to make wholesale changes of a team, but that is what Brazil chose to do, dropping the old and faithful, including the unfamiliar and the untried. Only Pele was there as a name to conjure with, but he was clearly still suffering from his Bulgarian wounds and when Morais compounded his agonies with two monstrous fouls Brazil were beyond redemption. By that time, however, Eusebio had proved that, for the rest of this tournament at least, he could wear Pele's crown with impunity. In the first half he had set up one goal and headed another; Rildo pulled one back for Brazil, but then late in the game Eusebio lashed in Portugal's third. He was a star, and it was as exhilarating to welcome him as it was melancholy to watch Brazil's departure, personified by the limping Pele, bowed and blanketed, crippled yet again for his genius.

Hungary followed Portugal into the quarter-finals by defeating Bulgaria 3–1, the latter's defence again uncharacteristically porous. The late Gundi Asparoukhov scored an early goal for Bulgaria, their only goal of the competition.

Two of the quarter-finals were ugly affairs, the third exhilarating, the fourth a disappointment by reason of its result. Of the two in the first category, England's match with Argentina was the worse, surely a candidate for the least attractive match ever staged at Wembley, a stadium already over exposed in this competition to uninteresting football. Possibly only the fact of England's victory prevented thousands from storming the box-office and demanding their money back. England played poorly, Argentina scarcely played at all — their efforts were concentrated on shirt-pulling, tripping, obstructing, kicking, provoking and bringing the game to a halt as frequently as possible. The net result was that the whistle never stopped blowing, the referee's notebook was overflowing with names and, shortly before half-time, the infamous Rattin incident took place in which the Argentine captain was sent off, refused to go and was only persuaded to do so after ten minutes of wrangling. His specific offence seemed negligible; it looked as though he was being made the scapegoat for the sins of his side. Against ten men England played no better, but thankfully Hurst, who had replaced the injured Greaves in the attack, headed a splendid goal after seventy-seven minutes and Argentina were removed from the lists. They threatened a 'Battle of Berne' invasion of the England dressing-room afterwards: the match would leave a sour note for years.

The encounter between West Germany and Uruguay was only marginally more appetizing. Two Uruguayans were sent off, and the Germans capitalized on their broken ranks to score three second-half goals to add to Haller's fortunate first-half deflection. It was this and a refused penalty which had caused the South Americans to run amok; a half-time scoreline of 2–0 to them would not, on the run of play, have been an injustice.

Up in the fortunate North, the Everton crowd witnessed a remarkable match in which North Korea, even more lively than before, were a goal up in a minute and not long after had scored two more. Reports that read Portugal 0 North Korea 3 were flashed to a disbelieving world. It could not last. Eusebio decided the mice had played long enough, scored twice before half-time (once from a penalty), added two more afterwards (including another penalty) and Augusto added a fifth. Eusebio's play was quite irresistible, but North Korea had certainly sent shivers down Portuguese spines and they had contributed to some splendid entertainment. Their long, ascetic preparation for the World

Cup had been well rewarded; what had been most impressive, however, was their capacity to learn, and adapt, as they went along.

The fourth quarter-final was disappointing in that it prevented the dreamed-of possibility of a Hungary-England confrontation in the Final, which would have been emotive to a degree. Russia defeated them 2–1, undeservedly, decided alas by a goalkeeping error. It was especially a pity as the Hungarians in full attacking cry were probably the most exhilarating sight this World Cup produced. Not by any stretch of the imagination were Russia an attractive side, and their semi-final was yawningly uninteresting. Chislenko, their most gifted forward was injured, then sent off, the Germans played cautiously, but they got their noses in front through Haller and later kept them there with a typically opportunist shot by Beckenbauer. Porkujan scored a late, meaningless goal for Russia. Only Yachin had seemed endowed, as ever, with charisma.

Charisma certainly attended the England-Portugal semi-final. Looking back to it through the grey mists of negativity that have cloaked Wembley internationals since, it seems to belong to a golden age. Perhaps it assumes a nostalgic greatness beyond its real worth, but the memory cannot help lingering over the assured attacking style of the English, their strength and composure in defence, the flashing counter-thrusts of the Portuguese, Eusebio's stealth and power aligned with the aerial cunning of Torres, and the sporting generosity of the losing side. No doubt if England had lost it would not have seemed so rosy; fortunately for once, they won worthily and well. After half an hour Bobby Charlton scored simply when Pereira only half-stopped a shot from Hunt. In the second half he scored again, majestically, striking Hurst's pass with fulminating precision into the corner of the goal. England were not yet home and dry; eight minutes from the end a bout of pressure on the England goal ended with Jackie Charlton punching the ball out from under the bar, and Eusebio scored once more from the penalty spot. The game closed on a knife-edge, with Portugal threatening an equalizer, Gordon Banks standing between them and success. It was a match of freedom and pleasure, and somehow or other it does not seem to have been repeated. Eusebio left the stadium inconsolable; he would score yet again from the penalty spot in Portugal's 2–1 victory over Russia in the third-place match, and go home with nine goals in his pocket.

As for the 1966 Final it has long since passed into the realms of national mythology. The story is too well known to bear long repetition, though the very mention of it brings back the sustained seesaw drama of the occasion, the nail-biting tension, the ultimate reward. At half-time 1–1, 2–2 at full time,

4–2 at the end of extra time – there was no imbalance in the teams, only a rare perversity in Germany's second goal and England's third which gave the match a contentious aftermath it did not deserve. West Germany made the mistake of scoring first, freeing England from their caution and preventing their complacency. Within six minutes Hurst had equalized with a beautifully timed header. Peters' close-range second-half goal seemed to have sewn it up for England until, with television commentators already triumphantly announcing that England were only ninety seconds away from the World Cup, West Germany equalized from a doubtfully awarded free kick. Many people, Jackie Charlton by all appearances among them, felt that Held had fouled Charlton, not vice versa.

Weber scored when the ball was crossed to the far post, and the teams were subjected to the rare and punishing ritual of extra time. It depended on fitness and spirit and the telling factor in this respect was the non-stop redheaded motion of Alan Ball. He covered every blade of that sapping pitch as if with relish, and he laid on the goal which Hurst scored to put England 3–2 ahead. Striking the underside of the bar, the ball bounced almost directly down, in English eyes over the goal-line, in German eyes the opposite. A Russian linesman awarded it. As the last seconds ran out Hurst ran through a German defence too exhausted and demoralized to bother, and completed his hat-trick, a record.

The victory was famous and, on the run of play, deserved. England

1

3

144

had won without wings and without Jimmy Greaves, fit but not selected. When such a player was omitted and Hunt was included, it was realized that work-rate and loyalty, rather than the uncertainties of genius, were to be more highly rewarded by Ramsey. Such a policy had paid off now: it would prove expensive in the future. Meantime England rejoiced as never since 1945, and for a day and a night

naturally believed they had the best team in the world. They certainly had the finest goalkeeper, a sterling defence, discoveries in Hurst and Peters, greatness in the two Bobbies, Charlton and Moore. The retina retains the image of the Charlton brothers collapsed on Wembley's turf and of Nobby Stiles, socks down and teeth absent, dancing like a dervish round the edge of it, a winner at last.

1. **The nadir for Italy. Pak Doo Ik's shot beats Albertosi's dive and the North Koreans qualify for the quarter-finals, Italy for the journey home.**
2. **In the quarter-final, the Portuguese defence stands rooted like statuary as Li Dong Woon scores North Korea's second goal.**
3. **After this shot the scoreline at Roker Park read Portugal 0 North Korea 3. It did not last. Portugal roused themselves from their slumbers to win 5–3.**
4. **A brave challenge ends. Augusto scores Portugal's fifth and final goal to seal their extraordinary quarter-final tie with North Korea.**

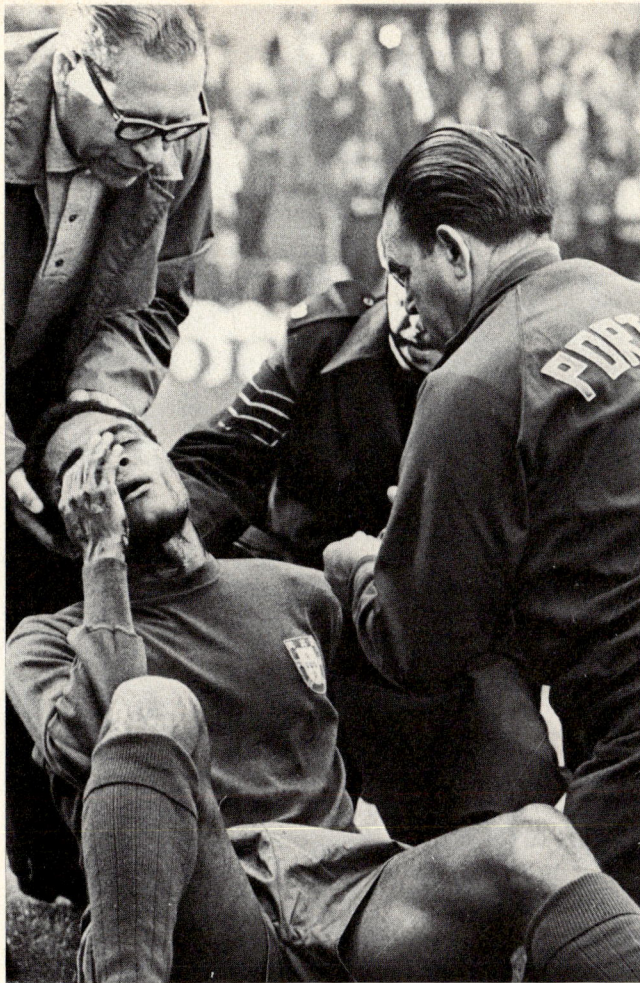

1. Augusto scored twice for Portugal in their group match with Hungary. This time, however, he was ruled offside.
2. Lev Yachin of Russia, one of the great goalkeepers of all time and still a powerful force in the 1966 World Cup.
3. Another goalkeeping giant. Mazurkiewicz of Uruguay saves one-handed against West Germany in their quarter-final at Hillsborough.
4. Eusebio, goal-scoring star of the 1966 World Cup, receiving attention during Portugal's match with Hungary.
5. 1966 Final. Haller exultant as his shot eludes Jackie Charlton and Banks, and West Germany are ahead.
6. The same match, and Hurst equally exultant as he equalizes for England from Moore's free kick.

1

3

2

ENGLAND 3 GERMANY W. 2

4

1. Gordon Banks commands the penalty area and fists away a West German attack in the 1966 Final.
2. Agony for England. From a doubtfully awarded free kick Weber equalizes for West Germany in the last minute of the World Cup Final.
3. Extra time about to begin. Moore and Charlton J. rest their limbs while England's manager tells his team to believe in their ability to outlast the Germans.
4. In the last minute of extra time Geoff Hurst breaks away from a bedraggled German defence and completes his World Cup Final hat-trick.

1970

MEXICO

Before the 1970 World Cup one of the more idiotic newspaper space-fillers was a computerized forecast of the result, which came out with the answer that England would beat Brazil 3–2 in the Final, after extra time. Such an absurd notion was both a symptom of the frenzied public interest that now surrounded the World Cup — it provided heavy newspaper copy for at least six months before it took place — and, more indirectly, a symptom of the way the game had moved. If it was thought possible to feed into a computer the salient factors of a football team, then football must have reached an advanced stage of mechanization. As far as England's recent performances were concerned, the newspapers could be forgiven for indulging in the experiment. The year 1966 had been seen to have bred an advanced, semi-automated style that was clearly going to risk even less to flair in Mexico than it had done in England. But the idea of extracting the principal ingredients of Brazil's football and handing them over to the mindless processes of a computer was completely laughable and, happily, Brazil proved it so. It is not impossible that, had England and Brazil met in the Final, the forecast might have proved correct — England came closer to defeating Brazil than anyone and, on chances created, ought to have done so — but it still defies reason to calculate the Brazilian performance in mathematical terms. What they produced in Mexico was what they had, in broad terms, produced in Santiago, in Stockholm, in Rio and, in essence at least, in Liverpool and Berne — football, unadulterated, spontaneous but skilfully planned, football, team football governed by the free rein given to the opportunism of its many artists. And, as far as that was concerned, no other side was within a mile of them.

The build-up to the finals was breathless, and much concerned with that phenomenon. There were arguments about heat and altitude. In the event none of the teams appeared to be greatly incommoded, having made careful preparations for the heat and allowed themselves time to acclimatize to the height. Possibly the single most damaging factor, for the European teams, was the timing of some of the matches — in the middle of the day — done to accommodate the European television viewers, a silly sacrifice that the players need not have made. European TV ratings would hardly have diminished if the matches had reached them in the middle of the night — the Mexican Olympics had proved that. The

watching world was football mad, madder than four years previously, and most of what they saw was worth watching.

The line up for the finals revealed some sad absentees and some curious newcomers. Portugal were out, having, like their principal team Benfica, temporarily declined; so were Hungary, eliminated by Czechoslovakia in a play-off. Thus renewed acquaintance with the talents of Albert, Bene, Eusebio *et al.* was disappointingly forestalled. Scotland had again fallen at the crucial hurdle, and so, astonishingly, had Argentina, defeated by Peru. Newcomers to the fold, with Peru, included the unpredictable representatives of El Salvador, Morocco and Israel. None were expected to reach the quarter-finals, and the chances of El Salvador

were thought to be even further reduced by presumed exhaustion after their 'football war' with Honduras. In Group I, played in Mexico City, they were matched against Russia, Belgium and the host nation, each of whom was favoured, in particular the Belgians, who had been runaway winners of their qualifying group and possessed outstanding attackers in Van Himst, Van Moer and Devrindt. The opening match between Russia and Mexico, resolved nothing, and informed nothing, except perhaps the pattern of refereeing to follow. After dire publicized warnings about foul play, about the conflict between Latin and North European styles of play and interpretation of rules, this opening game was severely policed and dull play was reduced to sheer boredom by the constant stoppages. But it worked well as a warning light, and

thereafter it could be claimed that this was a generally clean and sporting World Cup and the standard of refereeing, with one or two minor exceptions, was satisfactorily high. In the Aztec Stadium, neither Russia nor Mexico scored, and neither seemed much bothered with that.

Group II, in Puebla, was given a scarcely more impressive opening when Uruguay defeated Israel 2–0. The most significant feature of the match, and the most damaging to Uruguay's subsequent chances, was the injury to their star player, Pedro Rocha, in the first quarter of an hour. He would not appear again in the tournament. On the same day England began their programme in Guadalajara, playing a cool disciplined game in defence, obviously conserving their energies as if in trepidation of the heat and

the altitude. The forward line, however, did not exactly look penetrative, now based on a 4–4–2 principle which left the front-runners heavily exposed to some cynical Rumanian tackling. It was significant that the most potent attackers were Cooper and Newton until the latter suffered a crippling foul (one of several that went unpunished) and was replaced by Wright. Hurst scored the only goal with a calmly directed shot into the right-hand corner in the sixty-sixth minute. The only surprise of the day was the scoreline from Leon which read Peru 3 Bulgaria 2. Peru were a revelation and a delight, especially when compared with the Argentinians who might have been there in their place. They had public sympathy on their side at the outset, for a violent earthquake had devastated their country and the match was preceded by a minute's

silence. To begin with the Peruvians played as though surrendered to doom, and they had allowed Bulgaria to go two goals ahead through direct free kicks before they gathered themselves together and played with confidence and enterprise. Their attack was astonishingly lively, based on the Brazilian 4–2–4 and here the influence of Didi, who had become their manager, could be seen. Shots peppered the Bulgarian goal, at first wildly, later more accurately. Gallardo scored first, Chumpitaz levelled the scores with a free kick, the Bulgarians were bewildered by the onslaught and in a highly charged atmosphere Cubillas ran through and struck the decisive goal past Simeonov. The Peruvians in their joy clambered all over each other like a litter of puppies and had to be pulled apart by the referee.

Group IV nearly provided another surprise the next day when the unsung Moroccans led West Germany by a goal until the fifty-sixth minute. The Germans, uncertain of themselves, had, in the manner of others before when facing lesser teams, tried to be elaborate when simplicity would have done. As a result of their confusion, Morocco had scored in the first half and deservedly held that lead. It took the ageless skill of Seeler to pull the Germans back level and eventually, after sustained pressure, Müller won them two points. But Morocco had scarcely been inferior in ability, and their goalkeeper had performed miraculously. In Guadalajara Brazil began their assault on the trophy they intended to pouch for good with a dazzling display against Czechoslovakia, silencing their detractors, reassuring their supporters. They had, after all, changed managers at an alarmingly late stage, the future of Pele had been in doubt, the combination of Pele and Tostao questioned. But Zagalo had given them their head and the team played as if reborn. Admittedly the Czech defence gave them a freedom few others would allow, but the understanding of the forward line, the recovery of the defence after a frail beginning, gave cause for great encouragement. Pele scored superbly, cushioning a pass from Gerson on his chest and ramming it home on the volley, Jairzinho scored twice, Rivelino once from a devastating free kick — all this after Petras had silenced the stadium with an eleventh-minute goal (and subsequently fallen on his knees and crossed himself). Perhaps the most memorable moment of the game, indeed of the whole tournament, was an amazingly alert piece of opportunism by Pele. Almost on half-time he found himself in the centre circle with the ball, noticed that Viktor, the Czech goalkeeper, was some yards off his line, and unleashed a shot which whistled over the startled keeper and only just outside the post as he vainly clawed the air behind him. The World Cup was truly alive.

A disappointing Italy defeated an

even more disappointing Sweden by a single goal in Puebla, and Belgium brushed El Salvador aside 3–0 in the capital without ever looking the force they had threatened to be. Their next match would confirm a thinness of spirit, though it would be equally revealing of the Russian machine at full steam ahead. The Soviets for once had decided that the offensive could be more lucrative than the defensive and their forward line blossomed in rare style. Bishovets scored twice as they powered to a 4–1 victory, Lambert's goal for Belgium no more than a late, pale flutter. The two other Iron Curtain countries, Rumania and Czechoslovakia, met in Group III, and once more the Czech defence leaked badly, letting in the Rumanians twice after Petras had again scored early on. Peru continued in the same wayward and charming style when they faced Morocco, taking sixty-five minutes to break through and then scoring three times in ten minutes. With four points in the bag already their position looked rosy. As for Group II it witnessed another profoundly uninspiring display. Italy and Uruguay played out a goalless draw, meaningless and defensive, giving them each the point they sought. The six group matches in Puebla and Toluca would yield a total of only six goals.

The next day brought the long-awaited confrontation, for many the putative final — England v. Brazil. It was a fine game. England had to defy a hostile crowd — a noisy horde had laid siege to their hotel for half the night with the obvious intention of keeping the players awake — and intense heat. They played well and missed several chances; Brazil played well and took one of the two clear chances they had. The other, a header by Pele from a cross by Jairzinho, was pushed out by Banks in a save that was reflex bordering on the miraculous. (Constant replays of it on television made it lose some of its lustre.) Brazil were without Gerson, Felix was uncertain, the defence looked vulnerable, but England failed to exploit the opportunities they created for themselves. Lee, who never revealed his best form in the tournament, should have converted a perfect cross by Wright, Ball struck the bar, Astle, who came on as substitute, feebly shot wide when he had the whole goal to aim at. Brazil's goal when it came after fifty-nine minutes was typical of their style: Tostao controlled the ball over on the left, three England defenders converged on him, somehow he wriggled free to cross to Pele, who might well have shot. Instead he caressed the ball with his foot, feinted one way, and slid it the other, perfectly paced into the path of Jairzinho who crashed it home. Brazil were potentially always the more dangerous, but England had acquitted themselves with distinction — Charlton had played with renewed enthusiasm, Moore was superb, Mullery did a yeoman job in marking Pele. A draw would have been fairer.

On the same day, West Germany struck form. After conceding an early goal to Bulgaria, they scored five times, Müller registering his first hat-trick of the Cup, Libuda running wild on the wing. Bulgaria scored a second goal two minutes from the end, but it was too late to keep their interest in the competition alive. Their performances had been deeply disappointing, compounded in their last game when they could only manage a 1–1 draw against the Moroccans who had had no greater success but had shown considerably more spark. The deciding match of Group IV was, therefore, of importance only to discover who would meet whom in the quarter-finals. West Germany won it 3–1, another hat-trick by Müller, and Peru, by losing, were thus given the doubtful privilege of meeting the winner of Group III.

This proved, not surprisingly, to be Brazil, who were taken uncomfortably close by Rumania in their final game. Pele scored twice, Jairzinho once, but Rumania achieved what England had failed to do and with less ability, scoring twice and giving Brazilian supporters temporary cause for alarm. Felix was again a doubtful asset, the danger of creeping casualness in the team's play was there for all to see. Probably the absence of Rivelino and Gerson, very much the commanding general, had much to do with this. England, therefore, had to draw with Czechoslovakia in order to qualify. In fact they won, but it was poorly achieved — through a dubious penalty, coolly converted by Clarke — and the side seemed to lack any cohesion in attack. The strength of the side was too heavily weighted at the back, the front-runners forced

to run on unsupported, compelled to call on a talent they did not possess. Czechoslovakia looked more impressive than they had done before; they were unlucky to be sent home without a single point to their name and one hoped there would not be recriminations.

In Group I the host nation comfortably ripped apart the tattered defence of El Salvador, scoring four goals to the intense delight of the natives. To their even greater delight they later made sure of their quarter-final place by defeating Belgium 1–0, and the streets of the capital rang far into the night with quite disproportionate rejoicing, particularly as the goal was scored from an extremely doubtful penalty, hotly protested by the Belgians. All the same, Belgium had consistently played below their best and had not deserved to qualify. In the other game giant Russia came out top of the group by scoring twice against tiny El Salvador, but the defence of the latter won honours for itself, displaying the spirited energy of the doomed and keeping their goal intact until the fiftieth minute.

Sweden were another team who failed to live up to their promise, while Israel rose above theirs. The result was a 1–1 draw which, with hindsight, must have been a sore disappointment to the Swedes, for in their next match they defeated Uruguay with the only goal of the game, scored in the last minute by Grahn. Uruguay probably lost this on the grounds of temperament, for scurrilous rumours preceded the game concerning the referee and the possibility of a 'fixed' result. The official was replaced, the Uruguayans sulked and were thus lucky to reach the quarter-finals on the slenderest of goal differences.

They had nearly thrown it away in a fit of pique. In the last match of this group the proceedings ground to a thankful halt when yet another mindless and goalless draw was achieved by Israel and Italy — a pathetic display by the latter; obviously the ghosts of North Korea had not evaporated. They were top of the group, but with what cynical negativity had they achieved that status.

It is true that Italy's play had been partly governed by their failure to find their form. The inability of the much-publicized Riva to get the ball into the net was a worrying factor, and ill-feeling between Rivera and the Italian officials had deprived the team of the full-time services of their most subtly gifted player. So far he had only come on as a second-half substitute against Israel, and when Mexico and Italy

2

1. **The balloons go up in the Aztec Stadium, Mexico City, and the 1970 World Cup has begun.**

2. **A typically uncompromising tackle by a Uruguayan defender on Jairzinho of Brazil during the Mexico semi-final.**

lined up for their quarter-final in Toluca he was again absent. Mexico, supported like Chile had been eight years before, began as if believing they could do nothing wrong, Italy as if they could do nothing right, and when Gonzalez scored for Mexico after twelve minutes Italy looked doomed once more. They had never reached this stage of the competition since the war, and this time they had still not played as though they deserved to. Suddenly from somewhere they

151

found the coolness and the organization they had sought. They began to play as though time would give them its rewards; at half-time they were level through Domenghini; then in the second half Rivera came on for Mazzola, and the combination between him and Riva bore the fruit so many had prophesied, the one slight and intelligent, like a gazelle, the other a powerful direct machine boring in on goal. In the space of twelve minutes they scored three goals between them, and the chants of 'Me-hee-co' in the stadium subsided like a broken record-player.

An unpleasant match, pocked by some seventy fouls and unhappily extended to extra time, was served up in the Aztec Stadium by Russia and Uruguay. The latter were most unexpected winners, though the single goal by which they won was doubtfully achieved to say the least. Half the watching world could see that the ball crossed over the by-line before Cubilla crossed it for Esparrago to score in the last minute of extra time. Russia were nettled into uncharacteristically excited protest, with reason, but they had lost the match by allowing themselves to be frustrated by the needling Uruguayan tactics, and then demoralized by them. It was a boorish contest.

In Guadalajara Brazil and Peru produced exactly the reverse, the kind of confection only they knew how to concoct. Stern critics would comment that far too many goals came from unnecessary error, the less puritan were merely charmed by the evident enjoyment of the whole exercise. Peru were predictably beaten by the masters – who now had Gerson and Rivelino restored to fitness – but under Didi's wise instruction they had learned enough tricks to trouble his former colleagues. Brazil led 2–1 at half-time through Rivelino and Tostao, 4–2 at the end with a further goal by Tostao and a brilliant individual one by Jairzinho. In between Gallardo and Cubillas scored for Peru. The difference lay principally in Brazil's maturity, their ability to turn effervescence into icy calm, to score the goals when it mattered.

The fourth quarter-final was England's nightmare, a not easily forgotten episode. When the team arrived in Leon to face West Germany, Banks was suffering from stomach trouble commonly known as 'Montezuma's Revenge'. If Montezuma wanted any revenge, and the widespread anti-English feeling on the terraces suggested that he did, then in Leon he surely gained it. Peter Bonetti was told that he was appearing in his first World Cup match less than an hour before the start, not significant in itself for his ability was unquestioned, but a blow to the steady morale of the team who had always had Banks behind them and who had come to trust his reliability as if he were a deity. For an hour it mattered not a whit. England played better than they had done previously in the tournament,

scoring twice through Mullery (splendidly) and Peters. The Germans seemed broken, overrun by the confident English play in which Charlton, winning his 106th cap and thus becoming the most-capped England player of all time, was controlling the mid-field with all his old enthusiasm and style. Suddenly the match spun as if on a turntable. England, to the apprehension of their supporters, fell back into tentative defence and the Germans,

who had shown in the group matches their formidable powers of recovery, came surging forward. Grabowski took Libuda's place on the wing and played like a man inspired. After sixty-eight minutes Beckenbauer scored, a comparatively harmless-looking diagonal ground shot from the edge of the area which Bonetti, on a normal day at Stamford Bridge, would have picked up without effort. Here, unaccustomed perhaps

to the thin air and the increased speed of the ball, his dive was late, the ball sped under his body and into the net. However, 2–1 was no disaster and Hurst almost restored the gap with a brilliant header that slid agonizingly past the post. But Bell came on for Charlton, a poor exchange and a psychological lift to Germany – the man they admired most had been removed from the firing line. Eight minutes from the end Seeler scored a freak goal, a back-header that might have gone anywhere but looped over the stranded Bonetti and into the net. Hunter had come on for Peters, another mistake, substituting destruction for flair, and when extra time arrived the money was on West Germany. The inevitable Müller sealed it with a close-in volley and England could do nothing about it. They had lost a match they should certainly have won, because they failed to maintain the pressure, because they allowed the Germans the opportunity to rise from the ashes.

The Champions were out, to the undisguised pleasure of the South Americans. They had prepared themselves immaculately for the tournament, in playing ability and sophistication of tactics they were very likely the second-best team in the tournament, though the attack always looked short of scoring power. In four games they had scored only four goals. Their defence was overall the most assured to be seen, with Moore especially outstanding, playing with incredible poise considering the miserable charge of theft that had been levelled at him in Bogotá before the Cup began. Where they had lost most was off the field, where Ramsey's natural reticence was interpreted as arrogance bordering on xenophobia by the

1. A disappointing Sweden only managed a 1–1 draw with Israel in their group match. Here Larsson, the Swedish goalkeeper, gathers the ball at the feet of an Israeli attacker.
2. The goal-snatcher of the Mexico World Cup. Gerd Müller scored ten times in the tournament, three of them in this match against Peru.
3. An unedifying match which went to extra time was the quarter-final between Uruguay and Russia, Uruguay winning by a single disputed goal.
4. Uwe Seeler, veteran German striker, who disproved rumours of discord with Müller, heir to his throne, by striking up a highly effective partnership with him in Mexico.
5. Pele, restored to his greatness, in action against Czechoslovakia in Brazil's opening game of the 1970 tournament.
6. Bobby Charlton in uncharacteristic disarray, uprooted and sent flying by Brazilian defenders.

touchy Mexicans. Why after all had England arrived with their own bus? Was it thought the Mexicans couldn't drive? Such small matters, if played up by the Press, can rouse a nation to fury; for such reasons England were constantly jeered in the stadium. They were professional enough to deal with it, but it might none the less have made a difference.

The Italy-West Germany semi-final was a titanic struggle of constant ups and downs: five goals were scored in extra time, each one cancelling out the last until Italy finally pegged the defiant Germans down. Italy looked to be certain of victory until the very last minute of ordinary time when Schnellinger slid in to equalize Boninsegna's

goal scored as long ago as the seventh minute. In extra time Müller put Germany ahead, Burgnich pulled that back and then Riva put Italy in front with a fine shot. In the second period the tireless Müller headed Germany level again (his tenth goal of the series) only to see the game swing immediately to the other end, Boninsegna crossing from the left for Rivera coolly to pick his spot and drive it home. That was the last gasp, exhaustion stifled elation and disappointment, but possibly Beckenbauer's injury had cruelly affected Germany's chances. He had played the latter part of the game with his arm strapped to his chest. Without him the Germans would still achieve third place over

Uruguay, through a magnificent goal by the consistently dominating Overath.

Uruguay had, unsurprisingly, lost to Brazil in the other semi-final, though they had given them a fright with a freaky first-half goal by Cubilla. It was with evident relief that Brazil equalized late in the half through Clodoaldo, and thereafter they were relaxed enough to assert their superiority. Jairzinho scored yet another dazzling individual goal, and Rivelino's ferocious left foot made the scoreline a representative one at the very end.

The Final of the 1970 World Cup was something very special. It seemed all too short, as though we were in the presence of something very great but of its nature

evanescent. Italy were the willing participants in the arena, but though their play was as gallant and skilful as it was allowed to be, though their overwhelming defeat was entirely honourable, they were no more than foils for the brilliant Brazilian argument. Both sides were at full strength — but Rivera was once more mysteriously omitted, coming on as a late, meaningless substitute for the excellent Boninsegna who had scored Italy's only goal in the thirty-seventh minute. Brazil scored first, Pele rising to a high cross and striking it cobra-like with his head. It was a goal from the moment his feet left the ground. A score-line of 1–1 at half-time meant there was still an aura of suspended excitement about

1

154

the outcome. In part this merely disguised the feeling that Brazil were about to uncoil themselves and take the Italians apart, and the expectation of this was even more exhilarating than if the two sides had been locked in even combat. Brazil did just that, Gerson formidably in command of the mid-field, Jairzinho powerful and elusive on the wing, Tostao and Pele working together and slipping through the Italian defence like oil. Twenty minutes into the second half Gerson set the stadium alight with a remarkably struck goal, the ball flying into the net like a perfectly executed golf shot from outside the box. Almost immediately after this Pele, unselfish as ever, laid off the ball for Jairzinho to run

it in from close in and create a record for scoring in every round of the competition. It was all Brazil now, and Carlos Alberto's goal four minutes from the end had the sweetness of poetic justice, a beautifully timed shot on the run from the right, the captain meeting the ball rolled out for him by Jairzinho and driving it fiercely past Albertosi. It was one of the best goals of the tournament.

Brazil, Brazil, Brazil! The samba sounds filled the stadium, the daffodil and blue colours waved in the greatest fiesta they had known, confetti showered down from the stands. They had won the trophy three times and now could take it home for ever. Italy went back to Italy to be congratulated at last on a

post-war World Cup performance. Brazil went back to Brazil, to join the exuberance of Rio, the ball-playing jugglers of Copacabana, the greatest footballing nation of our time.

1. **Tommy Wright determinedly leaps over Paulo Cesar's challenge during Brazil's group match with England in Guadalajara.**
2. **The wonder save of the Mexico World Cup. Gordon Banks scoops away Pele's header when a goal seems a certainty.**
3. **The nearest England came to levelling with Brazil. Alan Ball's shot strikes the cross-bar with Felix beaten.**
4. **Francis Lee, pursuing the ball in typically direct style, mows down a West German defender during England's quarter-final in Leon.**
5. **England's challenge is finally buried as Müller rams home the deciding goal in extra time of the quarter-final.**

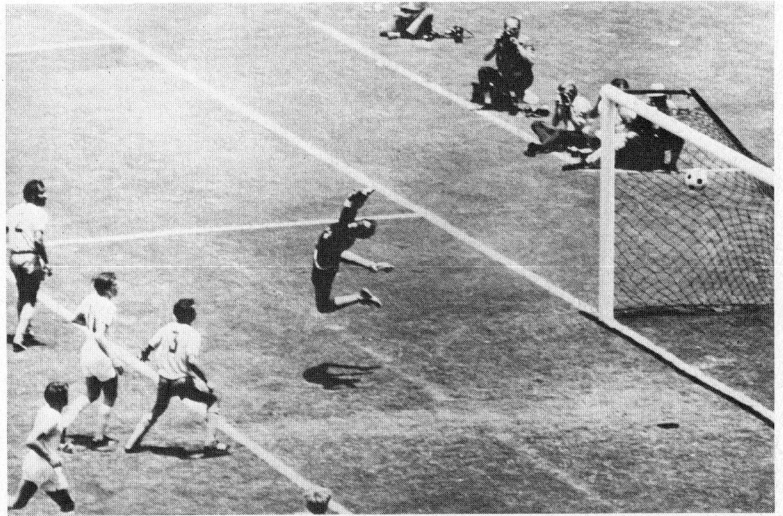

1. Extra time yet again, and the extraordinary see-saw patterns of the Italy-West Germany semi-final are completed by Rivera's goal, Italy's fourth.
2. Rivelino stopped with deliberate intent by a beaten Italian defender during the 1970 Final.
3. Carlos Alberto of Brazil wins the ball from Mazzola of Italy in the Mexico Final.
4. The picture that needs no explanation. Mexico City, 21 June 1970. Pele after giving Brazil the lead in the World Cup Final against Italy.

1974

WEST GERMANY

The pattern of 1970, when the World Cup finals were held in Mexico two years after the Olympic Games, is repeated in 1974, when West Germany stage the finals two years after the tragic 1972 Munich Olympics. As hosts, West Germany are automatic qualifiers, and are probable favourites to win, with Brazil as likely challengers. These two pages show international players who have delighted the world with their skills through the sixties and early seventies. As the 1974 finals are fought out many of them will be adding to their reputations as 500,000,000 spectators watch them on television sets all over the world.

1. Christian Piot (Belgium)
2. Paul van Himst (Belgium)
3. Jairzinho (Brazil)
4. Peter Shilton (England)
5. Mike Channon (England)
6. Allan Clarke (England)
7. Rodney Marsh (England)
8. Bobby Moore (England)
9. Roy McFarland (England)
10. Ray Clemence (England)
11. Alan Ball (England)
12. Johan Cruyff (Holland)
13. Rudi Krol (Holland)
14. Van Hanegem (Holland)
15. Florian Albert (Hungary)
16. Bene (Hungary)
17. Roberto Boninsegna (Italy)
18. Gianni Rivera (Italy)
19. Facchetti (Italy)
20. Luigi Riva (Italy)
21. Lou Macari (Scotland)
22. Pedro Rocha (Uruguay)
23. Karl Odermatt (Switzerland)
24. Franz Beckenbauer (West Germany)
25. Gerd Müller (West Germany)
26. Paul Breitner (West Germany)
27. Gunter Netzer (West Germany)
28. Dzajic (Yugoslavia)

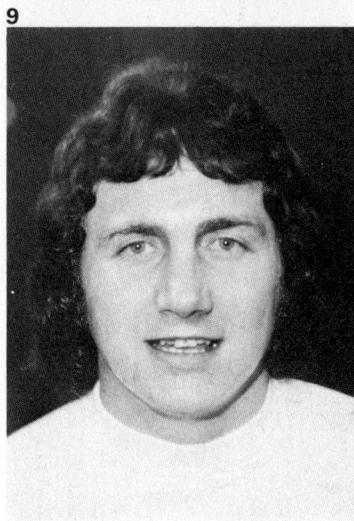

4

5

6

7

11

12

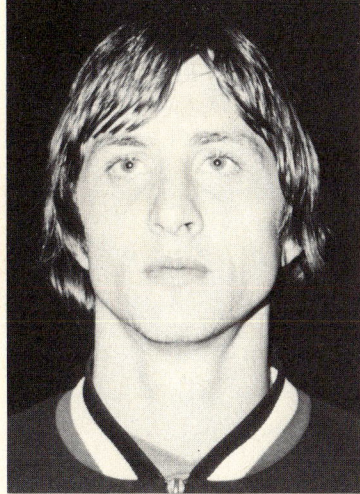

13

14

18

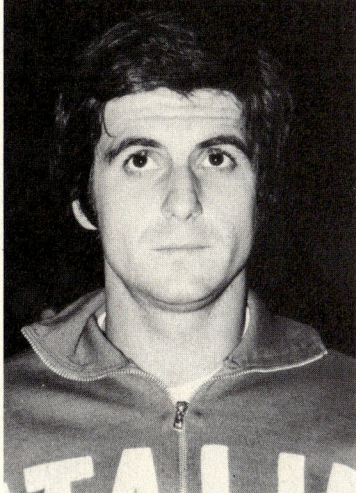

19

20

21

25

26

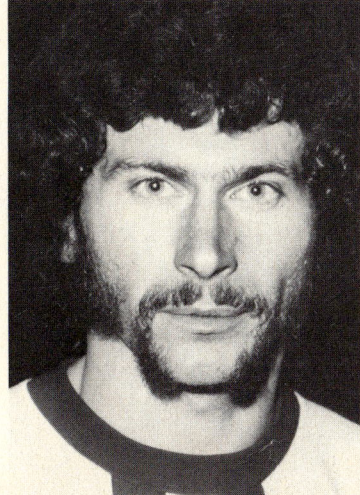

27

28

THE EUROPEAN GAME

Despair for Liverpool in the 1966
Cup Winners Cup Final. Held
raises his arms in triumph after
scoring Borussia Dortmund's
first goal.

THE EUROPEAN GAME

EUROPEAN CUP

In the summer of 1972 Ajax of Amsterdam, playing 'total football', won the European Cup. In the summer of 1972 West Germany, playing 'total football', won the European Championship. To the British public, goggle-eyed in front of their television sets and bloated from a surfeit of destructive home-grown football, the spectacle was exhilarating. It had been so long since they had seen that kind of football they had almost forgotten the taste of it. Now, within the space of three weeks, they had witnessed two major trophies decided by the openly committed attacking play of teams who had learned from the Hungarians of the fifties, the Brazilians of the sixties, from the great era of Real Madrid, and who still might hope to emulate them. Prosaic Russia, heavily weighted at the back, and cynical Inter Milan, still worshipping at the barren altar of *catenaccio*, were deservedly put to rout and with them, hopefully, went the idea that footballing rewards could be won by tactical systems that seek only to avoid defeat. The Germans and the Dutch played a fast-flowing attractive game, apparently based round the simple principle that ten members of the team should be creatively involved in both defence and attack, still disciplined by the outline of a system but free to improvise within it. By such means had West Germany, to a gasp of English astonishment, previously been England's masters at Wembley, with Beckenbauer and Netzer creating a playground for themselves in the middle of the field. By such means did West Germany become transformed in British eyes from a traditional footballing enemy to a team of superstars, thankfully conquering negative Russia. By such means did Ajax confirm themselves as the most exciting club team in Europe.

For those perched on the fence of political uncertainty Ajax's two successive victories in the European Cup were possibly the most potent argument they had yet heard for joining the Common Market. For those who care for such notions, their triumphs could be interpreted as an approximation to the European dream. As in the political arena, it took the carefully insular British a long time to come round to the idea of a European Cup. Now, of course, a club's ambition can reach no higher (unless it be to the ill-starred further stage of the World Club Championship), and winning the home League title has, rightly, assumed the most importance in the domestic season for it automatically grants access to the European Cup. And that competition has always remained a few grades higher in prestige than its younger cousins — the European Cup Winners Cup and the Fairs Cup (now called the UEFA Cup).

Ironically, the story goes that the European Cup owed its beginnings to an outburst of chauvinistic English journalism. It was actually the brainchild of Gabriel Hanot, football editor of the Paris newspaper *L'Equipe*, and it is sad that France should have sired both the World Cup and the European Cup and to date has won neither. When Wolverhampton Wanderers played Honved in December 1954, recovered from a 2–0 deficit and won 3–2, at least one English newspaper, for no logical reason, proclaimed that Wolves were 'Champions of the World'. They were nothing of the kind, and there was no basis to the

European Cup Final 1963. Eusebio on the point of unleashing the shot which gave Benfica the lead over AC Milan.

claim that they were – possibly English football journalists were indulging in some hysterical flag-waving at this so-called revenge for England's double drubbing by the Hungarians in the previous season. Hanot observed the headlines, pronounced them absurd as there was no competition to find the champions of the world, and set about organizing one. It was quickly found that the creation of a European club competition would be a more practicable first step. Publishing his proposals, he obtained early indications of favourable response from several quarters, within six months FIFA had been persuaded to approve the plan, UEFA had been appointed as organizers, and the first competition scheduled for the winter of 1955. So the Cup was born, its participants to be drawn from the winners of the domestic league titles, its matches to be played on a home-and-away basis apart from the Final which was to be contested on a pre-determined ground over ninety minutes.

The tournament was an instant success in almost every respect. People came in numbers to watch the games, forwards came forward in numbers to shoot at goal, even in the away games. It was like the infant days of the World Cup, a pleasing ingenuousness of attitude all too soon to be smothered by the uncertainty of adolescence, when teams would fear to attack away from home. A displeasing aspect of the first European Cup was that no English club was represented. Even though the Hungarian wounds were still open and bleeding, the Football League seemed to feel that no particular benefit could accrue from playing against foreign clubs and they forbade Chelsea, who had gallantly struggled to the League Championship title, to enter. Chelsea very feebly acquiesced. Scotland, however, who had a discreditably insular record in the World Cup, provided Hibernian and they proved worthy entrants, reaching the semi-finals with some splendid football before losing to the then formidable Reims without being outplayed by them.

It would have been fitting if Reims could have been the first winners of the Cup, in a Final which was played in Paris. They led 2–0, and then lost 3–2 to the irresistible Real Madrid. On 13 June 1956 the Spanish club clasped the European trophy for the first time; it wasn't until 31 March 1961 that another club held it aloft. Their amazing record in the intervening years is already part of football's folklore, a legendary team of multi-national talents, built around the extraordinary central pillar of Di Stefano, perhaps the most feared and admired player the game has known. Real Madrid had everything – money, support, a visionary president in Bernabeu, a super stadium (named after him), and the tentacles to draw in unique players from different corners of the world. But still the linchpin of their success was Di Stefano, and if he had not been so much the linchpin their success might have been yet greater, for some of the players the club netted from abroad could not respond happily to his autocratic presence on the field. Didi from Brazil and the great

Raymond Kopa, who played for Reims against Real in that first European Final, were two notables who stayed briefly and then fled. Puskas, too, when he arrived, might have found the partnership corrosive had he not wisely chosen to concede the limelight when he was in danger of capturing it. This was a decision which brought mutual benefit, for their inter-play and understanding became the highlight of that team's

many highlights, culminating in the wonderful double act they put on for the benefit of Hampden Park in 1960. This was the European Final when Real beat Eintracht of Frankfurt 7–3, almost certainly the greatest exhibition match the competition has seen. The memory focuses on the pair of them, perfectly in harness, setting up the goals for each other – Di Stefano tall, crisp, authoritarian, slightly severe, but wherever the play was concentrated somewhere to be found at the hub of it, directing it, destroyer, creator and executor; Puskas, short, tubby, with his perpetually dated hair style, scuttling through the middle, laying off the passes as if unravelling a string of pearls, swooping on the return to unleash his fulminating left foot. They scored all seven goals between them, and Eintracht were no walk-over.

Real Madrid won five times in a row; it is just possible that had disaster not struck, an English team might have shortened that run. Manchester United were the first club from England to enter the European Cup, in its second season. Once again the Football League, with its eyes blinkered and its feet

The incomparable Di Stefano scores Real Madrid's second goal in their classic European Cup Final with Eintracht Frankfurt in 1960.

firmly planted in the clay, refused permission to enter, or at least strongly advised against it. But Matt Busby's imagination had already been kindled by the European vista, and he was not a man to bow down before tame bureaucratic restrictions. He took his Babes to Anderlecht where they won 2–0 and then to Maine Road for the return — floodlighting was not yet

installed at Old Trafford — where they won 10–0. The legend of the new wonder team spread to Europe, though it was nearly extinguished by Borussia Dortmund in the next round. In the quarter-finals Manchester played the first leg in Bilbao, a snowy tie with predictable defensive errors. Atletico Bilbao won it by 5–3, and came to England knowing that United had to score three clear goals to defeat them. It seemed an almost impossible task, made more impossible by the home team's eagerness, their own undoing until finally they breached the Spanish wall. Viollet scored, Taylor scored, a play-off was in prospect, and then, in the last minutes, with the crowd frenziedly urging them on, their strength and fire and, above all, their style, were rewarded. Taylor crossed the ball for Berry to whip it home. United were through to face Real.

At that time Real were simply too good for them. Di Stefano and his superstar collection of aging mercenaries had too much wit for Roger Byrne's home-grown newcomers. Manchester went down 3–1 in Madrid, conceded two further goals in the return and, though they fought back with two goals of their own in the second half — one of them accredited to the new name of Charlton — the tie had clearly been decided. Real went on to beat Fiorentina in the Final. However the great hope that sprang from Manchester United's first venture into Europe was that they had banked invaluable experience for the future. The average age of the team was twenty-one years; Real Madrid were not in the first flush of youth (something which seemed to disadvantage them not at all) and Manchester, with that promise and that amount of time, could surely emulate them. So it was thought in the following season when, after a shaky beginning, they once more found their form and reached the semi-finals by splendidly holding Red Star to a 3–3 draw in Belgrade after winning the first leg 2–1. This time, it was felt, they might meet Real in the Final and earn their revenge. The dream, as is well known, was shattered in the slush of Munich; despite the great strength of reserves available at Old Trafford they could not do the job Busby had set out to complete. His ornament was broken; pieces remained, some of them priceless, but the argument over whether Byrne, Edwards, Taylor, Colman, Whelan and their colleagues would have matched, or later overtaken, the mastery of Madrid belongs, alas, to the realms of wistful conjecture. It took another ten years before Busby reached the European summit, and then it was with a team which, though gifted in many ways, belonged to slopes that were lower down the mountain than those of the original Babes.

Real's five European Cup wins were achieved at the expense of Reims (twice), Fiorentina, AC Milan and Eintracht. The last victory was the greatest and possibly for them the most satisfying, for only a few months previously they had been written off as past their best. At that time the new star in the Spanish firmament appeared to be Barcelona. In 1958–59 they won the Spanish Cup and League, their first season under the managership of the erratically brilliant Helenio Herrera. In March of the next season they were well on the way to still more spectacular success – top of the Spanish League (after a convincing defeat of Real), in the Final of the Fairs Cup, in the semifinal of the European Cup. Their progress to this stage had been impressive – a 6–2 win over CDNA Sofia in Barcelona after a 2–2 draw in Bulgaria, an overall 7–1 defeat of AC Milan, and then, in the quarter-finals, the trouncing of England's representatives for that year, Wolves. This was the season in which Wolves came within an ace of the double; their encounter with Barcelona was the most explicit exposition of the difference between what was supreme in English football and what was supreme on the Continent. Rather it showed the need for British clubs to explore deeper and more often in the European interior. Wolves came to Barcelona, predictably played their bread-and-butter game of the long ball backed up by honest sweat, the Spaniards let them come, dispossessed them, and danced through their exposed defence. A 4–0 defeat was bad enough; at Molineux it was made

disastrous by the head of Sandor Kocsis, ex-Hungary, who scored four goals himself in Barcelona's 5–2 win.

This was the beginning of the end for Wolves; it was also, ironically, the beginning of the end for Herrera. Buoyed up with success, Barcelona were due to meet Real in the semi-finals and on form, could be counted as favourites. Seven of their team had recently appeared in the Spanish national side, Real had clambered less convincingly up the European ladder that season, and they had been bothered by managerial ructions. But it was managerial ructions which decided Barcelona's fate – Herrera quarrelled with his superstar Kubala and with Czibor, omitted them from the team, Real Madrid, restored to form, conquered them 3–1 in the capital and 3–1 again in Barcelona, and Herrera was banished – to make more controversy, and more money, in Italy. It is perhaps worth noting with regard to Real's supremacy at the end of this competition, that their opponents, Eintracht, had defeated Rangers in their semi-final by an overall margin of 12–4, a memory that does not sit lightly on certain Glasgow breasts.

At this time, on the Continent, it seemed that almost

1

every successful team had a Hungarian somewhere in its make-up. Yet another expatriate from that country appeared in the headlines the year following Real's fifth win — Bela Guttmann, manager of Benfica. In that season Barcelona finally gained their revenge over Real, but instead of proceeding to their expected triumph in the competition, they were faced in the Final by the Portuguese side who, with the betting heavily against them, capitalized on feeble goalkeeping and a shrewd belief in themselves, and won a remarkable match by 3–2. For Barcelona it was a bitter blow, and, to date, their last substantial challenge for the trophy. For Benfica it was the beginning of the good life, and with the subsequent capture of Eusebio, the great life.

The next year, 1961–62, they won the European Cup again, and on the way secured two notable scalps — Tottenham Hotspur in the semi-finals and Real Madrid in the Final. Spurs were at the height of their powers, they had won the double and were on their way to a second successive FA Cup; in addition their team had been reinforced by the purchase of Jimmy Greaves from Italy. On their way to the

semi-finals they had played some spirited, skilful and courageous football, notably in an 8–1 thrashing of Gornik at White Hart Lane after being 4–2 down on the first leg. But when they faced Benfica in Lisbon they played with a disappointing naïveté, came home 3–1 to the bad, and not even the furious passions of their supporters (considerable in those days) could restore the deficit. Luck was against them, they conceded one goal and scored two, brilliant play went unrewarded. Benfica, wiser in the ways of Europe, withstood the challenge, and then confirmed their maturity by toppling a resuscitated Real 5–3 in the Final, a match notable for its remarkable shooting — Puskas, at thirty-six, scored all three for the Spaniards,

1. Not quite the great Real Madrid side of the late fifties which won the European Cup five times in a row. Pictured here is the team which reached the Final in 1962, but still containing the formidable talents of Di Stefano and Puskas.

2. The European Cup comes to Britain for the first time in 1967. The ball, thunderously struck by Gemmell, rests in the back of Inter Milan's net and Celtic are on the way to victory.

the young Eusebio two for the Portuguese. Golden days.

Benfica went on to three more European Cup Finals in the sixties, and lost them all, but their legend is fast and their reputation unscathed, not least by reason of their sportsmanship and the vivid open style of their play. In 1963, no longer managed by Guttmann, they succumbed to AC Milan in a Wembley Final. This match was something of a disappointment, partly because the stadium was less than half full. A European Cup Final between two foreign clubs was apparently still no great inducement for the British football fans. In this instance they did not miss a great deal, apart from a simply wonderful goal by Eusebio and two for Milan by the Brazilian Altafini, one of which was almost certainly offside. AC Milan played their customary unattractive *catenaccio*, but they had one great virtue, the young Rivera. Rivera is one of the most interesting players Italy have produced, in that he is somewhat different from the standard volatile footballer of that country. At a tender age he was an extraordinarily cool, intelligent general of the mid-field — indeed he may have matured too early for his own good, for he has suffered reproof, particularly from the national team selectors, for an individualism not over-laced with reverence. As a player, though, with his acute perception, composure and his superb footwork, he could even disguise the dross of *catenaccio*. When AC Milan won their second European Cup in 1969 he was again the potent force in mid-field.

Unsung heroes of that 1962–63 European Cup were Dundee. In the end they were convincingly defeated in the semi-final by the eventual winners, but to reach that point they had rattled up some impressive aggregates — 8–5 against Cologne, 4–2 against Sporting Lisbon, 6–2 against Anderlecht. Their strength lay chiefly in two men who would make bigger names elsewhere — at the back Ian Ure, at the front Alan Gilzean. Rangers, who succeeded them in Europe, did less well. On the edge of a gradual decline they met a Real Madrid similarly poised but less inclined to accept it. Age could not wither the power in Puskas's boot — he scored the only goal in the Glasgow tie and three of the six by which Rangers were crushed in Spain. Once more Real looked a good bet for the Cup, and when they just held on to defeat AC Milan in the quarter-finals and demolished FC Zurich in the semi-finals, the impression of a renaissance was vivid. In the Final they were faced by Herrera's new baby, Internazionale, about whom he had made prophecies of a similar extravagance to those with which he had launched his brief career in Barcelona. Once again his predictions were immediately accurate. Inter had fine individual players — Burgnich, Facchetti, Jair, Mazzola, Suarez (cunningly bought from Barcelona) — but their success was due to the efficiency with which they collectively locked up their defence, only breaking out when the opposition were stretched to indulge their individual talents in attack and score one of their rare goals. The

fact of the matter was that goals *against* Inter Milan were always rarer than goals *for*. Thus they had disposed of Everton by a single goal over two matches in the first round; thus their implacable organization was too much for the less drilled genius of Real in the Final, and the Spanish team's game was lowered to a state of unworthy confusion. Two unnecessary errors explicitly accounted for the 3–1 difference in favour of Inter, but overall they looked worthy of the margin. Who could master them?

The next year, in Europe, none. Liverpool came nearest, in their first year of continental involvement. They had progressed to the semi-finals by way of Reykjavik, Anderlecht and, on the fortunate toss of a coin, Cologne. When Inter came to Liverpool they were introduced to that unique and massive wall of sound which, in the vernacular, is called 'the Kop'. It was too much for them, and so were Liverpool's footballers, newly crowned FA Cup winners, at their most persuasively energetic. Liverpool, exhilaratingly, won 3–1; in Milan, absurdly, they lost 3–0 — absurdly because two of the Inter goals belonged to that category where disbelief simply cannot be suspended. A Liverpool supporter would say, to his dying day, that the referee in that match has much to answer for. Inter were therefore in the Final again, confronted by Benfica but played in their own San Siro stadium — on this occasion almost completely waterlogged. Fiercely partisan support and a single greasy goal, skidding through Costa Pereira's legs, won them the Cup for a second year.

A hat-trick of victories was denied them the next year — 1965–66 — by a new-look Real Madrid, not the potent force of the past and shorn of the great names who made that potency (with the exception of the ever-present Gento), inheritors of a tradition rather than creators of a new one. This was a narrowly won semi-final; the other was equally close, Manchester United once more throwing away their chance of glory by falling to Partisan Belgrade when they should have won, particularly after a superb display in the previous round. Then, ahead by only 3–2 after the Old Trafford leg, they had gone to Benfica and, incredibly, stripped the Eagles of their feathers in their own nest. Their 5–1 victory in Lisbon has gone down as one of the most dramatic upsets in European Cup history and the name of George Best was writ large on the Continent. As if in reaction, Manchester were over-casual against the Yugoslavs, and Eastern Europe had a representative in the Final of the competition for the first time. But they were not good enough for Real who registered their sixth victory.

The European Cup was eleven seasons old and only four clubs had their names inscribed on it, two from Milan, one from Madrid, one from Lisbon. In 1967 Glasgow Celtic brought honour to Britain and glory to their city by becoming the fifth, and it was their first attempt at the trophy. Their victory must have had a bitter taste for their great rivals, Rangers, who had already competed in the tournament six times, once reaching the semi-final. But Celtic, in that season at least, had something special because they won everything in sight and their European triumph over dreary Inter in the Final at Lisbon was a real triumph for the kind of vigorous attacking football they had

come to practise under Jock Stein. Inter may have been depleted by injuries but, after taking an early lead, they simply lacked both the spirit and the skill to withstand the Scots' assault. Gemmell's equalizing goal, a violently struck long-range shot, is unforgettable. Herrera moved on once more.

The next year emotion welled out of Wembley in great warm waves as Matt Busby's ship finally rode home. With the exception of the 1966 World Cup Final it is probable that no victory in the history of British football was more willed by the people than this one. Ten years after Munich he had avenged the fates, with a lesser team but with a greater glory, for

the struggle had been long. Three times United had reached the semi-finals; now at last they broke the barrier and having done that, and having also the advantage of Wembley for the Final, they were virtually propelled to victory over Benfica by popular support. The match had its agonies — United could not translate territorial advantage into goals, their only score in normal time coming from the unlikely thinning head of Bobby Charlton. Graça equalized, and Eusebio almost became an enemy of millions in the last minutes when put through clean on his own. But Stepney dived bravely at his feet, saved the shot with his stomach, Eusebio applauded him and became, of

1. Robson of Burnley stumbles as he is challenged by Seeler of Hamburg in their European Cup quarter-final, 1961.
2. Altafini scoring his, and AC Milan's second goal to clinch the 1963 European Cup for the Italians against Benfica.
3. Celtic attacking the Dukla Prague goal in the European Cup semi-final of 1967. Johnstone (left) watches as Wallace gets in a header.
4. Hero of the hour. George Best (Manchester United)

slips away from a Benfica defender during the European Cup Final of 1968, a game in which he scored a crucial, and brilliant, goal.
5. On their way to the Final, Manchester United just beat Real Madrid. Aston, Kidd, Zocco and Best dispute possession.
6. Ten years after Munich, Bobby Charlton has his hand on the European Cup at last, and the effort contained in that time is mirrored in his face.

3

6

course, the crowd's instant hero. Extra time was overwhelmingly Manchester's – George Best struck the decisive blow when he received a pass in a packed penalty area, controlled it, waltzed through the defenders, drew the goalkeeper, side-stepped him and slid the ball home. It was the work of a matador. Kidd, with his head, and Charlton, with a crushing volley, completed the ritual.

Manchester United deserved to win that year, not least for the heroics they had shown on the way to the Final. In the second round they had faced tough opposition in Sarajevo, in the quarter-finals they had desperately defended a slender lead in the snows of Gornik, in the semi-finals they had gone to the Bernabeu Stadium with a one-goal lead, seemingly lost it irretrievably by half-time and recovered quite astonishingly to draw there 3–3. A memorable, highly emotional match, capped by the spectacle of Foulkes, survivor of Munich, scoring the goal that took them to the Final. At Wembley, between the inexperience of Kidd and Aston (both excelling on the night) and the maturity of Crerand, Foulkes, Charlton and Stiles lay the adhesive brilliance of Best and, further uniting them, a wall of emotion a hundred yards thick. It had to carry them through; not so the next season, when the precise blades of AC Milan cut them down in the semi-final. AC Milan went on to outclass Ajax Amsterdam in the Final, Prati scoring a superb hat-trick, and it looked as though the Italian game would come back into a pre-eminence on the Continent.

In fact, the reverse happened. The next three European Cups belonged to Holland. In 1970 Feyenoord, though taken to extra time, outclassed Celtic in the Final. The Scottish team were

disappointing after a fine performance in the semi-final when they had defeated Leeds in both legs. Then, the following year, Feyenoord's great rivals, Ajax, won at Wembley against the outsiders Panathinaikos, who were managed by one of the legends of the competition, Puskas. The Hungarian's guiding hand was clearly as potent as his left foot had been, for on their road to the Final the Greek team eliminated Everton and then, in an extraordinary turn-round, Red Star of Belgrade. From Yugoslavia they returned after the first leg with a 4–1 deficit and against all expectations recovered from this with a 3–0 victory in front of their own crowd, thus qualifying on the away-goals principle. In the Final they showed themselves worthy aspirants for the title, but Ajax had plenty in hand.

Ajax's football, however, did not truly flower until

1. Leeds' year of near-misses. Their defence stands rooted in despair as Murdoch's shot bends the net and clinches Celtic's place in the 1970 European Cup Final.
2. Van Dijk scores the first goal for Ajax in the 1971 Final of the European Cup against Panathinaikos at Wembley.
3. Arsenal beat Grasshoppers of Switzerland 5–0 on aggregate in the European Cup of 1971–72. Grasshoppers' goalkeeper Deck makes a spectacular save.

the 1972 competition. Then, under their new manager Stefan Kovacs (who had replaced Rinus Michels) they began to enjoy themselves with 'total football', reaching their best form in the Final. *En route* they disposed of Arsenal in the quarter-finals, somewhat fortunately in the manner of their goals (two of which were helped in by Arsenal), but deservedly in the manner of their play. Arsenal, though hugely

173

competent, were simply by their nature unable to raise themselves to the same level. In the semi-final Ajax defeated a revived (under Jimmy Hagan's management) Benfica by a single goal and qualified to face Inter Milan, who owed their presence to a number of factors, not all of them directly related to football. In their second-round match against Borussia Münchengladbach, Boninsegna was felled by a Coca-Cola tin (surely a record), thrown by a drunken (on Coca-Cola?) spectator. Borussia, at the time leading 2–1, went on to win 7–1, but on Inter's protest the match was declared void, a replay ordered on neutral ground, and the Italians won by 4–2. In the quarter-finals Inter squeezed through on the away-goals ruling over Standard Liège. In the semi-finals they overcame Celtic after 210 minutes of playing time and no goals by winning the penalty kicks competition, a hardly more satisfactory eliminating process than the toss of a coin. Neither side, after two games of cynically defensive tactics, deserved to be in

1

a European Final. Thus the contest between Ajax and Inter took on all kinds of meaningful overtones, and, to the general relief, the result proclaimed a victory for the kind of football which could breathe life back into a game already dangerously near asphyxiation. *Catenaccio* was finally exposed as the graveyard of invention, doubly confirmed by the lonely but sophisticated threats which Mazzola and Boninsegna posed on the rare occasions they were allowed to attack. What might they have achieved with the kind of support that Cruyff enjoyed? He, fittingly, scored both goals. It was, as the saying goes, a night to remember.

1. Johan Cruyff of Ajax gets in a shot as Facchetti of Inter Milan tackles him. The European Cup Final of 1972: Ajax 2 Inter Milan 0. Cruyff scored both goals.
2. Ray Kennedy, 13 stone 4 pounds, body-checked by a Grasshopper! Arsenal beat Grasshoppers of Switzerland in the 1972 European Cup, but lost in the quarter-finals to the eventual winners, Ajax.

2

UEFA CUP

The European Cup Winners Cup and the Fairs Cup (once called the International Inter-City Industrial Fairs Cup, now known as the UEFA Cup) have always been but pale cousins of the European Cup, following in its wake and increasingly benefiting from its slipstream. They can still generate a considerable interest, though this may in recent years have been unnaturally inflated in Britain by reason of the relative success of British clubs in both competitions, particularly when compared to the moderate record in the European Cup. In the Cup Winners Cup the three seasons between 1970 and 1972 produced British winners; in the Fairs Cup the five seasons between 1968 and 1972 also kept that trophy on a British sideboard. But the comparative lack of glamour of this last competition is perhaps best summarized by Jackie Charlton's feelings after Leeds' tragic near-miss season of 1969–70. Falling at the last hurdle in the League and beaten at the last gasp in the FA Cup, Leeds were only left with the meagre crumb of qualifying for the Fairs Cup and Charlton's vocal disappointment at facing once again this third-rate tournament when only a few weeks previously the whole of Europe had seemed to beckon was a heartfelt cry with which it was easy to sympathize. In fact Leeds went on to win the Fairs Cup splendidly, their third Final and their second victory in the competition, defeating a fluent young Juventus side. Both legs were drawn but Leeds came out on top on the away-goals rule, having twice come from behind to equalize in Turin. It is sad that the Yorkshire club have not thus far been rewarded by one of the major European trophies because their highly professional side of the late sixties and early seventies could, on its day, produce more sustained, polished, football than any British club and might well have graced a European Cup Final with immense distinction. Injuries, continuous pressure at the top, and absurd fixture congestion, enough to cripple the bravest spirits, have probably caused them to falter when success was theirs for the taking, rather than any weak link in their talent.

1. Allan Clarke gives Leeds an early lead in the second leg of their 1971 Fairs Cup Final with Juventus.
2. Martin Chivers scores for Spurs as they eliminate Red Star Belgrade from the 1972–73 UEFA Cup.

In the early years of the Fairs Cup's history, Spain had a monopoly of victories – winning six times out of a possible eight, only AS Roma in 1961 and Ferencvaros in 1965 interrupting the sequence. But then the first two competitions, which took the absurd total of five years to play off, were confined not to club teams but to representative sides from cities which staged trade fairs, the rather curious basis for the Cup's inception. In 1958 Barcelona beat London on a two-legged basis, in 1960 they repeated the trick at the expense of Birmingham. Birmingham lost the following year to Roma. These were all matters of great unimportance, and successive Finals which saw Valencia defeat Barcelona, then Dynamo Zagreb, to be subsequently beaten themselves by Real Zaragossa were scarcely calculated to quicken the pulse. However, Manchester United, European semi-finalists *par excellence*, reached that stage, and fell at it, in 1965, overcome by the powerful Ferencvaros in a replay in Budapest. Ferencvaros went on to defeat Juventus in the Final. The next year, gathering momentum, the tournament produced two British semi-finalists and, unfortunately, two Spanish finalists.

Chelsea, who had done well to hold AC Milan in the third round (winning on the toss of a coin), were finally decisively beaten by Barcelona in a replay in Spain. Leeds, the other semi-finalist, also went to a replay in their tie with Real Zaragossa, and lost it on their home ground. Barcelona eventually won the Cup, both sides losing their home leg.

Leeds went a stage further in 1967, reaching the Final, but conceded two goals in Zagreb and the defences of the Dynamo side were too astutely marshalled at Elland Road for Leeds to be able to restore the balance. But they were rewarded the following season, in the Final marginally defeating a splendid Ferencvaros side who had earlier eliminated Liverpool. In wintry conditions the Hungarians had played magnetic football in the grand manner at Anfield, a performance which won the admiration of the Kop, who can temper partisanship with appreciative knowledge of the game in almost equal doses, the principle presumably being that any side which can beat Liverpool must be pretty good. So Leeds brought the Fairs Cup to Britain, and limpet-like it remained, moving to Newcastle in 1969 who

1

reached memorable heights in their Final against Ujpest Dosza, winning both at home and away, and overall by a 6–2 aggregate. In the previous round there had been a particularly unpleasant encounter with Glasgow Rangers whose fans invaded the St James' Park pitch for no palpable reason other than the fact that their team was not winning. Rangers fans would further disgrace themselves in European competition in 1972, provoking a minor riot in the Final of the Cup Winners Cup in Barcelona, a stupidity which may have seemed unimportant at the time because Rangers were victorious, but which subsequently caused the club's suspension from Europe for a year.

Arsenal gave first positive proof of their revival by capturing the Fairs Cup in 1970, disposing of Ajax in the semi-finals without undue difficulty and in the Final courageously recovering from a 3–1 deficit in Brussels to outgun Anderlecht 3–0 at Highbury. The next season they were somewhat less distinguished in losing to Cologne in the quarter-finals, but Leeds regained the Cup and Arsenal had much else to crow about. This was the last Fairs Cup; the 1971–72 season saw it renamed as the UEFA Cup and an all-English Final. At the tail-end of an over-long, over-crammed season Tottenham found the extra stamina to defeat Wolves, owing much to the formidable scoring power of Chivers whose two goals at Molineux were among the most spectacular of the season. In the semi-finals both teams had collected a famous scalp, Spurs thankfully defeating AC Milan who played an inexcusably unattractive game at White Hart Lane, and Wolves achieving a curious victory over Ferencvaros, in the course of which they had three penalties awarded against them and Parkes managed to save two of them. If converted they would have made the crucial difference.

1. In the 1966 Fairs Cup, Chelsea played AC Milan three times and did well to hold them, eventually reaching the quarter-finals on the toss of a coin.
2. Fairs Cup semi-final 1969. McFaul anticipates Penman's penalty and tips it round the post, and Rangers are denied the chance of taking the lead over Newcastle.
3. Consolation for the disappointments of 1970. Jackie Charlton celebrates Leeds' 1971 Fairs Cup victory in traditional style.

2

3

EUROPEAN CUP WINNERS CUP

The European Cup Winners Cup, as compared with the European Cup, probably owes its lesser charisma to three factors: firstly, it is younger; secondly, domestic Cup competitions in most European countries are of minor importance, having nothing like the kudos of the FA Cup; and, thirdly, the representatives who take part are not necessarily the best available, having given evidence of fortune in a knock-out tournament rather than of superiority sustained over a whole season. But it has intermittently given off bright sparks, brighter certainly than the Fairs Cup, and gradually, as with all three major European competitions, has gathered interest and grown in prestige. And for the clubs a win in Europe, of any kind, can always help to offset disappointments at home. A lowly position in the League table and early elimination from the FA Cup can be restored by a good run on the Continent, can bring back the disgruntled spectators for whom there is always, whatever the result, the curiosity value of seeing a foreign side perform on their team's park. These can provide some attractive oddities, and some upsets. Chelsea, for example, who had played magnificently to defeat Real Madrid in the Cup Winners Cup Final of 1971, found themselves faced early in the following season's competition by a team of amateurs from Luxembourg called Jeunesse Hautcharage. The Londoners ran up an aggregate of 21—0. In the next round they were rudely dispatched by opposition scarcely more distinguished than their predecessors, Atvidaberg of Sweden achieving a 1—1 draw at Stamford Bridge to win on the away-goals count. Chelsea might have scored a hatful of goals; instead they had surrendered the trophy.

Scotland almost scored an instant triumph in the inaugural year, 1960—61, of the Cup Winners Cup, Rangers defeating Wolves in the semi-finals and offering stern resistance to Fiorentina in the Final. But the power of Fiorentina's Swedish import, Kurt Hamrin, was decisive, and his goal in the away leg in which he beat three men near the touchline, cut in and smashed the ball home before tumbling among the

Great day for West Ham. Alan Sealey scores one of his two goals against Munich 1860 in the Final of the Cup Winners Cup 1965.

photographers was, as it sounds, quite extraordinary. This was the only year the Final was played on a two-leg basis; thereafter, like the European Cup, it was contested on a sudden-death basis on a pre-determined ground. The first of these was at Hampden, poorly attended by only 27,000, in spite of the great Real Madrid-Eintracht tie two years before. Presumably Fiorentina and Atletico Madrid did not contain the same stellar attractions (apart from Hamrin). A 1–1 draw in Scotland was resolved into a 3–0 win for Atletico in the replay in Stuttgart four months later.

The following year produced one of those delightful anomalies in which the mighty are almost humbled. Bangor City, a Welsh non-League club who had achieved the impressive feat of winning the Welsh Cup, proceeded to subject AC Napoli to a display of *hwyl* (if that can be applied to soccer), leading them 2–0 at home and holding them to 3–1 away. In the play-off at Highbury, their bubble finally subsided and they went down 2–1, but it was a close call for the Italians and not until the tie was over did the supporters of Naples learn of the humble status of their opponents. They reacted with predictable fury at their team and its officials.

At the other end of the spectrum Tottenham, with their great team still intact, played some wonderful football and crushed Atletico Madrid 5–1 in the Final in Rotterdam. In the three previous ties Spurs had accumulated aggregates of 8–4 against Rangers, 6–2 against Slovan Bratislava, 5–2 against OFK Belgrade. It reads almost like fiction compared with the lean scorelines of today. The pattern continued in 1963–64. Manchester United defeated Tottenham (winning 4–1 at home after being 2–0 down at White Hart Lane), Sporting Lisbon defeated Manchester (winning 5–0 in Portugal after being 4–1 down at Old Trafford), MTK Budapest defeated Celtic (4–0 in Hungary after being 3–0 down in Scotland), and, to cap it all, the Final between MTK and Sporting Lisbon in Brussels went to 3–3 after extra time. As if exhausted by mathematics the Portuguese side collected the Cup two days later with a 1–0 victory in Antwerp.

One of the golden days in West Ham's history is 19 May 1965. Playing, fortunately for them, at Wembley, they produced some truly entertaining football, of the kind that alarms their supporters with its tendency to present gift-horses to the opposition and then uplifts them with its capacity to create chances, all of which is part of their traditionally magnanimous style. Munich 1860 were a good side, West Ham were better on the day, particularly Standen in goal, and Alan Sealey splendidly scored the two goals which mattered late in the game. Earlier, Cardiff City had continued the Welsh tradition of irreverence by knocking out the holders, Sporting Lisbon, and almost getting the better of Real Zaragossa.

The following year Germany had revenge over West Ham when Borussia Dortmund eliminated them in the semi-finals. They went on to win the Cup, defeating a surprisingly ineffectual Liverpool — who had played well to beat Celtic in the semi-finals — in Glasgow, 2–1. A British-German Final, for the third successive year, also came about in 1966–67. 'Rangers rally in Nuremberg' might have been the headline; it wasn't enough and Bayern Munich won by the only goal of the match, scored in extra time. A hat-trick of German wins was forestalled when AC Milan comfortably outplayed SV Hamburg; then the Cup went east for the first time, Slovan Bratislava conquering Barcelona 3–2 in Basle. In many quarters this was a welcome victory, not least because of contemporary political developments in Czechoslovakia.

There followed the hat-trick of British victories, the first of them by Manchester City, an achievement which did not receive its fair share of publicity in Britain. In torrential rain in Vienna, even though handicapped by an injury to Doyle, they played with great character and skill to overcome a physically orientated Gornik 2–1. In very different conditions, under the balmy skies of Athens, Chelsea succeeded them as Cup holders. They already had a grasp on the trophy when they defeated Manchester City in the semi-finals; in Greece they rose to the occasion when faced by the legendary name, if not so legendary talents, of Real Madrid, holding out for a 1–1 draw and then finely winning the replay 2–1. They owed a great deal to Bonetti, even more to Charlie Cooke who played a mid-field role of such skill and perception he might well have been mistaken for one of the original Real greats. One of those, Gento, was still present opposite him, but no longer the irresistible force of old.

In 1972 Rangers played very well to capture the trophy, for they had a hard passage to the Final including a tough pair of games against Sporting Lisbon (a 6–6 aggregate eventually being decided in the Scots' favour on the away-goals rule), a cleverly achieved victory over Torino, and a convincing win over their old enemy Bayern Munich (who had beaten Liverpool). In the Final they acquired a three-goal lead by direct assault, and though Moscow Dynamo pulled a couple back, Rangers, whether helped or not by the arguable assistance of their supporters, held on for a deserved success.

184

3

6

1. Not a contest for a European trophy but a scene from Wolves' visit to Russia in 1955 when they played Moscow Spartak. Spartak also came to Molineux and were beaten in a memorable match.
2. League football in Hungary. Albert of Ferencvaros, in white, engaged in a heading duel with a Videoton player.
3. Bottles on the pitch at Anfield, but joy for Liverpool after they had beaten Celtic in the semi-final of the Cup Winners Cup in 1966.
4. Young about to score the first goal for Manchester City against Gornik in the 1970 Final of the European Cup Winners Cup, played in Vienna.
5. The great days of French football seem, alas, to be temporarily over. Nevertheless a capacity crowd witnesses this French Cup Final between Olympique Marseille and Bastia.
6. The Cup Winners Cup stays in Germany in 1967. Smith of Glasgow Rangers escapes the attention of Maier and Beckenbauer but misses the chance in front of the Bayern Munich goal.

EUROPEAN CHAMPIONSHIP

There are two other major competitions which involve European participation, but one of them, the World Club Championship, is best left forgotten, for its history is regrettable and its future uncertain. In recent years the two-legged ties have become notorious as brutally physical battles, having almost nothing to do with football and for this the South American clubs must bear a heavy burden of the blame. Suffice it to say that in 1972 it was a great restorative of values to see Ajax's beautiful football triumphant in Amsterdam after they had been boorishly kicked round the field in Argentina, and to see Cruyff walk off the field with both his legs still attached to his body.

The other competition is the European Championship (formerly the Nations Cup), which began by seeming to be just another competition but has grown into an event of some importance, a kind of half-way mark between World Cups. It possibly has a high nuisance rating because of the heavy fixture commitments of clubs, but it can provide an opportunity for reassessment and experiment in the national teams before the final run-in to the next World Cup. The first competition struggled on for two years, 1958–60, with no British participants and scarcely any interest. Russia emerged as the winners over Yugoslavia. In the second competition, 1962–64, England ingloriously succumbed to France early on; Spain defeated Russia in the Final. In 1966–68 the World Cup formula of qualifying groups was adopted, and the tournament offered the opportunity for quick revenge after World Cup defeats. England, in an atmosphere of considerable hostility, were beaten in the semi-finals in Italy by Yugoslavia. Poor Nobby Stiles (poor Nobby Stiles?) was hounded by the crowd as if he were the devil incarnate. It was no doubt of some satisfaction to the Italians, after their abysmal showing in the World Cup, when they defeated Yugoslavia in the replay of the Final. Italy had earlier eliminated Russia on the toss of a coin, which was a somewhat contentious method of arbitration.

The Championship really only acquired stature and wide public interest in 1971–72. Played over a much shorter period it provided the opportunity for reasonably sustained competition at international level. England qualified for the quarter-finals at the expense of Switzerland, Greece and Malta, and came face to face with their World Cup *bêtes noirs*, West Germany. The year 1966 had been one thing, 1970

another, and 1972 offered the chance to settle the issue. A quite irrational over-confidence in the British Press preceded the first encounter at Wembley, a feeling which no doubt ebbed swiftly from those experts as within ten minutes it was clear that this was a new, superbly organized and individually gifted West Germany, no longer to be haunted by the psychological spectre of English superiority. England for their part chose a tired unco-ordinated team, virtually bankrupt of attacking ideas and too uninspired to execute those they did have. The match, as football, was a revelation. For England it was a nightmare and plainly a 3–1 deficit was irrecoverable in Berlin. A shoddy match there resulted in a 0–0 draw, which some considered an English achievement. In fact, with the destructive players that Ramsey picked, a 0–0 draw was probably the only conceivable result.

The West Germans went on to defeat Belgium in the semi-finals, while Russia beat Hungary. The Belgians were possibly the second-best team in the tournament — they splendidly outplayed Italy in the quarter-finals, but at a cost. Van Moer had his leg broken in the most tasteless of fouls. For that alone the Italians deserved their welcome of rotten vegetables at Milan airport. The injury to the Belgian forward seriously weakened them against the West Germans, but their threat for the future looked potent and their style of play had much in common with their German conquerors and with their near neighbours in Amsterdam.

The Final was poetic justice, pure and simple. As a contest it barely existed, as an exhibition it was priceless. The West Germans scored three times, though the figure was largely meaningless — it might have been doubled or trebled so pronounced was their superiority. The memory relishes the spectacle of their three central pivots — Beckenbauer, cool at the back, gracefully distributing, then bursting through to attack; Netzer, streaming forward, master of the calculated pass; Müller, bustling at the front, deadly in execution. One of the goals stands out in illustration — Beckenbauer produces a defence-splitting pass, the ball is switched across to Netzer, his shot from the outside of his vast boot bends past Rudakov and thuds against the bar, Heynckes retrieves and his fierce effort from the right forces Rudakov to a plunging save at the opposite post, the ball runs loose again, Müller closes in like a terrier, controls it, sweeps it home. At that moment for West Germany Munich 1974 looked safe as houses. At that moment for England the long haul upwards should have begun — not just towards that pinnacle but towards 'total football', as played by the best teams in Europe.

Farkas scores Hungary's first goal in the first leg of their Nations Cup quarter-final tie with Russia in 1968. Russia reached the semi-finals on a 3–2 aggregate.

Müller, for once in his own penalty area, helping Breitner screen the ball from Bell and Lee while Maier waits to gather in the European Championship quarter-final, Wembley 1972.

The sixth Hungarian goal in the match that began the modern preoccupation with sophisticated tactics. By changing the role of the centre forward with such success, Hidegkuti, seen scoring with arms raised, caused a re-examination of the roles and deployment of players in all positions. England 3 Hungary 6, Wembley, 1953.

TACTICS MANAGERS FINANCES STRESSES

DEVELOPMENT OF TACTICS

Football tactics and strategy have changed radically over the years. The disposition of players around the pitch has altered and the functions and objectives of players in individual positions have changed. This has led in turn to a confusion in terminology — an old-style centre half's duties were similar to those of a deep-lying centre forward of the fifties; what are usually called centre halves these days could more properly be described as centre backs. New terms have proliferated: *verrou*, *catenaccio*; in despair, perhaps, simple numbers are used to describe styles of play: 4–2–4 or 4–3–3.

None of these terms is quite adequate. Really sophisticated observers sometimes use expressions like '4–2½–3½', which seems to be elaborating to the point of absurdity. Players do not take up positions on chalk-marks on the pitch, as actors might in a studio, and the ebb and flow of a game rarely permits a pattern to be imposed on a team's performance to the extent that journalists sometimes claim.

However, trends can be discerned, and the development of strategies traced from the earliest days to the present. Figure 1 shows what might be called the 'classical' formation, since it is that traditionally used to describe players' positions and to decide the numbers they wear on their shirts, although in fact few teams nowadays actually play in such a formation.

This was not the first dispensation of players to become popular. Around the 1860s when the modern game was developing, the accent was very much on dribbling, and British teams would usually be found playing eight forwards, one half and one defender, as in Figure 2 (goalkeepers can be ignored in these discussions, since their position, of course, has always remained static). One can imagine that the ball was followed around by packs of forwards like an exaggerated version of the way schoolboys learn the game these days, except that then there was more hacking, tripping and bodily contact in general. The leading players earned the title 'The Prince of Dribblers'. R. W. S. Vidal of the famous Wanderers was the best of these, although as his style depended to some extent on deflections from opponents and barging through, he was quite unlike the latter-day 'Wizard of Dribble', Stanley Matthews.

The half back in this formation was properly named — he really was a 'half', half attacker and half defender. His function was vital to the success of a team, and the next stage in tactical thinking was to duplicate him, a forward being pulled back, so that the popular formation became 1–2–7, as shown in Figure 3.

The Scottish club, Queens Park, was the first to realize the value of the principle of 'letting the ball do the work'. Their players discovered that better progress could be made on the field if they passed the ball from out of the general mêlée to a team-mate standing aside. They therefore spread themselves around the pitch to a greater degree, pulling another forward back to a full-back position. Slick passing and combined play gave Scotland a superiority over their opponents in early internationals and led to a recognized Scottish style, which was quickly copied all over Britain. Indeed, in his novel *The Card*, published in 1900, Arnold Bennett gives Preston North End the credit for inventing the passing game. Figure 4 shows the Scottish formation of the 1870s.

Once the principle of passing was well established, it is clear that long through passes and diagonal passing from wing to wing could make life very difficult for the full backs. The half backs were still by no means defenders, but supporters of the attack — what we might nowadays call midfield men. So the trend continued.

Another forward was pulled back and the distribution shown in Figure 1 became the norm.

This pattern lasted for about fifty years, and became so accepted, that although it has been superseded time and time again many clubs still identify their players in their programmes by means of it. As has been said, the terminology is still widely used, and we might say, for instance, that the inside left performs a mid-field scheming role, which means that he is playing as the old attacking centre half would, or that the centre half and right half are twin stoppers, which means that they are fulfilling the roles of the old-style full backs. It was the function of the full backs in the classical formation to block the centre route to goal while the wing halves, playing wider, curbed the two wingers.

An upheaval in the established formation was caused by the change in the offside law in 1925. Since 1866 a player had been adjudged to be offside if there were fewer than three players (one of whom was usually the goalkeeper) between him and the opposing goal line when the ball was played. Around 1910 full backs discovered that a more effective way of stopping attacks than dispossessing the forwards was to move craftily upfield at opportune times and catch them offside. Notts County are generally 'credited' with the invention of the off-side trap. But it was 'Big Bill' McCracken, a member of the Newcastle side that dominated the early 1900s, who perfected it. One of the great full backs of the day and an Irish international, McCracken was one of the game's thinkers. He so organized his defence that forwards couldn't find a way through. It happened that some games were stopped on average every two minutes for offside. The fans became as frustrated as the forwards. Pressure for a change in the rules grew, and in 1925 the FA acted. Two possible alternatives were considered: the number of opponents required between the attacker and the goal-line could be reduced to two, or the area of the field in which a player could be offside could be reduced. One trial match was played, in which each method was tried for one half, and the FA chose the former, not without criticism. It is interesting to note that in the Anglo-Italian Tournament, a strange and much-ridiculed competition begun in the sixties, a combination of both methods is used, and a player cannot be offside except in the opposing penalty area.

Once the offside law was changed goal-scoring increased dramatically.

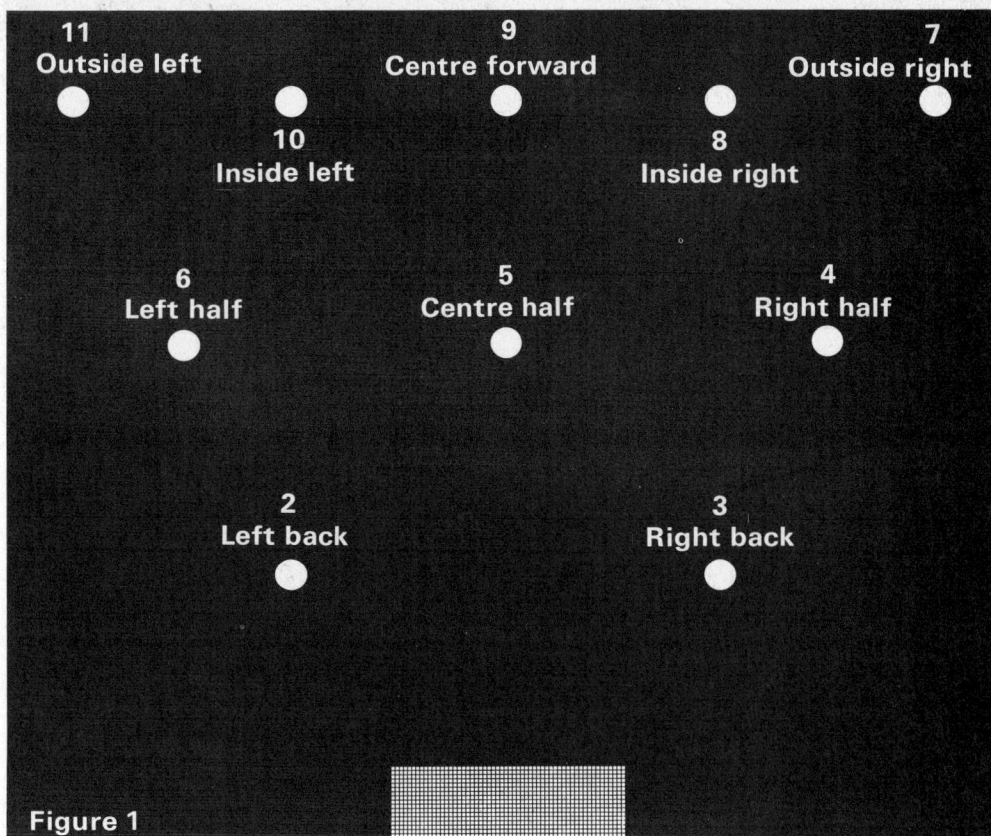

Figure 1

In 1924–25 76 goals was the highest total for a first division side; in 1925–26 exactly half the first division teams beat this total, 102 being the highest. In 1926–27 Middlesbrough scored 122 second division goals, and George Camsell himself registered a record 59 for the season. Dixie Dean next year scored 60, a record which still stands. The immediate effect of the change in the law was that the number of goals scored increased by about a third.

Centre forwards scored prolifically. Heading, an art not thought worth developing in the early days of football, was now an essential part of a centre forward's technique – Dixie Dean in particular scoring many close-range goals with headers of precision and tremendous power. The idea of giving the centre half the completely new role of 'stopping' the centre forward was first developed by Charlie Buchan, who persuaded Herbert Chapman, his manager at Highbury, to try the system with Arsenal. Chapman was a moderate player, but a dynamic, single-minded manager, once banned from management when Leeds City, his club, was wound up in 1919 after alleged illegal payments to players. Chapman's suspension was lifted after two years, and he took over Huddersfield Town, making them the most powerful side of the twenties. They won the League Championship three times running from 1923–24 to 1925–26, the first time this feat had

been performed. Huddersfield were also second in the next two seasons, but in their third Championship season Chapman had left them to make Arsenal one of the greatest club sides ever. Arsenal had entered the first division by the back door, being elected when football resumed after the First World War and the number of first division clubs was increased from twenty to twenty-two. Before Chapman arrived, the club had won no honours, and as a matter of policy did not spend greatly in the transfer market. Chapman reversed both traditions. The first player he bought was Charlie Buchan, an inside forward from Sunderland.

After a match at Newcastle, which Arsenal lost 7–0 (the Newcastle centre

Figure 1 The classical formation.
Figure 2 The usual formation of the 1860s.

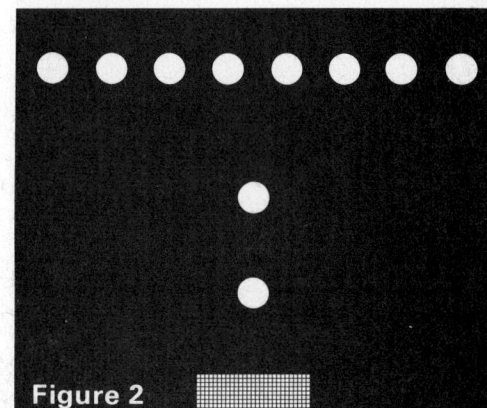

Figure 2

forward was the fabulous Hughie Gallacher) Buchan suggested that the centre half should be dropped back to the last line of defence and that an inside forward (he had himself in mind) should also be pulled back to provide the link between defence and attack, as in Figure 5. Chapman agreed to try the plan, although not with Buchan as link-man (his goal-scoring talent was needed forward). As the system became accepted and copied many teams withdrew both inside forwards, leaving the spearhead centre forward and the two wingers as the last three fully committed strikers. The forward line thus resembled a W, and with the full backs moving wider to mark the wingers, the whole system became known as the WM formation (see Figure 6).

Arsenal and Chapman were extremely successful with this method. Arsenal won the Championship four times in five seasons, being second on the other occasion, and became the second club to win the title three years in succession. Chapman bought and trained the right players to suit the play: Herbie Roberts, the tall stopper, known as 'Policeman' Roberts; fast, scoring wingers, Bastin and Hulme; and the schemer *par excellence*, Alex James. Arsenal did not mind defending. The opposition was lured forward into a defensive web, and succumbed to a fast breakaway goal. The legend grew: 'Lucky Arsenal.'

Arsenal's success inevitably meant that other teams copied them. However, they lacked the requisite flair. Buchan, Chapman and Arsenal have much to answer for: British football became stereotyped, declined as a spectacle, and became defensive and sterile of ideas. Also, because foreign teams failed to achieve the results against British sides that their football often deserved, it became complacent.

On the Continent, the third-back game was not followed so slavishly, and there were notable advocates of a more open, purer style. A wealthy Viennese, Hugo Meisl, studied soccer in England, Hungary and Italy, and dedicated his time and fortune to Austrian football. His lieutenant was Jimmy Hogan, an unremarkable player in Britain, but destined to be one of the greatest coaches of all time. Meisl brought Hogan to Vienna in 1912, where he made the 'Scottish style' into the 'Austrian style', with the attacking centre half as the basis of his philosophy. For years after Britain had abandoned this style and Hogan had moved on elsewhere, Austria continued to follow his teachings with great success. In 1931 an Austrian

Figure 3   The popular pattern of about 1870.
Figure 4   The Scottish formation of the 1870s.
Figure 5   Charlie Buchan's stopper centre half plan.
Figure 6   The WM formation.
Figure 7   The 1953 Hungarian deep-lying centre forward plan.
Figure 8   The 4–2–4 formation.
Figure 9   The 4–3–3 system. The full backs are encouraged to overlap.

1. Bill McCracken (Newcastle United), exponent of the offside game, in 1912.
2. Charlie Buchan (left), inventor of the stopper centre half, shakes hands with Fred Keenor before the 1927 Arsenal v. Cardiff City Cup Final.

team known as the *Wunderteam* beat Scotland 5–0 in Vienna, and in 1932 was unluckily defeated 4–3 by England at Stamford Bridge. It also beat Germany 6–0 and 5–0, and Switzerland 2–0 and 8–1. This team, in the 1934 World Cup, lost 1–0 to the eventual winners, Italy, in the semi-final. A member of the *Wunderteam*, Walter Nausch, was Austrian team manager in 1952, when Austria drew 2–2 with England at Wembley. He was still advocating the principle of an attacking centre half, and in Ernst Ocwirk had one of the best, as well as one of the most attacking, ever.

Hogan taught the basic skills and strategies; his players trained with a ball to improve their control. This elementary idea was anathema to British clubs, who trained their players to build up their strength and stamina, believing that British players' skills were innate. Even after the Second World War Danny Blanch-flower was to speak out about this insularity. It was the despair of Hogan, who had spells as a manager at Fulham and Aston Villa, both very short, although with Villa he was successful. These clubs had no time for fine theorizing. Hogan's talents were more appreciated in Holland, Austria, Hungary and Germany; scorned in his own country, he did much to spread the highest class of soccer on the Continent.

Another great continental supporter of the attacking style was Vittorio Pozzo, manager of the Italian teams which won the World Cup in 1934 and 1938. Pozzo, a friend of Hugo Meisl, had studied in England in the early days of the century, and became an admirer of British football, and particularly of Charlie Roberts, the Manchester United and England attacking centre half. Pozzo's greatest asset was his skill in inspiring the volatile Italians to produce their best when it mattered. A psychologist in the matters of a footballer's form and temperament, Pozzo used persuasion, patriotism and flattery to good effect and was a much-respected father figure to his teams. The style Pozzo preached was based on an economical attacking game; he eschewed frills and elaborations in favour of directness. He was critical of the stereotyped third-back game, and the battering-ram type of centre forward — his players were mobile and their attacks, based on long passing, were swift and fluid. Pozzo died in 1968, aged eighty-two. He lived long enough to see Italian football paralysed by over-caution and ultra-defensiveness.

British football, secure in the knowledge that home teams could always beat foreigners on their own soil (it was 1950 before Scotland lost at home, 1953 for England) continued to believe in the soundness of its tactics. In fact, the tradition of home invincibility had lasted so long that continental sides arrived with an inferiority complex.

In retrospect it is clear now that an accomplished team which could overcome this handicap with a good start could win. But in the event, the finality with which Hungary shattered English pride in 1953 was traumatic. The basic tactic was simple. By withdrawing the centre forward to a deep-lying position and refusing to allow him to indulge in the formal battle for high crosses with the centre half, the Hungarians threw the English defence into confusion. The Hungarian centre forward was Hidegkuti, a converted winger. If Johnston, the English centre half, came forward to meet him, paths were opened to goal for the deadly inside forwards, Puskas and Kocsis. If Johnston stayed back, Hidegkuti was

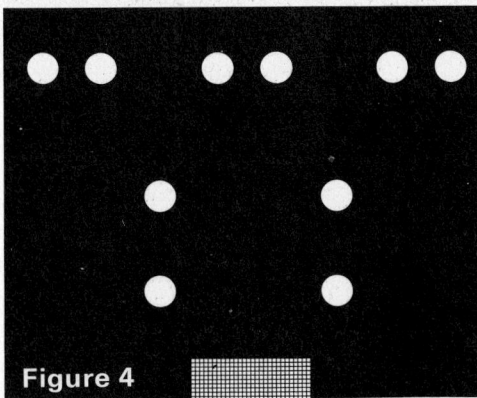

Figure 4

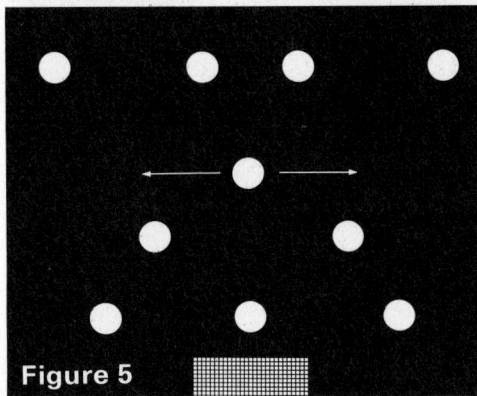

Figure 5

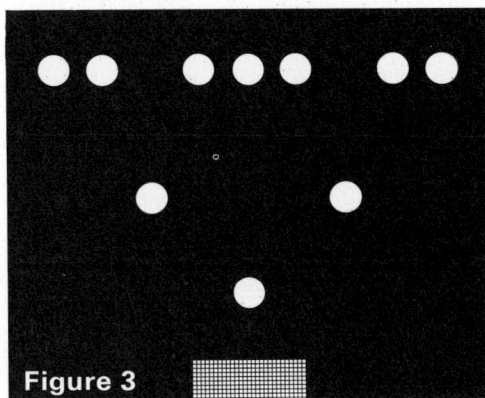

Figure 3

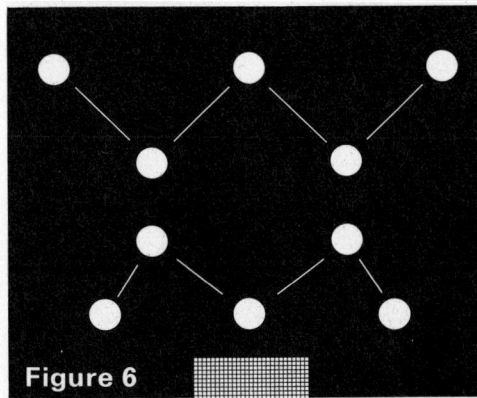

Figure 6

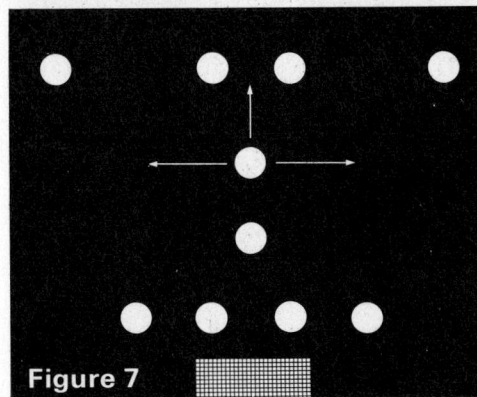

Figure 7

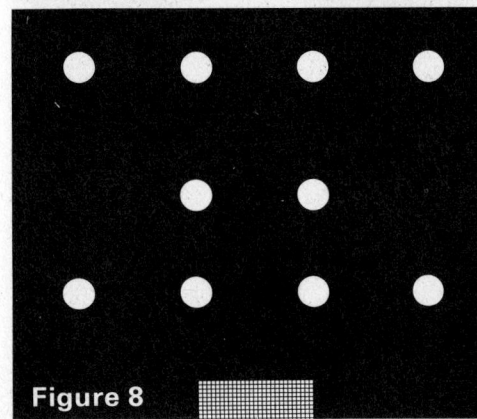

Figure 8

beginning of this chapter that methods rarely can be described properly by simply stating a team's basic deployment of players. This was nowhere more true than with the 1953 Hungarians. Each footballer combined team play with individual brilliance. Boszik played a smooth, polished game. Hidegkuti's runs from deep positions demonstrated skills not met before by most of the Wembley crowd. Sandor Kocsis was the nearest approach to the accepted prototype of a centre forward, but he allied the usual heading and shooting power with considerable ball control. Above all, there was the great Ferenc Puskas, whose left foot was lethal, and whose right foot was reserved for standing on. For years it had been recognized that a great player must have two feet. Another British canon had to be revised after the Hungarian match.

Hungary confirmed the form and convinced the remaining sceptics with a 7–1 annihilation of England in Budapest in 1954. England's right back was Alf Ramsey, whose patriotism

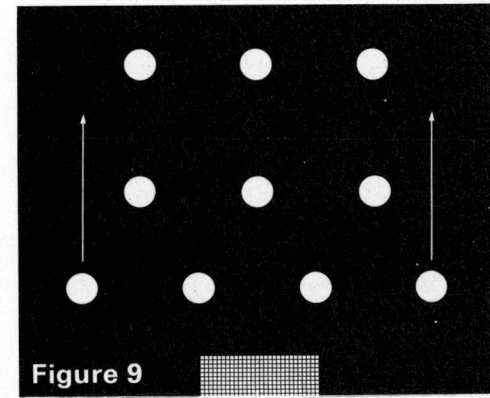

Figure 9

unmarked and could advance on goal with the ball at his feet. A quick wall-pass or two and the way was clear for a shot.

Another legend much cherished by the British was that for all their cleverness at ball control, continentals could not shoot. A tremendous shot by Hidegkuti to open the score in the second minute exploded that myth. With a centre forward to control the mid-field, Hungary could strengthen their own defence by withdrawing a wing half to become a second central defender. Their method contained the seeds of the soon-to-be recognized 4–2–4 combination. The formation they used against England is shown in Figure 7.

The fact that soccer observers failed to attach a formula of the 4–2–4 kind to the Hungarian style is probably due to the fact that the team was composed of great players who refused to be stereotyped; successful improvisation was very much a key to their dominance. It was said at the

received a blow from which it fully recovered in 1966. English pride generally was more quickly assuaged by calling the Hidegkuti plan the 'Revie plan', after Don Revie, who copied it with much success.

The term '4–2–4' became a part of every fan's language after Brazil had won the World Cup in 1958. It was clear that Brazil had two wingers, Garrincha and Zagalo, and two strikers in the centre, Vava and Pele, who shared eight of the ten goals Brazil scored in the semi-final and final. Zito and Didi played in mid-field in front of a line of four defenders. The simple formation is shown in Figure 8.

The 4–2–4 formation, because of Brazil's success, became very popular. It is a very fluid system, enabling attack and defence to be performed in depth. An attacking method frequently used is the overlapping full back. The full back is encouraged to initiate attacks by advancing up his wing, overlapping the mid-field man,

Figure 10 The Swiss *verrou* system: the bolt.
Figure 11 *Catenaccio*, as it might be used against 4–2–4 opponents.
Figure 12 The defensive screen, or mid-field sweeper, as practised by Beckenbauer.
1. Alex James (Arsenal) playing against Newcastle in 1933.
2. Manager and tactician Vittorio Pozzo (white hair) and World Cup winning Italy in 1938.

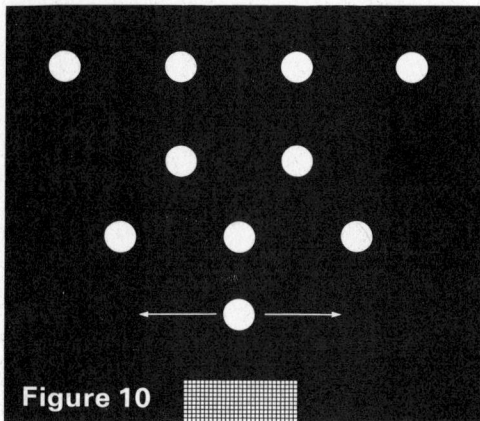

Figure 10

who drops back to cover him. The last goal of the 1970 World Cup competition, and one of the finest, was scored by Carlos Alberto, the Brazilian right back, who moved up to convert a pass from the opposite flank.

Brazil have continued to use either 4–2–4 or 4–3–3; or, most often, have improvised brilliantly somewhere between the two. Their 1970 formation had Jairzinho and Rivelino on the wings, with Pele being joined in the centre by Tostao. Clodoaldo and Gerson formed the mid-field link. The system demands stamina and fitness from the two men in the centre, and a variation is to reinforce the mid-field by pulling back a forward, thus making the 4–3–3 formation (Figure 9). This is, of course, more defensive than 4–2–4, and can lead to dull play as three forwards can often be frustrated quite easily by a well-organized defensive four. The overlapping full back is a necessary instigator of attacks in this system. It must be admitted, however, that the method used by the great attacking Brazilian sides since 1958 has leaned towards 4–3–3, as the left wingers Zagalo and Rivelino have tended to play behind the line of the other three attackers.

But then Brazil's strength lies in great individual flair, which cannot be defeated by defensive deployment alone.

Before the Second World War, Switzerland, who over the years have produced few great players but have achieved a fair measure of success by intelligent attacking tactics, developed a system known as *verrou*, or 'the bolt'. It was based on the old classical formation of the attacking centre half, with the full backs defending the centre and the wing halves the wings. One inside forward was pulled back to play alongside the centre half, but the method differed from 4–2–4 in that one full back played *behind* the other, as in Figure 10. This ensured double marking for the opposing centre forward, blocking the most direct route to goal, through the centre. The lone defender in the back line could also move to either wing to deal with dangerous situations; he was a 'sweeper-up' at the back. The system looks more defensive than 4–2–4, but in fact the Swiss encouraged the wing halves to attack when possible, and generally played an attacking game.

Not so the Italian clubs, however, who took over 'the bolt' in the fifties,

and transformed it into the depressingly defensive *catenaccio* system, which makes Italian league football so unattractive to watch. It began when the wealthier Italian clubs, backed by industrialists, imported star forwards, initially from Scandinavia. The reaction of the poorer clubs was to attempt to cancel out the opposition's star attacker by detailing a man to do nothing else but mark him closely throughout the game. This is a tactic which can be used with success whenever the opposition has one particularly dangerous man. When Johnny Haynes was the 'general' of the Fulham side in the late fifties,

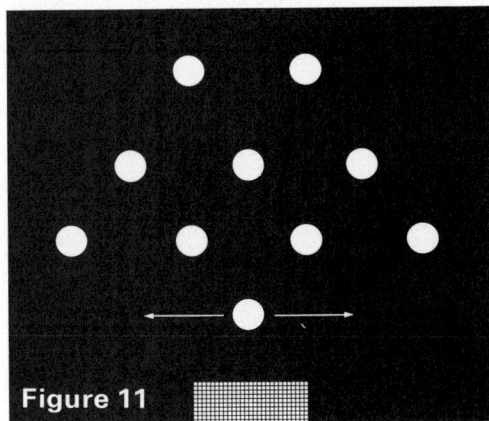

Figure 11

West Ham United would play Andy Malcolm, who could not command a regular place in their side, merely to shadow Haynes. England used the tactic when in the World Cup of 1966 Stiles was used to shackle Eusebio of Portugal, and also in 1970 when Mullery was set to nullify Pele. In the 1966 World Cup Final Beckenbauer of West Germany closely marked Bobby Charlton, but this was a mistaken policy, since Beckenbauer's own great talents were wasted in a negative role.

In Italy, the man given the close-marking task was an *additional* defender, which meant one less forward. Sometimes, two of the opposition were closely marked, and there was another depletion of the forward line. The weaker clubs found that the system worked amazingly well. Even against the best opposition a situation of stalemate could be enforced, and with a breakaway goal games could occasionally be won.

Eventually defenders were given the task of closely marking *all* of the opposition forwards, and an extra defender was used at the back, as in the *verrou* system, to cover all the other defenders. *Catenaccio* was born. It is not a system which can be expressed in numbers, as the number of close-marking defenders depends upon the number of opposition attackers. Against a formal 4–2–4, a team playing *catenaccio* would play the 'free' back (called in Italy the

libero, also known as the 'sweeper'), four close-marking defenders, probably three men in mid-field (to mark the opposition's mid-field men and provide a link for themselves) and two attackers. Figure 11 shows the rough alignment.

With only two attackers, specialist wingers who patrol the touch-lines disappear. Goals are usually scored through breakaways. In Italian football since the fifties one breakaway goal has often been enough to win a match. The stronger sides, caught in the web of *catenaccio*, were forced to adopt the system themselves to ensure against the solitary breakaway, and Italian domestic football became strangled in a wholly defensive philosophy.

A form of sweeper who is not entirely defensive and who is not the last line of defence, has recently made an impact on soccer tactics. Leading practitioner is Franz Beckenbauer, at last reaching his niche as one of football's great figures. Beckenbauer is the epitomy of 'class', displaying unhurried elegance and panache in every move. Not used to his full capacity in the 1966 World Cup, he was more of an influence in Mexico in

1970, where his goal put West Germany back in the game in the quarter-final against England, and his skilful attacking from mid-field positions did much finally to overcome the holders.

It was in the Finals of the European Championship (formerly the Nations Cup) that Beckenbauer found his true role. Too good a player to be given the duties of man-to-man marking or even of defensive sweeping, Beckenbauer operated as a sweeper both in front of and behind the defence, being a defensive screen and a springboard for attacks. The West German formation is shown in Figure 12, although the

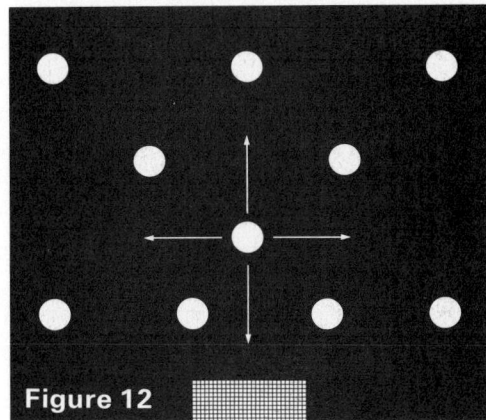

Figure 12

German method is to encourage all players to commit themselves individually to attack or defence as the situation demands, a policy known as 'total football'.

Bobby Moore, another great footballer whose talents have been a little inhibited by defensive duties, took on new life when he began the 1972–73 season as an advanced sweeper for West Ham United.

Most modern football teams play to a system based on one of those so far described. Systems are not rigid, and the flow of a game is likely to impose its own demands. But every footballer must know his role before a match starts, and managers define such roles by means of these formulae.

They are but part of the requirement for success. A sensible system for a team manager to choose would be one that takes account of the strengths and weaknesses of the players asked to employ it. The same applies to the style of play within that system. But other factors unrelated to systems are important, for instance each player's psychological attitude, his confidence, his fitness, his team-spirit.

All these matters are the province of the manager. Heroes when things go well, hated by the fans and sacked by the Board when they go wrong, managers are at once vulnerable and influential.

1. Dixie Dean, of Everton, outjumps the original 'stopper' centre half, 'Policeman' Herbie Roberts, of Arsenal, and Eddie Hapgood.
2. A top-of-the-table Italian league match in 1967. Mazzola (Inter Milan) shoots, with Bercellino, Cinesinho and Del Sol (Juventus) in attendance. The score was 1–0 to Juventus, a frequent score when *catenaccio* is played.
3. Franz Beckenbauer of West Germany, a constructive centre back.
4. Terry Cooper, of Leeds United, one of the best overlapping full backs, beaten on this occasion by Peter Osgood of Chelsea. Gary Sprake saved in the 2–2 Cup Final draw of 1970.

INFLUENTIAL MANAGERS

Herbert Chapman has been mentioned already as perhaps the most successful manager there has been in English football. A rival of the thirties who refused to use the stopper centre half was Major Frank Buckley of Wolverhampton Wanderers. Major Buckley's forte was the discovery and development of young players through his scouting system. Most of the players in his fine team of the thirties were home-bred; what is more the sale of other players from the 'nursery' brought Wolves over £100,000, a big sum in the days when £14,000 was the record transfer fee. Buckley caused a sensation by injecting his players with secretions from monkeys and having them regularly visit a psychologist for confidence boosting. Despite all the sales Wolves still finished runners-up in League and Cup in the last season before the war.

Stan Cullis, Wolves captain, was the last attacking centre half in English football until Jack Froggatt, a converted left winger, revived the tradition for both Portsmouth and England in the fifties. After the war, Cullis, a disciple of Buckley, took over the managership of Wolves with great success. Wolves won three Championships before 1960, and in the 1959–60 season almost brought off a hat-trick of wins plus the elusive League and Cup double. Wolves style was based on long passing and fast attacking and was spectacular to watch.

In the 1949–50 season Tottenham Hotspur won the second division of the Football League, and the following season they won the Championship itself. They used an exciting new method which came to be known as 'push-and-run', and the presiding genius was Arthur Rowe. The philosophy was simple. The team in possession was the team on the attack, no matter where the ball was. Spurs' players were instructed to pass the ball immediately and move into new positions. Short, fast, simple passes were the order of the day, from the full backs through to the centre forward, and the men were available to carry out the method to perfection: Alf Ramsey, Ron Burgess, Eddie Baily. Possession was so important that Ramsey frequently passed back to goalkeeper Ditchburn rather than make

a risky pass upfield (an unusual tactic at the time); Ditchburn would throw out rather than punt into no-man's-land. Spurs' superiority was absolute, but the team grew old together and the right replacements were not forthcoming. Rowe himself had a nervous breakdown and Spurs declined until their resurgence under Billy Nicholson, one of Rowe's team. For two brief years, Arthur Rowe had guided one of the greatest of all club teams. The current side with the nearest approach to the 'push and run' style is Ajax of Amsterdam, the European Cup-winners of 1971 and 1972. Nicholson's 1960–61 Spurs became the first team in modern times to achieve the 'double', but his influence was not as great as Rowe's, and it was Rowe who had brought Blanchflower, the inspiring leader of the 1960 side, to Tottenham. Nevertheless Nicholson bought shrewdly and is one of the most successful of present-day managers. He made Spurs his life, and helped by coach Eddie Baily, another member of Rowe's team, gave his players a singleness of purpose and a collective spirit which has kept them near the top throughout the sixties and seventies.

A post-war British manager whose triumphs arise from his capacity to inspire something between respect and love from his team is Sir Matt Busby. His Manchester United players have included some talented men whose temperaments and styles have led to incidents off and on the field: George Best, Paddy Crerand, Denis Law, Nobby Stiles. His sides have experienced ups and downs, but by his unswerving support of his players, his understanding of their private problems and his faith in their natural styles and talents, he has found that they have repaid him by reaching the heights on several auspicious occasions. When Busby took over United in 1945, the club had a blitzed ground, a stand and offices destroyed by fire, no training facilities and a large overdraft. In 1948 they won the FA Cup in one of the finest of all Finals. Between 1946 and 1951 they were runners-up in the League Championship four times, and between 1951 and 1957 they won it three times. In 1956–57 a young team, on the threshold of outstanding achieve-ment, lost the League and Cup 'double' only through an injury to their goalkeeper in the Cup Final. Roger Byrne, Eddie Colman, Duncan Edwards and Tommy Taylor were already outstanding players. All were killed, with others, in the Munich air crash. Busby himself almost lost his life. His footballing spirit should have

been broken. But astonishingly, United, with a new side, were in the Cup Final the following year, were runners-up in the Championship the year after that; in 1962–63 came another Cup win and in 1964–65 another League Championship. In 1968, after yet another Championship, came Busby's greatest success, the winning of the European Cup. Truly, his record equals anybody's.

Another manager who inspires affection is Bill Shankly of Liverpool. Champions in 1964 and 1966 and Cup-winners in between, Liverpool were one of the strong sides in the sixties and promise to be even better in the seventies. Shankly retains his faith in attacking wing play (perhaps not difficult for a man who has had Callaghan, Thompson and Keegan on his books and who played behind Finney). He prefers a rugged style of play befitting a man with his craggy features and mining background. Shankly is so much 'Mr Liverpool' that it is strange to remember that his considerable playing skills were exercised for Preston North End and Scotland.

Most consistent English side since they gained promotion to the first division in 1964 have been Leeds United. Between then and 1972 they were Champions once, five times runners-up; Cup-winners once, twice

---

runners-up; three times winners of the UEFA Cup or Fairs Cup, once runners-up; eternal challengers for the 'double'. Don Revie is an all-round manager. A tactician and shrewd buyer in the transfer market, he, too, inspires loyalty in his players, and is loyal to them. It is noticeable that he loses no opportunity to praise Norman Hunter at a time when that player's technique is being questioned. Not always satisfied with the treatment he received as a footballer, Revie takes pains to ensure that his own players have every consideration.

Jock Stein is a Protestant who manages the predominately Catholic Glasgow Celtic. Glasgow's Protestant club is, of course, Rangers, and the two sides have dominated the history of Scottish football. Stein, who was a Celtic captain in the fifties, took over the managership in 1965, since when Celtic have not only eclipsed Rangers by winning the Championship a record seven times running, but have become the most successful club in Britain. In 1966–67 Celtic won every competition which they entered, in the process becoming the first British club to win the European Cup — the best season any club has ever had. Celtic play the traditional Scottish passing game with the accent on attack; their European Cup Final victory over Inter Milan, apostles of defence, was acclaimed with satisfaction all over Europe. Stein, like Busby, has always got the best from his players, especially the temperamental ones like Gemmell and Johnstone, and the veterans, like the much-travelled goalkeeper, Simpson, and Auld, who had been sold to Birmingham before Stein brought him back and made him an essential part of the Celtic strategy.

Being a constant inspiration to their sides is difficult for managers with television and the Press seeking controversies in all their actions and statements. Some, like Brian Clough and Tommy Docherty, seem to court publicity. With strong personalities and dogmatic views, it seems impossible for these two to avoid upsetting some of their players some of the time. Clough has had more success than Docherty, winning the 1972 Championship with Derby County; the seventies will show if either can achieve success over a long period, as Busby and Stein have done. Malcolm Allison is another whose outspoken views get maximum coverage, and it will be interesting to see if he can achieve at Crystal Palace the success he had as assistant to Joe Mercer at Manchester City.

A different style of manager is epitomized by Ron Greenwood and Dave Sexton. Two of the best coaches in the country, these men are theorists whose achievements are based on concentration on the basic skills and strategies. Quietly spoken, they are not popular as television pundits, a fact which has done nothing to hinder their work at West Ham and Chelsea. Bertie Mee, of Arsenal, is a successful manager whose utterances are more ordinary than visionary, but the record of his club speaks for itself.

Harry Catterick has known the heights and depths with Everton, a team supported with religious fervour. Championships in 1963 and 1970 and a Cup victory in 1966 punctuated some disappointing seasons. Catterick relinquished his duties as team manager in 1973, after developing a cultured style of attacking play. He is a critic of the robust 'they shall not pass' philosophy and a supporter of the referee's get-tough campaign. What Everton have lacked for consistent success is the 'needle' attitude necessary in the English League. Catterick has never been afraid to buy, sell or drop top players to suit the needs of the team, and his replacement of the idolized Young by the inexperienced Royle led to his being injured when angry fans forced him to run the gauntlet and jostled him on his way to the coach after a match at Blackpool.

When Stanley Matthews was transferred from Stoke, he said he would like to return to end his career there, where he was a local idol and where a previous move to transfer him had resulted in mass protest meetings. It was, therefore, no stroke of genius when manager Tony Waddington brought Matthews back to Stoke. Results and gates improved, and Waddington developed the theme by buying other players supposedly nearing the end of distinguished careers. Nearly all had an extended Indian summer — McIlroy, Dobing, Eastham, Banks. In 1972 Stoke won their first major honour, the Football League Cup. It was astute buying, but there were precedents. Buchan returned to Arsenal after sixteen years to help mould the great side of the late twenties and early thirties. Arsenal later had great service from veterans Ronnie Rooke and Joe Mercer. More recently Dave Mackay in his last playing years inspired Derby County, and Celtic's success with Auld has already been mentioned. It is a ploy which might be used more often.

A problem facing some clubs and managers is the degree to which the football team is associated with the town. Its success then becomes a matter of civic pride and pressures on the club are magnified. Burnley, for instance, a town with a population of no more than 77,000, has a greater footballing tradition than, say, York,

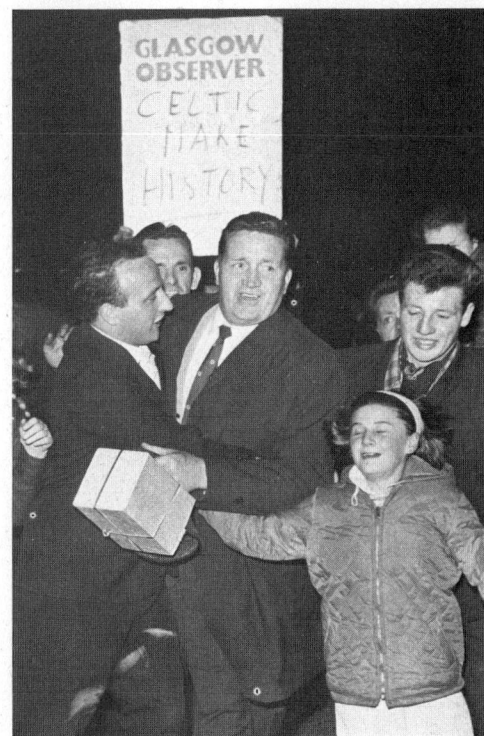

which has a much larger population. Burnley players are local heroes, to be met and recognized around the town, and the club is a local amenity. Its successes and failures, and the standard of its football, are in a small measure part of the quality of the townspeople's lives. Club chairman, and its driving force for some years, is local butcher Bob Lord. A man of dogmatic views, Lord will attack over-robust tactics in opponents and unfair Press reports with equal indignation. His cause is football in Burnley, and the need to preserve sympathy between club and community is an essential part of it. Therefore ex-Burnley players Jimmy Adamson and Harry Potts were given managerial posts, earlier heroes demonstrating

1. **Arthur Rowe managed Tottenham Hotspur in their successive second division and Championship winning years, 1949–51.**
2. **Jock Stein made Glasgow Celtic the first British European Cup winners.**
3. **Bertie Mee brought success back to Highbury when more illustrious names had failed. The big smile is flanked by the League Championship Trophy and the FA Cup, both won by Arsenal in 1971.**
4. **The joys of managership. A warm welcome for Jock Stein at Glasgow Airport.**

Blackpool appointed Stan Mortensen as manager with the same object of retaining a link with the golden days. Bolton Wanderers have twice tried Nat Lofthouse in the post. Bolton's post-war managers also include Jimmy Armfield, an ex-Blackpool player, and Jimmy McIlroy, who played for Burnley, while Blackpool had successes under Joe Smith, a great Bolton forward of the twenties. Lancashire teams view each other with mutual respect. However, these days the abolition of the maximum wage permits richer clubs to attract the best players more easily, the proliferation of the motor-car allows fans to travel further to watch the best, and teams with great histories but comparatively small resources like Burnley, Blackpool and Bolton will decline as the teams in the cities of Manchester and Liverpool will thrive.

A manager with the opposite problem – local apathy – was Jimmy Hill, who in 1961 took over at Coventry, a city with a population of over 250,000, most of whom were reluctant to go anywhere near the turnstiles. Hill's initial job was therefore one of public relations, and nobody could be better suited to it. He improved the facilities at the ground, installed an electronic results board, held Sunday trial matches. He invited the public to come and see what was going on, changed the club colours to sky-blue, began a 'sky-blue' radio programme for waiting spectators, ran 'sky-blue' vans round the city, publicized the 'sky-blue' excursion trains to away matches, improved the programme (it was displayed at a design exhibition), opened fêtes, invited boys to the ground for an autograph session, talked to the Press and encouraged his players to do the same. It was all good copy for the papers, and it won hundreds of column-inches and thousands of supporters. The enthusiasm was infectious, and playing success came, too. The club moved from the third division to the first in six years. And then Hill left, to continue talking to even larger audiences on television.

1. **Sir Matt Busby with the splendid Coupe des Clubs Champions Européens: the European Cup in Manchester United colours.**
2. **A manager managing. Stan Cullis at his Wolverhampton desk in 1964, the year he lost his Wolves job. He later managed Birmingham City.**

The Inter Milan sides of the 1960s who won the European Cup twice running playing *catenaccio* were managed by Helenio Herrera, a Frenchman who previously had been successful with several clubs in Spain before being sacked by Barcelona after a defeat by Real Madrid. Herrera was a disciplinarian who looked after his players as if they were schoolboys, on occasion supervising their food and their leisure. Before big games, players would be taken from their families for several days to train together. A year after Inter's defeat by Celtic in the European Cup Final, Herrera was allowed to go to Roma. He also managed the Spanish national side, but did not achieve the results he had with his club sides.

The manager who brought West Germany to the front in post-Second World War soccer was Sepp Herberger. West Germany did not take part in the 1950 World Cup competition, being excluded from FIFA membership, but they won the Cup in 1954. Because in an early match they lost 8–3 to Hungary their ultimate win has been dismissed as a gigantic fluke, but in that match Herberger had cunningly played reserves, being confident that West Germany would nevertheless qualify for the quarter-finals. A truer indication of their strength was the surprising 6–1 defeat of Austria in the semi-final. In the Final, West Germany first showed their great capacity for fighting back by winning after being two down. Herberger's teams played in a similar style to English sides, with the accent on speed, long passing, directness and total physical commitment. This basic game earned West Germany good results in the 1958 and 1962 World Cup competitions and in 1966 they reached the Final in England. In 1964, Helmut Schoen, for long assistant to Herberger, had taken over, and West Germany again had a splendid World Cup in 1970, when Schoen's influence began to take effect. Schoen improved on Herberger, and outstripped Ramsey, by concentrating on adding ball-playing skills to the side's toughness

1

2

and determination. His use of
Beckenbauer has already been
discussed, and his choice of veteran
striker Seeler to play alongside new
golden boy Müller in the 1970 World
Cup, when they were said to be
unsympathetic to each other, provided
personal successes for both of them.
West Germany's improvement can be
measured by their results against
England. Having failed to beat them
until 1968, they then registered three
victories running, eliminating England
from the World Cup and European
Championship in the process. In the
early seventies West Germany were
the best side in Europe, and only
Brazil could rival them in the world.

Sweden, despite regularly losing her
best players to wealthy foreign clubs
(particularly Italian) has a surprisingly
good international record since the
Second World War, largely due to a
Yorkshire coach, George Raynor.
Raynor, with limited resources, was
adept at planning different strategies
for different matches. In the 1950
World Cup, Sweden, as an amateur

side with Raynor's protégé, Jeppson,
at centre forward, eliminated mighty
Italy and finished third. In 1958, as
professionals, with their stars recalled
from Italy, Sweden reached the Final.
Raynor's outlook was old-fashioned in
1958 in that he preferred skill to
work-rate, and old heads to human
dynamos. Sweden have played good
attacking football, and Raynor and his
teams have deserved their good results.

South American countries are noted
for great players and teams rather than
managers, perhaps because soccer
there is more dominated by politics,
and managers consequently more
vulnerable; perhaps, too, because
players depend more on individual
flair than managerial organization.

In 1958 Vicente Feola, the team
manager, imposed a 4–2–4 formation
on his Brazilian side, and the great
talents of such as Zagalo, Garrincha,
Didi and Pele were directed into
productive channels. Brazil at last
achieved the results their skills
deserved. Feola was not an innovator,
however, as he copied the method

from the Rio club, Flamengo. He was,
moreover, but one of a managerial
team. Brazil prepare scientifically for a
World Cup tournament, and the
players are attended by doctors and
psychologists. Conditions for the
World Cup Finals in Sweden had been
studied in detail the year before by
Dr Gosling, a Brazilian strong man.

Brazil won the 1962 World Cup
under Aymore Moreira (Feola was ill),
but in 1966, again under Feola, were
disappointing, winning only one match
and failing to reach the quarter-finals.
There were valid excuses (Pele was
cynically fouled and injured in two
games), but Feola had to go, and his
place was taken by Joao Saldanha, a
soccer writer and broadcaster. He
attempted to strengthen the defence
by using a sweeper and saw Brazil
comfortably and impressively through
the 1970 World Cup preliminary
rounds, but his outspoken views were
not to the liking of all the Brazilian
hierarchy, and after remarks about
Pele he was replaced three months
before the finals by Mario Zagalo of

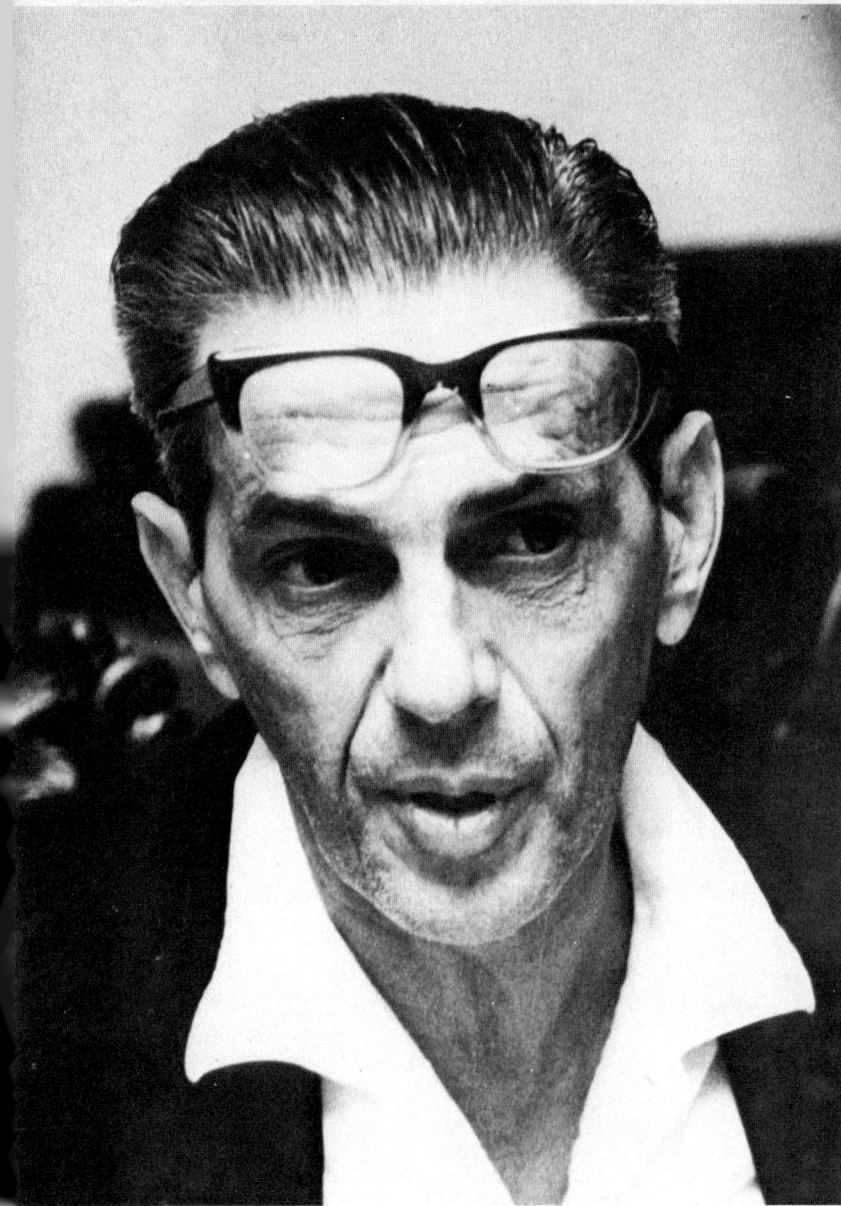

1. **Sepp Herberger managed the West German team in their 1954 World Cup triumph.**
2. **Helmut Schoen took over from Herberger as West German team manager, and won the 1972 European Championship.**
3. **Joao Saldanha lost his job as Brazilian team manager just before the 1970 World Cup finals.**
4. **Mario Zagalo took over from Saldanha and won the 1970 World Cup with Brazil.**

the victorious 1958 and 1962 sides. Zagalo reverted to the old formation and won the tournament, with Rivelino playing in much the same way as Zagalo himself had in earlier triumphs.

Another Brazilian player of 1958 and 1962 who was managing a team in the 1970 World Cup Finals was Didi, who managed Peru. Didi organized the highly individualistic Peruvians into a 4–2–4 combination, much like the Brazilians had been organized in 1958. Peru played like a slightly less talented Brazil — strong in attack, prone to error in defence and always exciting to watch. They reached the quarter-finals, where Brazil defeated them.

The most discussed manager of recent times is Sir Alf Ramsey. His methods have never met with universal approval, but in 1966, when England won the World Cup, none could deny that he was successful, and few were inclined to question his policies. When in 1970 England lost the World Cup to Brazil, criticism became fashionable, but even so it was directed as much against alleged mistakes in the use of substitutes in the quarter-final with West Germany as against his overall philosophy. In 1972, West Germany knocked England out of the European Championship, and Ramsey's detractors increased.

Much of the controversy which surrounds Ramsey arises from his personality. Basically a self-contained man, Ramsey does not seem to need friendship. He has a temperament which questions the motives and behaviour of others, particularly journalists, and thrust into the lime-light, he developed a mild persecution complex. To function, he needs the complete respect and loyalty of his players, and this he has undoubtedly achieved (it is his greatest strength) by offering them respect and loyalty in return. This can be shaken. In New York in 1964 Moore slipped out of the England team's hotel for a quiet drink with some friends. Ramsey was annoyed, and relations between the two men were cool for a while. However, Moore's undeniable dedication and professionalism are the qualities Ramsey most admires and the two later became very close. Ramsey has said, 'There's another Alf Ramsey on the pitch in terms of Bobby Moore.' Jimmy Greaves, on the other hand, was never forgiven for suggesting that it was no great thrill to join the England party for special training if there were no intention to pick him for the team. Alan Hudson and Colin Todd also suffered Ramsey's

wrath for declining to go on an England Under-23 tour, and were banned from internationals for two years. Ramsey saw these players' actions as threats to his authority and to his single-minded building of team-spirit and if one accepts his style of managership, one must accept his reactions as correct.

Ramsey needs his dignity. This leads him to affect a careful deliberate style of speech, and because he is less concerned sometimes with what he is saying than how he is saying it, he is misunderstood. His 1970 remark, 'I don't think we can learn a lot from Brazil', was probably meant as an expression of his faith in his players and their talents. Seen like that, it is not altogether reprehensible, but seen as blind chauvinism and an unwilling-ness to learn it makes his critics despair. Certainly Ramsey is often reluctant to see things as they are and needs to rationalize, at least in public. But this is common to all managers, as well as politicians and others in public life.

Alf Ramsey accepted the England managership at the end of 1962. He took over from Walter Winterbottom. Winterbottom's record as England manager for sixteen years was good: England lost only 27 of 137 matches during that time. Winterbottom was a coach and theorist who continues to do much for sport and soccer. He was unlucky in that the improvement in standards all over the world became clear during his managership, and English fans and critics lost patience with home sides unable to assert their long-presumed superiority. His cultured manner made him appear aloof. The mere fact that he removed his spectacles to be interviewed was enough to cause distrust in the man in

1. Ferenc Puskas managed Panathiniakos, European Cup finalists from Greece in 1971.
2. Didi, star Brazilian forward of the fifties, managed Peru in the 1970 World Cup finals.
3. The thinker. Manager Dave Sexton of Chelsea.
4. Two soccer knights and a soccer gentleman. Sir Alf Ramsey, manager of England, Bobby Charlton and Sir Matt Busby, ex-manager of Manchester United.
5. Alf Ramsey sympathizes with Bobby Brown, Scotland's team manager, after England's 3–1 win at Wembley in 1971. Brown was later replaced.
6. Ramsey in happy mood at a training session.

the street. Of more importance, his courtesy and charm were old-fashioned in a football context and were no help in communicating with players. The main rational arguments used against him were that he could not establish a settled side and that many of his selections were eccentric and proved wrong. This was unfair, because he was saddled with a selection committee.

Ramsey took over as a powerful team manager with sole responsibility for selections. He had been a good player, was reputedly a player's man who spoke a player's language and was welcomed as the strong man who would get things done. He had, after all, taken Ipswich Town from the third division to the League Championship in a few years, one of the unlikeliest of soccer's success stories.

Ramsey began well, with a string of wins, and gradually built the team which won the World Cup. What has become accepted as the Ramsey style — a defensive 4–3–3 or even 4–4–2, without wingers — actually developed fastest during the 1966 World Cup Finals. It is easily forgotten that conventional wingers Connelly, Paine and Callaghan played in the first three matches (Paine in particular played well) and that Greaves played in as many matches as Hurst. Perhaps these selections were Ramsey's last deference to the old order. He believes it wasteful to play wingers who by definition are on the edge of the action and he prefers forwards like Hurst who get into the thick of things

1. **Bill Shankly, popular manager of Liverpool.**
2. **Shankly, near the end of his career as a Preston North End player in 1949, is outjumped by Doug Lishman of Arsenal.**
3. **The mercurial and itinerant Tommy Docherty was manager of Queens Park Rangers for a few days in 1968 and met Alan Harris and Barry Bridges, whom he had transferred from Chelsea two jobs earlier.**
4. **Docherty was Scotland's team manager when this picture was taken in 1972, but he later left Scotland for Manchester United.**
5. **Harry Catterick, Everton manager, in the summer of 1968, after one of Everton's better seasons.**
6. **Billy Nicholson tells some of his Spurs players how to beat Aston Villa in the 1971 League Cup Final. Spurs won with two goals from Chivers (left).**

5

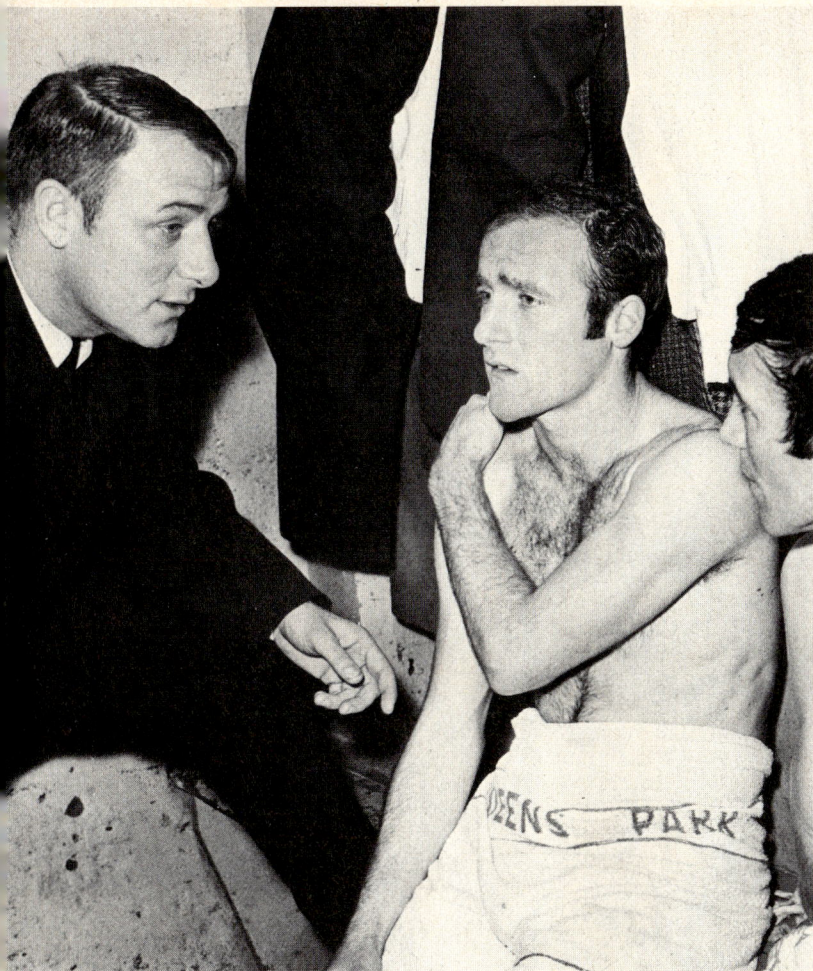

rather than forwards like Greaves whose effectiveness comes from avoiding the scrimmages.

Ramsey's playing style did not suggest the managerial style to come. As a player Ramsey brought culture to the position of full back. He was incapable of the physical intimidation that was the stock-in-trade of many other full backs of the time. However, he was obviously impressed by it, because as a manager, it is his faith in hard players that has won him most valid criticism. He threatened to resign when an FA committee suggested Stiles should be dropped during the World Cup, claiming Stiles was not a dirty player. In the European Championship return match with West Germany, when England needed to win by two goals to stay alive, Ramsey picked Hunter and Storey, both hard destructive men ('but fair' says Ramsey). He claimed he needed players who could win the ball in mid-field, although these were not the players who could do much with it, even if they won it, particularly as there were only two forwards to convert possession into goals.

Ramsey shows no urgency in the search for ball-players. His team has not developed since 1966. The World Cup was won once, but it will take new policies to win it again. Ramsey has built an England squad, and given it team-spirit, determination and confidence; it may take another man to give it flair.

1. 'Where are all the spectators?' might have been Jimmy Hill's reflection when taking over at Coventry City.
2. Two ex-wing halves with Lancastrian backgrounds became manager and team manager at Coventry in 1972: Joe Mercer, an old Everton player, and Gordon Milne, who played for Preston and Liverpool. Their thoughtful, constructive attitude was soon in evidence in Coventry's play.
3. Ron Greenwood, a cultured centre half with Chelsea, an enthusiastic FA coach, and an apostle of attractive football as West Ham's manager.
4. Malcolm Allison, a winner of cups, holds Manchester City's League Cup in triumph in 1970.
5. Brian Clough, as a forceful Middlesbrough centre forward in 1958, before injury cut short his career.
6. Brian Clough, equally forceful as Derby County's manager in the seventies.

2

3

5

6

FINANCES

Several developments since the Second World War have considerably raised the status of British footballers. The financial rewards of star players are astronomical compared with those of their predecessors. On the other hand, the demands made on them have increased and new stresses and strains have become apparent.

Footballers began to be paid in the 1870s. The first professional is sometimes said to be James Lang who claimed to be paid by Sheffield Wednesday when he joined them from Scotland in 1876, but it is likely that other players were being quietly paid at about the same time. The FA frowned on payments and banned Accrington in 1883 for paying a player. Major Sudell, President of Preston North End, then admitted he did the same and Preston were disqualified from the 1884 Cup competition. However, it was clear that many clubs were making payments and later in 1884 the FA allowed payments for lost wages. At the same time they banned Scots from the FA Cup competition, a move to stem the luring of Scots to English clubs with money. In 1885 the FA lost the battle completely and professionalism was legalized.

Steve Bloomer, in the 1890s, was paid 7s 6d a week by Derby County, and this was an average wage of the time. In 1901 wages were restricted to a maximum for the first time; the amount was £4 a week. In 1910 it was raised to £5. The maximum wage was increased to £9 in 1920, but then reduced in 1922 to £8 for the season and £6 in the close season. Incredibly, this maximum remained until 1947! To put these figures in perspective, players earning the maximum before the Second World War were considerably better off than most working men (£3 10s was a respectable wage in the thirties), but were not in the same class as public entertainers of the stage or screen.

The Players Union had been operating since 1907, but had no real success before 1947, when a minimum wage, as well as a maximum, was fixed. A player over twenty years old earned between £7 and £12 in the season and £5 and £10 in the summer. The maximum crept up over the next few years until in 1958 the last maximum wage was imposed; it was

£20 in winter and £17 in the summer.

The Players Union became the Professional Footballers Association in 1958 and led by an enthusiastic chairman, Jimmy Hill, campaigned very forcefully and skilfully for the abolition of the maximum wage. In 1961 the Football League (the FA ceased controlling wages in 1910) capitulated, and professional football became overnight a very attractive career.

The abolition of the maximum wage was approved by the richer clubs as much as by the players. After the Second World War there were suspicions that many clubs were making illegal payments to players to keep them happy. Such great clubs as Arsenal, Manchester United and Sunderland were subject to FA investigations.

Before restrictions on wages were lifted, it was possible for the stars to earn extra money outside the game, mainly from articles and books, opening shops and fêtes and occasionally from advertising. Nat Lofthouse, whose career ended simultaneously with the rise in wages, earned a little extra by advocating Andrews Liver Salts. However, many players whose great deeds were performed in the forties and fifties have cause to regret the maximum wage. Tommy Lawton, for instance, who played for England twenty-three times between 1939 and 1949, could not earn more than £8 a week for most of that time. Even his fees for internationals were usually only £10. He could earn small bonuses (averaging about £1 per league point, plus a little more for Cup runs) and occasional benefits, but these were not obligatory, and many players never received a benefit. It is clear then, that Lawton did not earn big money from football. In his autobiography, he defended the maximum wage, claiming that football was a team game, but undoubtedly he suffered from the system. His fame led to jobs inside and outside football for a while after his retirement, but he eventually experienced financial difficulties which happily modern players will avoid. These were alleviated for him when in November 1972 a testimonial match was played between Everton and a Great Britain team. Wilf Mannion, the last of whose twenty-six international appearances was in 1952, became a labourer, and must have mused many a time as he clocked in in the early morning on the £100-a-week salaries paid nowadays to players with half his talent and achievement.

In an effort to earn salaries commensurate with their fame and drawing power, some players left

England. In 1950 Neil Franklin, one of England's best centre halves, went to Bogota to play in a Colombian League outside the jurisdiction of FIFA. Charlie Mitten also sought riches in Bogota. Both men shortly returned to the English League.

Transfer fees have rocketed with salaries and with the rewards open to clubs who win places in European competitions.

In 1905, the first £1,000 transfer, of Alf Common from Sunderland to Middlesbrough, was investigated by an FA Commission. In 1908 a limit of £350 was set on transfer fees, but this was lifted after only four months, as clubs found ways to circumvent it. At the Second World War, the record transfer fee was still only £14,000, paid by Arsenal to Wolves for Bryn Jones. After the war fees rose more quickly. First British club to pay over £100,000 for a player was Manchester United, who paid Torino £115,000 for Denis Law in 1961.

Italian clubs are the world's biggest spenders on the transfer market, often paying big fees for players from other countries. As long ago as 1962 Juventus paid £200,000 to Real Madrid for Luigi Del Sol, and in 1963 Roma paid about £240,000 for Sormani, a record which stood for a long time. Current record is about £400,000 paid to Varese by Juventus for a Sicilian, Pietro Anastasi, in 1968. Strangely, few of the players who have joined Italian clubs at immense fees have proved outstanding in international football. Inter Milan tried to buy Pele for £300,000 but, not surprisingly, he was not allowed to leave Brazil. Transfer fees are not disclosed officially, and the figures quoted are journalist's estimates, admittedly based on inside information.

British players, who until recently were not allowed any share of the transfer fee in Britain, began to go to Italy in the fifties for large signing-on fees. John Charles, in 1957, received about £10,000 for signing for Juventus from Leeds. Leeds received £55,000. In 1961 Gerry Hitchens received a similar sum from Inter Milan, as did Denis Law and Joe Baker from Torino. In the fifties two players who had played for Charlton Athletic as amateurs, Swede Hans Jeppson and Eddie Firmani, a South African of Italian descent, were paid £18,000 and £5,000 respectively to play for Genoese clubs Atalanta and Sampdoria. Both were later transferred, for £60,000 and £80,000, to other Italian clubs.

South American players have also received big money for signing for Italian clubs. Sivori, from Argentina, Schiaffino from Uruguay and

1. **Bryn Jones became the most expensive pre-war footballer when George Allison of Arsenal paid Major Buckley of Wolves £14,000 for him in 1938.**
2. **Neil Franklin, of Stoke City and England, just before he went to Bogota.**
3. **Wilf Mannion was forced to become a £12-a-week labourer after his days as a sophisticated inside forward with Middlesbrough and England.**

Amarildo from Brazil, all received over £20,000. Spanish players Del Sol and Suarez, when joining Juventus and Inter, received £47,000 and £59,000 respectively to sign on.

British players are now permitted to receive five per cent of domestic transfer fees, provided they have not asked for the transfer themselves. Tony Hateley, who began playing with Notts County and eventually returned there via Aston Villa, Chelsea, Liverpool, Coventry City and Birmingham City for combined fees approaching £400,000, improved his own bank balance on the way. The £225,000 Derby County paid in 1972 for full back David Nish earned Nish over £10,000 for himself.

It might appear from this that soccer players who are transferred are likely to earn more from the game than those whose loyalties keep them at the same club throughout their careers. One method of rewarding the latter is to offer them contracts incorporating bonuses for long service and this sometimes leads to dissatisfaction among the younger players. Arsenal use such a scheme, and it was a cause of Charlie George being on the transfer list during the 1972–73 season. He thought his salary should be more on a par with those of the older players.

Much of the British footballers' improved status arises from the court case George Eastham fought in the early sixties. Previously clubs were under no obligation to transfer a discontented player. Under the retain-and-transfer system they could effectively freeze him out of the game merely by paying him his old wage. Eastham found himself in this unhappy situation, and with the help of the Professional Footballers Association challenged at law Newcastle United's right to hold him. He won, and in 1963 the retain-and-transfer system was held to be a restraint of his trade. A player now can renegotiate his contract whenever it expires, and if he and the club cannot agree to a new one, he may appeal to the League and if necessary to an independent tribunal. If the club agree to a transfer, he may even appeal against the fee demanded.

Players' incomes nowadays bear no relation to those of only twenty years ago. George Best, for instance, first arrived at Manchester United when he was fifteen years old. When seventeen he played his first game in the first division. Within a year he was earning £100 per week. Before he was twenty-one he owned his first boutique. Best, because of his youth, his looks, his apparent unconcern with authority, and the publicity with girls, became a teenage hero of pop-star proportions,

requiring a staff to answer his mail. He turned down an offer of several thousand pounds to make a pop record. Advertisers required him to endorse their products. Soon he bought another boutique and a share in a shoe shop with his friend Mike Summerbee, of Manchester City. He made films, had a television series and lent his name to numerous newspaper and magazine articles. He built a much-publicized £30,000 house, full of modern gadgetry, like a television set (rented!) which disappeared up the chimney when not required. In his mid-twenties Best's earnings from all sources were estimated at about £50,000 a year.

Bobby Moore, England's captain for many years, does almost as well. Earning over £200 per week directly from soccer, he can make far more from outside the game. A similar sum comes from sponsoring products. The footballer's traditional commercial interests in clothes and sports equipment put Moore into the £30,000 a year class.

Most of the top stars in England's 1966 World Cup-winning side boosted their earnings, for a year or two at least, into something approaching £20,000 a year.

Before the boom in salaries, it was axiomatic that well-advised footballers learned a trade in preparation for the time in their careers when they had to give up the game. A sound business head still works wonders. Francis Lee entered the wastepaper business when still a second division player with Bolton Wanderers. The business now has a payroll running into double figures, and Lee has branched out into the usual journalism, boutiques, advertising and hairdressing. With outside interests bringing him in three or four times the £10,000 or so he earns with Manchester City, it is a wonder he can still play football with such verve and enthusiasm.

Tom Finney, a contemporary of Lawton and Mannion, had the good fortune to be a plumber. Although his football, spread over many years and taking in seventy-six appearances for England, earned him no more in total than Best or Moore make in a year, he ploughed much of it back into his plumbing business, and now a fleet of vans operating around Preston testify that this very popular player will be well off for the rest of his days.

A footballer need not be a world-class player to make a handsome living. The pool into which Arsenal players put their outside earnings arising from their 'double' victory in 1971 was worth several thousand pounds. On the other hand, an average player in a lower division, with an unsuccessful club attracting small gates, might never earn £40 per week. Overall average wage for professional soccer players in Britain is about £60 per week.

Clubs encourage players to perform better with bonus systems. Traditional method is bonuses for wins and draws, but these have been restricted to £4 per win and £2 per draw in the League with similar small sums for Cup victories. More remunerative are bonuses based on positions in the League at various stages in the season; a player in a Championship-winning side might earn over £1,000 in such bonuses. Another form of bonus is based on the gate — say a £1 bonus for every thousand spectators over a given number.

On the Continent and in South America players have been earning large salaries and bonuses for longer than British players. In Italy, particularly, top players have been earning £20,000 a year for many years. Pele, in Brazil, is a vast one-man business, employing managers and lawyers. His income is about £150,000 a year. Bonuses offered to South Americans are huge. In the 1966 World Cup in England, the Argentine players would have received £5,000 per man had they won the Cup, and the Brazilians in 1970 did receive £7,000 per man plus shares and expensive gifts.

After the 1966 World Cup Bobby Moore challenged in the High Court the right of the Inland Revenue to tax his bonuses of approaching £2,000 and won, the Court deciding that these were in the nature of a testimonial. In 1972 Bobby Charlton received a testimonial, which included a match with Celtic, and Charlton's testimonial exceeded £30,000. Jimmy Greaves was also granted a testimonial, the centre piece of which was a match between Spurs and Feyenoord. Clubs may arrange testimonials for players who have been ten years with them — however, if the club arrange the testimonial the sum is taxable as earnings. To avoid tax the arrangements must be made by an outsider — usually, in fact, a committee of friends.

Television provides an income for players who can talk about the game. One of the first players to appear regularly was Wally Barnes, who became a BBC-TV commentator. Jimmy Hill became very successful as the leading soccer commentator on Independent Television and Paddy Crerand, Derek Dougan and Bob McNab appeared frequently with him. Dougan also has his own programme in the Midlands. Managers Revie, Mercer and Allison have been regular

television pundits. Bob Wilson has a television spot. Danny Blanchflower was employed by CBS in America to help explain football when it seemed likely to get a big following there after the 1966 World Cup.

Managers share in the new affluence. Top managers' salaries in Britain exceed £10,000 a year. This again is small beer compared to fees paid on the Continent. Helenio Herrera, for many years a top manager in Spain and Italy, moved from Inter Milan to Roma in 1968 at a salary of about £67,000, paid into a Swiss bank and therefore tax-free. His earnings, at times, have exceeded £100,000 a year.

Continental clubs are often backed by local industrialists. The Juventus club in Italy, for instance, has been supported for years by the giant Fiat motor company. The Dutch club PSV Eindhoven is the sports club of the international company Philips Electrical. 'Bubbly' provided the backing for the French club Stade de Reims for many years, the money coming from a rich champagne producer, but soccer interest has declined among the perverse French, and the financial support ceased. In Eastern Europe the army has 'sponsored' soccer by offering posts to the top players. Famous army clubs are Dukla of Prague, CDNA of Bulgaria and Honved of Hungary, the club of 'Galloping Major' Puskas.

Bulgarian railways support Lokomotiv Sofia and the many Dynamo clubs in Europe are connected with state-run electrical industries.

Despite all this, football club finances all over the world are very precarious. In England many clubs receive income from football pools, supporters' clubs and generous directors, but the bulk of the income is the money taken at the gate. Players' salaries take nearly three-quarters of this. Indeed, with some clubs the wages bill exceeds the gate money. All too often the difference between profit and loss in any given season's trading depends upon the transfer deals.

Club finances are complex. They are not run on usual commercial lines. There is a limit (seven and a half per cent) on the dividend that is allowed to be paid to shareholders, but clubs seldom pay a dividend anyway. Many own property, often in the form of houses. Clubs that own their own ground are wealthy, as professional grounds are usually in prime development areas. It is not difficult for these clubs to get overdrafts. Most clubs in Europe operate by courtesy of their banks, and if all loans were withdrawn overnight the soccer industry as it is now would collapse.

Financial troubles afflict clubs of all sizes, but of course the smaller clubs have more difficulty in overcoming

1

216

Their income from gates and
their resources in players and property
are less, the overdraft consequently
more limited, and many skirt the edges
of bankruptcy continuously.
Accrington Stanley were forced to
retire from the League in 1962
because of rising debts.

Most third and fourth division clubs
in the English League lose money
every season, often as much as
£20,000. Charlton Athletic, a London
club with a great history — in the top
four in the first division in all three
seasons before the war and Cup-
winners since — found themselves in
the third division in season 1972–73.
They lose about £40,000 a year, and
their bank overdraft considerably
exceeds this figure. They have suffered
from having a ground with the largest
capacity in the Football League
(75,000 packed in to see a Cup tie in
1938), but, in S.E. 7, with poor
communications. Needing a gate of
about 17,000 to break even, they
averaged just over 10,000 in the
second division and about 7,000 in
the third. It is clear that the club
cannot exist for ever in its present
circumstances.

A method some clubs employ to cut
costs is to trim their staffs to a
minimum. Portsmouth, in the sixties,
were among the first to employ a
first-team squad only, with about
fifteen players on the books.

Newport County trimmed their
wages bill in 1971 to £24,000, but
even with their landlords (the local
council) waiving their rent they still
lost money and increased their
overdraft.

Brentford have shown that gloom
need not be total. In the fourth
division in 1969–70, their gate receipts
totalled £47,000, about £15,000 less
than was needed to cover the wages
and expenses bills. There had been
talk of a merger with West London
neighbours Queen's Park Rangers, a
club who themselves were at one
time grateful for the support of John
Bloom, the washing-machine
millionaire. Brentford were 'rescued'
by a group of supporters, and engaged

1. Charlie Mitten (dark shirt), who
   went to Colombia in the fifties,
   attempts a centre in the 1948
   Cup Final.
2. George Eastham, soccer
   litigant, beats Robson and
   Clark of Newcastle to a cross.
3. Helenio Herrera, who earned
   vast sums as a manager in
   Spain and Italy, whistles at a
   baffled Mazzola while training
   Inter Milan.

217

Frank Blunstone as manager. He cut the staff to a minimum and bought and sold cleverly on the transfer market. Brentford have since made a profit each season, have nearly wiped out the overdraft and have even gained promotion to the third division. It is pleasant to record, too, that Queen's Park Rangers reached the first division in 1968, and although promptly sent back again, repeated the feat in 1973 despite the transfer of Rodney Marsh, the crowd's hero.

The benevolent director is the man who as much as any other has allowed British soccer to continue as it has for so long. Support from industrialists has been mentioned as a factor in continental football; in Britain, the local businessman who buys a seat on the Board by means of such things as interest-free loans to the club asserts a great influence. He is not above criticism: being an enthusiastic amateur he naturally wants a hand in the running of the club, often much to the scorn and fury of the professional manager and players. He operates at all levels of football. The presence of a member of the Moores family of the great Littlewoods pools and mail-order company on the Board must bring comfort to Everton well-wishers. Chelsea's Board includes a representative of the Mears building family; it was a Mears who bought a site originally from the Great Western Railway and built the Stamford Bridge Stadium on it. Just as Mears owns Chelsea's ground, Harold Needler, chairman of Hull City, owns Boothferry Park. A quarry-owner, Needler bought the ground after the war, and has since made huge investments in the club, including a settlement of shares in his quarry business worth a couple of world-class players. Much of the money has gone in improvements to the

1

2

3

ground and its facilities, making it one of the finest in the country. Playing success has not yet followed, nor the gates which only follow success, but at least Hull City are equipped for a boom and may yet become a power in the land.

Just as football clubs are restricted in the dividends they pay (or more often fail to pay), so they are not allowed to pay director's fees. Therefore rewards to these men come from the kudos, the local fame and the pleasures of associating with the players, and only indirectly, perhaps, from increased business.

1. Gerry Hitchens, of Aston Villa, sought his fortune in Italy in the sixties.
2. Charlie George was dissatisfied with his Arsenal wages in 1972, and went on the transfer list.
3. Pietro Anastasi, £400,000 worth of footballer, equalizes for Juventus at Leeds in the 1971 Fairs Cup Final. Gary Sprake and Jack Charlton are beaten. Leeds United won the Cup on the away-goals rule.
4. Denis Law scoring with a header. He had a lucrative spell in Italy in the sixties.
5. George Best made a fortune from soccer before the game went sour for him.

4

5

STRESSES AND STRAINS

The financial set-up in British football has led to many more games being played each season. In an effort to increase a season's aggregate gates the Football League introduced in 1960 the Football League Cup. At first it was spurned by some leading clubs, who did not enter, and it was not until the 1969—70 season that all the League clubs took part.

Sponsored competitions began in the sixties. The Watney Cup is played at the beginning of the season between eight Football League clubs who qualify by being the previous season's top scorers. Eight Scottish teams compete for the Drybrough Cup. The Texaco Cup is contested by English, Scottish and Irish League teams. The Anglo-Italian Cup concerns English and Italian clubs.

European competition has added greatly to the number of games played in a season since Hibernian first took part in the European Cup in 1955—56. Each season nowadays about a dozen English and Scottish clubs are engaged in one of the three competitions. With World Cups and European Championships taking place every four years, plus the Home International Tournament, a leading player is likely to be required to play in half as many games again as he was in the fifties.

Games are of more significance, too. There is less of what is called 'end of season stuff', where two mid-table teams play out a lethargic ninety minutes with nothing very much depending on the result. Now bonuses or places in European competition are often at stake.

There is more of a spotlight on the players, as more are required for international squads at senior and under-23 level. There is more transfer activity, which means that any promising youngster is liable to be assessed by a visiting manager or scout at any time. There are more televised matches — several each weekend

1. **Derek Dooley's playing days for Sheffield Wednesday ended at Preston with a bad injury: he became Wednesday's manager.**
2. **The man who made soccer pelvis-conscious. Alan Mullery returned to Fulham from Spurs in 1972 after pelvic injury.**

and usually one during the week also. All this encourages players to give of their best at all times.

Consequently physical and psychological pressures build up. Most-publicized player in this respect, as in many another, is George Best. Best has 'disappeared' more than once when he should have been playing football, on one occasion turning up in London with an actress. Television cameras have followed him into night spots. His problems (or perhaps lack of them) with girls are legendary. His private life has been so exposed that it is understandable that he has felt the need on occasion to flee. He built a mansion, but who could expect him to sit in it in solitary splendour? His erstwhile landlady, Mrs Fullaway, is the best-known landlady in the country, interviewed by Press and television: 'And this is the chair George actually used to sit in.' Best returned to Ireland after his first night at Mrs Fullaway's as a fifteen-year-old. His absence then was hardly news even to Manchester United supporters, but his flight to Spain at the end of the 1971–72 season when he should have been in Troon to play for Ireland was front-page news. When traced, Best announced his retirement from football, aged twenty-six. He claimed that the pressure on him had forced him to drink, and that he was a physical and mental wreck. Best later announced his desire to play for a London club, but once more returned to Manchester United. The mansion, however, was sold, the buyer enjoying his moment of reflected glory when interviewed (of course) on television.

In the 1972–73 season, United reached the foot of the first division table and morale slumped. Manager Frank O'Farrell was sacked in favour of Tommy Docherty, and Best's antics received again the blaze of publicity. Some United players were quoted as being unsympathetic towards him, and he was left out of the team.

A great player like Best is subjected on occasions to rough opposition tactics on the field. On the whole Best overcomes them very successfully, but

George Best resists Mike Bernard of Everton, with Howard Kendall moving in. This was August 1972, after Best's return from an escapade in London. Later, Best and Manchester United vowed not to play with each other again, and Best went off to Acapulco, put on weight and talked of the unbearable pressures of being Britain's most famous footballer.

his open disgust at referees who do not 'protect' him has led him into trouble. On one occasion he threw mud at a ref, on another knocked the ball from a referee's hands. He shows contempt, too, for the game's aged rulers, once arriving late for a disciplinary meeting after missing a train. Best is probably surfeited with football and disillusioned. He must be disappointed that with Northern Ireland he may never play in the World Cup finals, the great international show-piece in which he could conceivably prove himself to be as great as Pele, and earn similar international acclaim. It is to be hoped he regains his inspiration, and shows his best form on British pitches in seasons to come, for undoubtedly he is one of the greatest footballers ever.

The end of the 1971—72 season provided much evidence of strain in footballers, apart from George Best's defection. Don Revie announced that some of his Cup Final players were not fully fit; the team won the Cup but were unsuccessful in the Championship the following week when losing to Wolves. Geoff Hurst broke down in training for an international match with West Germany. England players presented Sir Alf Ramsey with a letter to the effect that they were too tired to go on a summer tour for England — the tour was cancelled. Colin Todd withdrew from an Under-23 tour because of fatigue. He only earned himself a ban from internationals. Francis Lee, a chunky player who gives the impression of being an unworried extrovert, spent several days in hospital suffering from complete exhaustion. Professional Footballers Association chairman Derek Dougan said that the League must introduce reforms to streamline domestic competitions, as there was an intolerable burden on the players of top clubs. League secretary Alan Hardaker seemed unimpressed.

The mental strain is not difficult to appreciate. In the twelve years or so that a footballer is at the top he packs the triumphs and despairs that another man might experience in a life-time's career. He might change his employer and his home three or four times, he will be promoted to the first team or to the national team, he will be dropped (equivalent, perhaps, to being sacked), his mistakes will be in the papers, he will be watched at his work by thousands, he will be sometimes abused, he will suffer industrial injuries periodically, and he will know that at the first sign of weakening powers another will take his job — there is no kicking upstairs or backwater sinecures for footballers. All sportsmen know that mental attitude

is a vital part of competitive sport. It is as easy for the mind to crack as the body. It must be added, in parenthesis, that most top footballers have profitable businesses to run outside the game. They thus add the normal worries of business executives to the strains of playing the game: ulcers may accompany bruises.

Physical strains are even more obvious. Many doctors have commented on modern soccer stresses, among them Tottenham Hotspur's medical adviser, Dr Brian Curtin. Dr Curtin has said that many modern footballers will be burnt out before they are thirty. He has detected arthritis and other signs of strain in footballers in their early twenties.

Dr Neil Phillips, honorary medical officer to the FA, has spoken of both the mental and physical problems and has predicted nervous collapses for footballers in the near future.

Conditions such as tennis elbow have been known to the general public for years. What is less known is that top sportsmen in any sport are likely to contract all sorts of deformities and incapacities earlier in life and more frequently than non-sportsmen. This is due to strain being put on the joints over a long period. Footballers are particularly susceptible to arthritis of the hip. The joint shifts slightly and is not necessarily painful at first. Perhaps a year later the player will feel the effect; perhaps ten years later he will be seriously incapacitated.

Blackburn Rovers paid West Ham United £25,000 for youth international Martin Britt, a fee which eventually worked out at about £4,000 a game. Britt was found to have arthritis of the knee, which began probably with an injury in a practice game.

A more famous soccer casualty was Derek Dooley, who burst on to the scene in the 1951—52 season when he scored forty-six goals in thirty games for Sheffield Wednesday. Before his talent could be assessed with certainty, his leg was broken at Preston, gangrene set in and it was amputated.

Many retired footballers suffer with muscular complaints late in life. One contributory cause may have been the old-style heavy studded boot. A player

Peter Osgood (dark shirt) was on the Chelsea transfer list for two weeks in 1971 for lack of effort: Colin Todd (Derby County), seen challenging him, was banned from international football for two years in 1972 for withdrawing from an England Under-23 tour. He claimed tiredness.

may turn at speed 100 times in a match, and with studs digging into soft ground ligament and cartilage injuries must inevitably follow. Players nowadays wear lighter boots and shinguards, and a new PVC boot with the studs on a revolving disc may alleviate strain still more.

But the biggest cause of serious physical injuries is the crowded soccer programme. Players do not get the opportunity to rest properly after what begin as minor injuries. Many arthritic ex-players owe their present condition in part to attempts to build up muscles by exercise when rest would have been more beneficial. These were errors of medical practice or diagnosis. Today the errors are more likely to be of soccer expediency.

Pelvic disorders made the headlines in the 1971–72 season. Both Alan Mullery and Bob McNab missed a large part of the season after suffering what appeared to be at first minor strains of the groin. Players with minor strains are tempted to try to 'play through them' in order to keep their place in the side, and all that that implies: security and bonuses against a possible spell of obscurity in the reserves. Unfortunately the only cure is all too often rest. Playing on leads to chronic conditions and longer absences through injury. Mullery eventually announced his retirement

1

from international football and left Spurs for his previous club Fulham.

There are three crises facing British football: player's stresses, violence inside and outside the ground and falling gates. The last two are connected and are as much a matter for sociologists to study as soccer legislators. The first is the most important, and its remedy is in the control of soccer itself. The number of games in a season must be reduced, perhaps by cutting down the teams in the first and second divisions and reorganizing the third and fourth divisions into regional leagues again. Futile competitions like the Anglo-Italian Cup must go. The League must act, perhaps encouraged by the Professional Footballers Association. Jimmy Hill and George Eastham have changed soccer in the past — is it now Derek Dougan's turn?

1. Francis Lee playing against Scotland in 1971. At the end of the 1972 season Lee recovered from exhaustion in hospital.
2. Derek Dougan (right) of Wolves, chairman of the Professional Footballers Association, fails to prevent John Dempsey, Chelsea, clearing the ball.

Asa Hartford (dark shirt), whose transfer from West Bromwich Albion to Leeds United was called off in November 1971 when the Leeds medical revealed a hole-in-the-heart condition. Hartford is seen playing for Scotland later in the season in a tussle with Emlyn Hughes (England).

INDEX

Figures in **bold** type indicate illustrations

Acknowledgments

The photographs in this book are from the following sources:
Argus South African Newspapers Ltd.
Associated Press
Auckland Star, New Zealand
Owen Barnes
Barratt's Photopress
Camera Press
Central Press Photos
Co-Press-Studio, Amsterdam
Czechoslovak News Agency
Fox Photos
George Outram and Co. Ltd.
Graphic Corporation, Accra
Interfoto, Budapest
Keystone Press Agency
Liverpool Echo
C. De Meuro
Paul Popper
Press Association
Radio Times Hulton Picture Library
Sportapics
Syndication International
Thames TV
A. Wilkes
A. J. Winder

Acknowledgment is also due to Sutton United Football Club for permission to quote from the club programme.

Bibliography

SOCCER – A PANORAMA Brian Glanville Eyre and Spottiswoode, London, 1969
ASSOCIATION FOOTBALL (in four volumes) edited by A. H. Fabian and Geoffrey Green Caxton Publishing Company Ltd, London 1960
PICTORIAL HISTORY OF SOCCER Dennis Signy Hamlyn Publishing Company Ltd, Feltham, Middlesex, 1968
40 YEARS IN FOOTBALL Ivan Sharpe Hutchinson's, London, 1952
CENTURY OF GREAT SOCCER DRAMA John Cottrell Rupert Hart-Davis, London, 1970
MY TWENTY YEARS OF SOCCER Tommy Lawton Heirloom Modern World Library, 1955
WORLD CUP '70 Hugh McIlvaney and Arthur Hopcraft Eyre and Spottiswoode, London, 1970
SOCCER COACHING THE MODERN WAY Eric Batty Faber and Faber, London, 1969
100 YEARS OF THE FA CUP Tony Pawson William Heinemann Ltd, London, 1972
FOOTBALL MAN Arthur Hopcraft Collins, London, 1968
BRITAIN VERSUS EUROPE Roger Macdonald Pelham Books, London, 1968
WORLD FOOTBALL HANDBOOK (Annual) Compiled by Brian Glanville, Mayflower Books Ltd, London
ROTHMANS FOOTBALL YEARBOOK (Annual) Queen Anne Press Ltd, London